Just14

By Andy Dale

A fictional take on the events of the 1980-81 season

and a tribute to fourteen true Villa legends

Released 15th July 2015

Copyright

Front Cover Design & Illustration

by Gary Dillon - www.dillonart.co.uk

Thanks to

The wealth knowledge supplied by

Frank Holt and Tony Butler

The endless support of my partner Rachael

The Football Association for letting me use all the

Results & Tables

Dedicated to

Four very special men

Jack Dale (Grandpa), Len Cox (Grandad),

Howard Hill (Ultimate Villa Fan)

and Harold Dale (Best Dad)

Introduction

Everyone has a favourite year. For me it has to be 1981. For many it was a memorable year: Botham's Ashes, the Yorkshire Ripper, the Brixton riots and the wedding of Charles and Di. For me 1981 was the year when fourteen remarkable men earned a place in my heart forever; the same year I turned 14.

The only problem is, I am a football fan and we don't live in years, we live in seasons. So this is the story of a teenager, 'The Villa' and a lucky radio during the 1980-81 season.

Chapter One (August)

Even with his head snapped off Brian Little is still the best player on the pitch. A delicately swerved pass from 'Sid' and a wonderful finish from the 'headless' Little, chipped in from the left-hand edge of the penalty box. 2-0 to Aston Villa, surely this is going to be the day? Just three minutes to go and victory is in sight. Disaster! A cracking sound as I move my knee back. I look down and see an all too familiar sight. Lying on the pitch, no longer attached to his base is Alex Cropley. My Aston Villa Subbuteo team are yet again a man light. The Airfix glue will have to wait, there's a game to be won. A game of real significance because I (Jonathan Stadler, aged 13) am about to beat my big brother for the first time EVER. Des Bremner wearing the Villa white away strip will have to play instead, but it doesn't feel right. The No. 10 Cropley was so perfectly weighted.

The importance of this Subbuteo game cannot be underplayed, as this is a Villa – Wolves grudge match, as well as my brother against me. Despite my great hopes for 1979-80 (last season) the Lions (Aston Villa) finished 7th, a place and a point below the Wolves. What was worse, the Wolves had also won the League Cup. I know, I stood behind the goal as Andy 'Traitorous'

Gray rolled the ball (with its snazzy red stripe) past Peter Shilton in the Forest goal. My first ever trip to Wembley, the spiritual home of football, and I see my brother's team win a cup. Yes, I cheered surrounded by an end full of delirious Wolves fans, but it wasn't supposed to be like that. I was pleased for my brother (Mark), Dad and my grandad back home, but why wasn't it the mighty Villa?

A mistake by Jimmy Rimmer as his base comes unexpectedly detached from his rod and the lead is halved. Why isn't the pinger on the oven going off – surely it must be full-time? My arty brother had painted his team recently and it was George Berry, with his afro, who Colin Gibson had just collided with just inside the shooting area. Surely my wall and Jimmy (now firmly refastened to his rod) can keep it out? Just seconds later I am getting the large white ball and Jimmy from my net. I don't think Peter Daniel, or my brother, have ever hit a better free-kick than that one. Now we get the loud pings of the kitchen cooker. One day I will beat him but today I will have to settle for a draw.

Now it is time to tune my lucky radio into BBC Radio Birmingham and let the 1980-81 football season begin.

Wolves and the Villa are both away first game. The Villa are at Leeds, who had finished mid-table the previous season and Wolves are by the sea at Brighton & Hove Albion. Brighton are not a very good team so Wolves should win, although Mark claims that they are Wolves' bogey team, a point emphasised by

Brighton being the only side to do the 'double' over Wolves last season.

Despite trying to appear confident I have a bad feeling about this season. I have stuck on my bedroom wall my 'Roy of the Rovers, My Team Performance 1980-81' poster ready to mark off every result. I have decided this season to use my new red Paper Mate biro. It will only be used for filling out this chart. Also, ready for the new season is my 'Shoot League Ladders'. I'd spent the previous night carefully pressing out all 92 team tabs. Apart from a slight rip in West Ham United and a total beheading of Grimsby Town it had been a job well done. I just hope that after three games I will be able to place the Aston Villa tab higher than the Wolverhampton Wanderers tab. Of course, to start with they are placed in alphabetical order, so Villa are second, with only Arsenal above us. If only the season finishes that way. I am distracted by my fixture list that I'd copied from the Express & Star. Our final game is at Arsenal so now I am daydreaming of the two teams meeting level on points, joint top of the table. Deep into injury-time and Villa are awarded a penalty. Gordon 'Sid' Cowans against Pat Jennings. Cowans runs towards the ball. This to win the League for Aston Villa?

My daydreaming is interrupted by my brother announcing that we are going to listen to the matches on the big stereo unit tuner in the front room. I protest, I want to listen to it on my lucky radio; the small battery one that I got from my grandad in 1977, the last time Villa won a trophy. Mark was always dismissing the powers of my lucky radio, but when it was on, the Villa rarely lost. Of course, I would have to do without it for half the games next season, because next season my parents are finally buying me a season ticket. A chance to see every Villa home game. Next season can't come fast enough. Just hope we don't get relegated this year like in '67, the year I was born. No, in Ron Saunders we trust, even if he did sell Andy Gray to blooming Wolves. Anyway, my lucky radio will save us.

Where the hell is my radio? I've looked everywhere for it, even behind the settee. Kick-off is fast approaching. Mark's probably hidden it. The teams are announced and at Elland Road defender Allan Evans is missing for us. Our big Scottish centre-half, he used to be a forward. Instead Eamonn Deacy from Ireland is going to play. Deacy is the player who wrote to Villa a few years ago asking for a trial.

Sadly my favourite player, Brain Little, is so injured that he even failed the medical to play for Birmingham City. So the Villa have a new striker called Peter Withe. He played for Forest when they won the league, but has been playing in Division Two with Newcastle. Mark says he used to play for Wolves and he was rubbish. But Ron Saunders paid half a million pounds for him last week. That's a third of an Andy Gray, or half a Trevor Francis. At 29 he's quite old. At least he has got 19-year-old Gary Shaw alongside him. Gary Shaw is far too pretty for a footballer but could be a great star. He is the only Villa player I have ever seen score a hat-trick live. It was against Bristol City.

The 1980-81 season was off. Listening without my little radio is worrying though. I am nervous, my hands are clasped around a piece of my mum's best Wedgewood. Come on the Villa! As I am thinking about having a go on Guess the Goals, with a guess of 18, comes the first Radio Birmingham 'Goal Horn' of the new season. It's only 3:02 and they're going off to Elland Road. It's a goal in the Villa game. Disaster! Leeds have scored already. A penalty given away by flipping Eamonn Deacy. I can tell Mark's trying not to laugh. Is this a sign of how the season is going to go?

Half an hour into the games and no more goals in the Villa game, lots of talk of Leeds domination. Wolves are losing to Brighton. Birmingham are winning the local derby against Coventry and no goals yet between the Baggies (West Brom) and Arsenal. Whatever happens at least it's still the holidays. So no ribbing at school on Monday. Just don't lose by too many Villa, please.

Half-time approaching and my brother's finally given in and retrieved my lucky radio from a cupboard in the dining room that is normally just reserved for the posh glasses used at Christmas. Mark says, "Now you can see that it isn't lucky and has no effect whatsoever on the result". We turn off the stereo tuner and switch on my little, yet powerful, radio. It's already tuned into BBC Radio Birmingham on the Medium Wave. As I turn up the volume the sound of the goal horn bellows out. Where's the goal? Is it a Wolves equaliser or just a goal in Walsall's Third Division game? No, it's back at Leeds. My lucky radio has struck gold within seconds. Super winger Tony Morley with a great goal has put the Villans level. Seconds later I am entering the name of Tony Morley in the Goalscorer section on the 'My Team Performance' poster and colouring in one square.

Into the second-half and the Villa with the help of my lucky radio have taken full control of the game. The Radio Birmingham reporter is full of praise as we are pushing for a winner. It's quarter past four, I can hear my Roy of the Rovers comic is being pushed through the letterbox, as news comes through that golden haired Gary Shaw has given Aston Villa the lead.

Twenty-five minutes later and Shaw's goal is enough to give Villa an away victory and their first two points of the season. Wolves have lost 2-0 at Brighton. So maybe now Andy Gray is regretting upsetting Ron Saunders. Arsenal have beaten West Bromwich. All in all a pretty good day. Just a pity there is no school on Monday. Time now to read about Tynefield City's Scottish keeper, Gordon Stewart, in 'Safest Hands in Soccer' and see if he did save that penalty. So glad they finally dumped the 'Smith and Son' strip from Roy of the Rovers.

9:24pm Wednesday 20th August 1980

Gary Shaw and my radio did well tonight. Shaw scored the winner in our 1-0 home win over Norwich. He scored in the second-half. Wish I had been at Villa Park under the fantastic AV flood-lights. At least Allan Evans was back alongside Ken McNaught at the heart of the defence. Perhaps Evans and

McNaught can become the centre-half pairing for Scotland in the next World Cup. Hopefully this time England will get there too and we won't have to call support the 'Jocks'. Never known my Dad cheer a Scottish goal like he did that Archie Gemmill one against Holland. Well, I suppose we were in a caravan at the foot of Ben Nevis at the time.

Just shaded in a green square for Gary Shaw's goal on my wallchart. Have to try to calculate the league position on the League Performance section. There is a picture of Albion's Cyrille Regis celebrating a goal on it. Haystacks from school would like that. I think we are 4th. The first league tables are never until after three games. Two games two wins is a perfect start.

Better get some sleep now. Dad says we are leaving at 6:30 in the morning to beat the traffic. Looking forward to sailing my rubber dingy in the sea.

1:42pm Saturday 23rd August 1980

Villa have the chance to be top of the league when the first league tables come out tonight (if we can beat Manchester City) and we are away on holiday. Why do my parents always insist on going on holiday when the season's begun? It isn't that I am against the family holiday, but how can I give it my full attention when my mind is focused on what's happening at Maine Road? This year we have come to Bournemouth. It is quite a posh chalet up the top of a hill with access to a fairly clean outdoor swimming pool. Best part is we have to go down a cliff railway to get to the beach. It's a lovely sandy beach and so far it's been really an okay holiday - although we only got here yesterday. With my brother, Mark, now sixteen, it could be our last family holiday so I am not complaining too much. Anyway, there's a colour telly in the chalet and I've got my own little room. The TV can't get BBC 2 and there is a very shaky picture on ITV but it was good enough to watch On The Ball during lunch. We missed Football Focus because of being on the beach. They did mention the Villa game, but it was all about how rubbish Man City are doing. City are bottom of the league and whilst the Villa have won both opening matches City have lost both of theirs. City manager Malcolm Allison is in his second spell as manager. He has signed a lot of players for loads of money. It was him signing Steve Daley from Wolves, for a fee my grandad said was totally mad, that allowed Wolves to steal Andy Gray from us. Malcolm Allison has sold players like Peter Barnes who always seemed to play so well with Steve Coppell in Mark's England Subbuteo team.

Mark doesn't know, but I've got my lucky radio with me on holiday. I sneaked it in the bottom of my sports bag. No hope of listening to it this afternoon though as Mum has just announced we are all going Pony Trekking in the New Forest. Apparently it starts at 2.30 and lasts TWO HOURS. At least we should be back in the car for 5pm. We're out of range of BBC Radio Birmingham, but one of the stations in Dad's new Morris Ital car is bound to have the football scores on. The car was brand new on 1st August. We received loads of looks driving down to

Bournemouth. The good thing is that since Dad got his new Ital the Villa have won every game. Maybe it's a lucky car. I like the car. It even has metallic paint and a go-faster stripe. There is one thing wrong with the new car though. The registration letter at the end is 'W'. As Dad pointed out on the day he brought it home, 'W' is for 'Wolverhampton Wanderers'. If he had only bought it a week earlier it would have been 'V' for Villa. But it was fun to have it on 1st August.

I am mounting a horse (far too big for a pony) called Colin with no idea whether Peter Withe has passed his fitness test or not. Mum is looking slightly nervous on a horse named Moses. Mark and Dad appear more relaxed on their horses. Also their hats seem to fit better than mine. I think I overestimated the size of my head and now I am struggling to see. Things are not going too well for my mum, as Moses has started to gallop off. It is either a total lack of control by my mum, who's a school teacher, or Moses has major problems with knowing his 'lefts' from his 'rights'. Whichever it is Moses is a very naughty horse and my petrified mum is now tightly clinging to his neck. Compared to Moses, Colin's a saint and my only difficulty is my lack of vision and low hanging branches. It does seem a long way from the ground.

Bravely allowing Colin to trot now, but my imagination is working overtime on what might be happening up in Manchester. Are the Villa on their way to being top of the league? Hope nobody noticed me singing, "We Are Top of the League". I am suddenly distracted by a girl on a horse coming towards our group. She looks familiar and is smiling at me. She is absolutely lovely. Short brown hair, big eyes and even a sign of some breasts under her blue sweater. While all of our group's helmets are either too small or way too big, this girl's fits perfectly. Perfect like her bottom that is just going past. It was a mistake to follow her bouncing bottom as she goes past and it results in me being whacked full on the nose by a very spiky branch I had totally failed to spot. Despite being in considerable pain I have retained my composure and Colin is staying calm. It's as if he is concerned for the state of his rider.

Back in the Ital and Dad is frantically trying to tune the radio in to Radio 2, but the New Forest is not ideal for radio reception. Finally we hear the name Gary Shaw. It gets better because he passes to Peter Withe. So the big man is playing. Just as Mum is moaning about pain in her shoulder from her ride on Moses the commentator says, "Withe just inches from his hat-trick". So Villa have scored at least two, and surely with only about ten minutes left are about to go top of the league. More crackle. My brother leans over to fiddle with the car radio knob. Now we have left the trees the reception is better.

With the loud noise of the crowd there's news that Ray Ranson has scored for Manchester City. We are winning though, 2-1 with just five minutes left. Mark is frantically trying to find out the Wolves score against the Baggies. Disaster!! Sometimes in life joy can turn to despair so fast. The news of a Dennis Tueart goal has done just that. The Manchester City player (who I had once swapped Eric Gates for in my Soccer Stars 1978 sticker album) has surely stopped the Villa winning and stopped us going top of the league.

The Villa game has ended 2-2. Despite my best efforts to be in a cheerful holiday mood I am struggling to prevent the build-up of tears. In contrast my brother seems pleased with a Wolves draw at Ron Atkinson's Albion. Or maybe he is just pleased we aren't top of the league.

11:12am Wednesday 27th August 1980

Today is my first visit to Villa Park of the new season: Leeds United in the League Cup. This is a bonus as we were supposed to still be on holiday in Bournemouth. We had to come home early because our Grandpa (Dad's dad) was taken ill while we were away. Dad says Grandpa is improving now so to make up for not finishing the holiday he will take me to the game tonight.

Dad tends to take me to Villa Park about four times a year. Normally when there is a game on a week night in the school holiday. My first game was near my tenth birthday. We played Middlesbrough and Gordon Cowans scored the only goal. I remember we stood in the Holte End quite near the front. It was just mind-blowingly brilliant. I still have the programme under my bed. It cost 15p. This season it has gone up to 35p so not sure if my dad will buy me one.

It has been a long Wednesday having to go into Wolverhampton to 'Buxton and Bonnets' with Mark to buy a new school blazer while my parents were looking after Grandpa. Maybe I should have admitted to Mum that I didn't actually try the blazer on.

It seems ages until we are finally on the M6 off to Villa Park. Maybe this will be the season we win the League Cup again. I had stayed up to watch us win it on Sports Night in 1977, thanks to Brian Little in the second replay. When I was seven I'd listened to Ray Graydon missing the penalty and then scoring the rebound against Norwich in 1975. I have the clippings from the Sports Argus for both triumphs. So about time we won it again. After all Villa have won the League Cup more times than anybody else. We even won the very first one. As well as winning the FA Cup the most times. Mind you, if Andy Gray hadn't have scored that winner for Wolves in last year's final then Forest would have won the League Cup three times as well. I wonder if I will manage to get to the final this year if Villa get there. It is mad that the only Wembley final I have attended is with the Wolves. Surely the fact that I am going to see them in the first leg of the second round will go in my favour.

The M6 is busy as always, but soon from Spaghetti Junction to our right we can see the majestic Villa Park and the amazing AV floodlights. So glad we have these special floodlights instead of the sort all the other teams have. Even though it's a nice summer's evening you can tell the floodlights are already on.

Ready for my first chance to see Peter Withe. Going down the Aston Expressway, how many other teams have their own Expressway. As always we hit lots of traffic. Still over an hour-and-a-half until kick-off so no need to worry. We park up and two lads start running towards the car. The one is a bit fat and is beaten to the car by the other lad. The fastest lad offers to mind the car. Dad offers him 10p. To the lad's disappointment Dad says he will give it him when he returns. Then another car pulls in slightly further down the road and the two boys go racing off. This time the fat boy gives the other lad a quick nudge and sends him flying. I think it is a fair shoulder charge, but Dad shakes his head in disgust.

We take my favourite walk through the grounds of Aston Hall. Probably because it always means I am about to see my heroes in claret and blue. There are several games of cricket going on as it is a lovely sunny evening. Sadly too hot to wear my woollen scarf, but I have pinned by Villa rosette to my blue Adidas tee-shirt. Aston Hall is a very old building where I think the Lord of Aston lives or one of the Bendall family that owns the club. I'm not sure which. It looks in need of a little repair. I like the way everybody is walking one way through the grounds all heading to Villa Park. There are a lot of leaves on the trees today so as we walk past Aston Hall we can only see glimpses of the magnificent stadium. Surely one of the best grounds in England. Certainly the best one I've been to. Although Wembley is impressive but Villa Park oozes character. This isn't the time for reminiscing, though we need to get to the ground. Kick-off's at 7:30 and it is nearly 6:20 already.

As we walk through the trees the breath-taking sight of the Trinity Road Stand comes into view. I am sure that however many times I see this vision it will always send shivers down my body. The Trinity Road Stand really is the best architecture I have ever seen with its regal central staircase and pointed brick roofs either side. One side saying 'Aston' the other 'Villa'. The symmetry of the two words of great name is fantastic. The way both have five letters and one starts with 'A' and the other ends with 'A' is all part of the Aston Villa magic. In the centre above the staircase is the historic Villa badge. The yellow lion with the motto 'Prepared' underneath. I am certainly 'prepared' to shout my heart out this Wednesday night. Part of me wishes we were going in the Trinity Road Stand but I am a real supporter and real supporters stand in the Holte End.

I haven't been since March, when Mark took me and we stood in the North Stand Enclosure with the away fans (Wolves). It wasn't a happy experience as Villa surprisingly lost 3-1 to a Wolves team containing many reserve team players. It was only four days before their League Cup Final. Maybe fitting that my next visit to the great ground would be for me to see Villa take the first step (hopefully) on the road to League Cup glory.

Soon Dad and I are standing on the enormous terracing of the Holte End. Like so many other fathers and sons were doing. This really is male bonding at its finest. Probably I was the only one there with a Wolves supporting father. Even so he will soon be cheering on the mighty Villans against 'dirty' Leeds. We always stand about a third of the way up. Quite central, but in the left-hand side. This gives an ideal view just above the top of the red caging. We are early enough to get a crush-barrier to lean against. All we have to do now is hope that somebody really tall doesn't come and stand in front of the barrier.

The Villa have no injuries. So it is the normal eleven. Eight English men, all of which I think Ron Greenwood should be watching, and three from Scotland. The three Scots are Allan Evans, Ken McNaught and Des Bremner. Bremner was the one that my Dad always says has a funny way of running. Allan Evans is very Scottish. I heard him on ATV the other night and couldn't understand a word he said. Ken McNaught played against us for Everton in the 1977 final before Ron Saunders signed him. That was the Final that took us three games to win. But at least it meant I got to stay up late. What a goal Chris Nicholl scored and I still remember that bloke in the eye-patch handing him the cup. Maybe he will be there again this year to hand it to Dennis Mortimer. The FA Cup might be the best cup to win but you only get little medals for winning that one. You get silver tankards for the League Cup. I know what I would rather have on my fireplace and you can drink from a tankard.

This game isn't quite as easy as I was hoping and Leeds have had quite a bit of the ball. But there is only one team going to win. Soon we are all cheering. It is winger Tony Morley who has scored the goal. His proper name is William Anthony Morley, so not surprised his parents called him Tony. I mean they couldn't really call him Willy. Mr Saunders signed him last summer from Burnley and I think at the time nobody had heard of Tony Morley. He has been the best player tonight.

Walking back through the park the 1-0 win, Dad seems to be trying to dampen my hopes of glory. He is saying that a one goal lead is not going to be enough to take to Elland Road next week. This Villa team though are unbeatable, well unless they play Liverpool of course. All I really want now is for Villa not to lose before I have to go back to school next Monday. I am not looking forward to that anyway especially as I am moving class.

12:29pm Saturday 30th August 1980

Saturday before my return to school and we are in Buxton and Bonnets changing my new school blazer. Mum has decided it is too tight. Need some charcoal grey trousers as well. They always look black to me.

I hate school uniform shopping! Why are we doing it on a Saturday lunch time? What about Football Focus? It was bad enough missing Swap Shop. We must talk Dad into finally buying a video recorder. Everybody else at school seems to have one. Including Mark Felbury and his dad's a binman. I am sure last year's blazer would still fit. I mean, I don't have to fasten all of the buttons. I am getting really hungry now, but if we go to eat at the 'Golden Egg' we won't get back for On The Ball. Whose idea was this? Mark jokingly suggests we might not get back until after 3:00 so I won't have my lucky radio.

Mum says I need new shoes. I hate having new shoes at the best of time. They always comment on how wide my feet are. I can't help having wide feet. I do a lot of walking around. This time though whatever pair they give me first, I will say they fit perfectly. I have to get back for 3pm. My football team needs me. We have to beat Coventry City. We should do, Coventry never beat us. We are, according to Gerry Daly in this week's Shoot, their bogey team. But Ron Saunders will still demand the players give 110%.

It seems we have to go to Clarks for shoes, as Mum says no other shoes fit my extra wide feet right. Bet there will be tons of kids there all trying school shoes on. I wouldn't mind but when we get to school we have to change into our pumps because of all the precious new carpets. Mum spends ages trying to find me a pair. At least as I wait I can see Football Focus in the distance on one of the TVs in Rumblelows. I'm sure that looks like Jim Blythe the Coventry goalkeeper. Perhaps he is saying how scared he is of facing Peter Withe. Wish I was in the Holte End today. Dad said he would try and take me again soon, but not today. I wonder what colour Coventry will play in. I can't see them wearing their sky blue kit. Quite like their Admiral kit though with its trendy tramlines. Mark painted the stripes on the Coventry Subbuteo team. Maybe they will wear their horrible chocolate brown one instead.

The first pair of shoes I try on have a horrible dotty pattern down the side and the left foot feels like it is being squashed in a vice. But time is ticking so I tell my parents they are perfect. I even manage to walk in them across the shop. With my teeth firmly clenched. It takes nearly seven minutes to pay for them. I used the stop watch function on my digital watch to time the very slow assistant. If the Coventry right-back is half as slow, then Tony Morley might score a hat-trick. I can hear the Holte End now shouting, "Morley for England".

My parents seem to have deliberately spent the last three hours in slow motion. Yes, we needed to eat, yes, it was nice to see my grandad (Mum's dad) and yes Snowy needed rabbit food, but I need my lucky radio. It is now 3:32pm and we have just got home. Although BBC Radio Birmingham has been on at both my grandad's and in the car the Villa have failed to score. It has been, as the reporter keeps saying, all Aston Villa but no goals.

In my small bedroom I am sitting on top of my Aston Villa duvet just waiting for the goal horn to sound. It has happened several times as Wolves, Albion and even the Bluenoses (Birmingham City) scored. I can hear Mark's cheers as Wolves go two up against Crystal Palace. If the Villa lose they could be level on points and goal difference with the Wolves. Oh we need a goal, but it is now 4:30pm. Just ten minutes to go. And just forty-and-a-half hours until I am back at school. Where have the last seven weeks gone?

Will be good to see the gang again especially if Villa can score. Pincher and Spud will be definitely smiling with the Wolves winning. Haystacks will be jumping on our backs after West Brom have won at Brighton. The battle of the Albions. Blooming Ron Atkinson is too good a manager for them. At least Tucker and Noddy will not be gloating, it looks like Walsall are going to lose to Brentford. Mind you being a Saddlers (Walsall) fan they never really get to gloat. I wonder why they don't support a proper team. I mean it is fine to have Walsall as your second team. At least they aren't glory hunters, like Rushton and Bellington supporting flaming Liverpool; just because they win all the time. I can't believe Kenny Bellington is going to be in the same form as me this year. He should have been expelled last term for piercing Sharon Chester's right ear during French. Never heard a girl scream so loud and the blood squirted everywhere.

Full-time at Molineux and a 2-0 win for the Wolves. That gives them 5 points. So a goal-less draw for the Villa at least keeps us a point ahead of them. Looks like fourteen goals is going to win on Guess the Goals today. I was too late to enter this week, but would probably have gone for sixteen because I thought the Villa would score a few. Just as I am going downstairs to retrieve my Roy of the Rovers comic from the letterbox I hear the dramatic goal horn. Obviously one of the games hadn't finished. Although the tuner is on downstairs and I am more down the stairs than up, I turn and run back up to my bedroom. I need my lucky radio just in case. "Deadlock broken in last minute at Villa

Park", the presenter announces. I freeze and hold my breath. On moments like this the whole school week can depend. I don't need to hear the reporter's words. The noise of the Villa fans is enough for me to know we've won. Two more points, a superb start to the season. My triumphantly raised arm sends my Villa lamp shade spinning as I jump on my bed. I stop to listen to the final report. The goal had been scored by the new Villa wonderboy Gary Shaw. His 3rd goal of the season. I sing out loud (if not very tunefully) the Gary Shaw song, "Gary Shaw, Gary Shaw, Gary Gary Shaw, he gets the ball he's bound to score, Gary Gary Shaw".

That night instead of reading straightaway the adventures of Roy Race and how he is struggling to cope now that Penny has left him, I have to work out the new position of everyone in the First Division so I can put all the team tabs on my Shoot League Ladders correctly and also to mark in red on my Villa Season Performance chart where we now are. I hoped we would be second but we are actually 3rd. I could claim joint top but with goal difference we are definitely 3rd. Ipswich, managed by Bobby Robson, who everyone seems to rave about, are top and then come Southampton. If only we had Kevin Keegan. At least we are two places above Bellington's Liverpool. Bet he has never been anywhere near Anfield.

Unbelievably ATV have highlights of Walsall against Brentford on Star Soccer tonight. I was hoping they would have gone for the Villa V Coventry Midland derby. It's obvious that

Gary Newbon doesn't like the Villa. Looks like Alan Buckley scored again. I wonder if one day the Villa will have a Player Manager. Perhaps Gordon Cowans could take over from Ron Saunders. Maybe 'Sid' is too quiet, but I could imagine Peter Withe doing it. Who was the last Villa manager with a beard?

So the end of August and a great month for the Villa and not too bad for me. Just dreading going back to school. If I stay on to the sixth form I will still have five more years of this.

End of August Top of Division One			
1.	Ipswich Town	Pl: 4 Po: 7	+7
2.	Southampton	Pl: 4 Po: 7	+5
3.	Aston Villa	Pl: 4 Po: 7	+3
4.	Sunderland	Pl: 4 Po: 5	+5
5.	Liverpool	Pl: 4 Po: 5	+4
6.	Forest	Pl: 4 Po: 5	+4

Villa August League Results	
16th Leeds (a)	2-1 Won (Morley, Shaw)
20th Norwich City (h)	1-0 Won (Shaw)
23rd Man City (a)	2-2 Draw (Withe 2)
30th Coventry City (h)	1-0 Won (Shaw)

Chapter Two (September)

Just my luck, first day back at school waiting for the 702 school bus and it is raining. New blazer's getting wet and new shoes are cutting into my feet. They're like Tony Hart's knife slicing through Morph. How I am going to survive the whole day I have no idea. Especially considering my lack of sleep. I spent the whole night watching the digital numbers on my radio alarm clock click through. Just didn't want the hour digit to keep changing. Also my ham sandwiches were too frozen this morning to be able to prise open to spread 'Branston' on. They are going to be so dry at lunch time and I have prawn cocktail flavoured crisps. The worst thing is knowing this day will probably get worse. Wouldn't be surprised if I end up with double French first lesson on the new timetable. Just hope I get Miss Cresswell for History again. She is so hot and has the best smile. As well as smelling really nice. You can always smell where Miss Cresswell has been in the corridors.

It is 8:55 and the 702 still hasn't reached school. What's the point of a school bus that's always late for school? It is so embarrassing always arriving late to registration. I am not even sure where my form room is this year. I think it is above the

Science block. Frances Coulton is in my form and sitting three seats away, but I remember what happened to the last person who tried to speak to her before 10am on a Monday morning. Anyway, she seems to be too busy trying to cut a slit in the side of her skirt. Maybe her new one is too tight like my shoes. I would take them off but probably struggle to get my feet back in them. The new first years look so tiny. I am sure they will grow into their uniforms. They look nearly as petrified as me and I am starting my third year.

Great, I am the last one in the form room. Frances Coulton must have known a quick way in. Only four of my classmates from last year have moved with me. Seems the reason for me having to move is because I have been put into the top Maths group. If I had known this was going to happen I would have deliberately got a few questions wrong in the Maths test. How come Kenny Bellington got to be in this class? I didn't even think he knew his two times table. Obviously helps having your dad on the school governors. At least this is only my form class so should get to be with the gang later.

It's Tuckers' birthday on Thursday so he will be the first of us to turn fourteen. We call him Tucker because his name is Peter Jenkins. Just like Tucker off Grange Hill. All of the 'Local Gang' have clever nicknames. Mine is 'Hugh'. It was Haystacks' idea as my name is Jonathan. So he shortened it to John (which I hate being called) and then it made him think of the Midland football commentator Hugh Johns off Star Soccer. That's why I am

'Hugh'. I quite like it even if it does sound a bit Welsh. Sounds like I should be a character on Ivor the Engine.

Our form teacher this year is a new teacher to the school, a Mr Walker. Strange looking man whose left eye appears to be two inches lower than his right one and he has a ginger beard. Oh and no earlobes. Probably about my dad's age, but he's inappropriately wearing a brown leather jacket. I wonder what subject Mr Walker teaches. He is not very organised and seems to be struggling to find a red pen for the register. Maybe I should offer to lend him one of the new red pens from my Abba pencil case. Too late, he has gone to find one. He could be some time as I am pretty sure the directions that Wendy McGregor has just given him for the stationery store cupboard will bring him out just behind the swimming pool instead. All the girls are rushing to the window to see if they can see him walking across the car park. Or more likely so they can ogle at the workman who is fitting the new bicycle shed in a very tight vest top. I guess the rain must have stopped now.

The day has got worse. Bellington has decided to come and chat to me. He seems keen to tell me graphically about three Villa fans he met on holiday and how he beat them all up. He is gloating about how the seeping blood matched the Villa fans red and blue shirts. I am trying to tactfully remind this ignoramus that the great Aston Villa play in claret, not red, but it is going way over his head. Bellington has decided instead to start mocking my Abba pencil case. Claiming that only girls like Abba. He is foolishly challenging me to name ten Abba songs. All the class are now listening to our conversation. Obviously my Abba pencil case is suddenly more appealing than the tight vested workman. I am in a no-win situation here. Yes, I can easily name ten Abba songs, but then that will make me in Bellington's eyes a 'girl'. I am always up for a challenge though. So I am now claiming I can name twenty Abba songs. My hope is that Mr Walker returns before I finish listing them. Sadly when I get to the 20th Abba song (which is the recent number one, 'The Winner Takes It All') Mr Walker is still missing. Obviously lost deep inside massive school.

Kenny Bellington has now found his infamous compass and is sadistically stabbing each eye of the four members of Abba on my pencil case. I can just about cope with Benny, Björn and even Agnetha, but Anni-Frid is just too much. Especially as after putting his compass through Anni-Frid's right eye it also pierced one of my blue ink cartridges inside. Quickly the blue ink is soaking through the white cloth of the pencil case. Abba are turning blue! Nobody is helping me. I feel completely isolated. I can feel tears approaching my eyes, but I can't show weakness. I am trying in vain to laugh it off. I even try joking it is Everton blue, but my eyes are definitely watering up. Bellington is enjoying the attention of the whole class and less than an hour into my third year I am about to burst into tears. Biting my lip trying desperately to prevent a complete flood. Bellington is now complaining about having ink on his hands and is using his sharp compass to try to get me to apologise for this.

Lizzy Fellows is the only one defending me. She is trying to ask Kenny Bellington to stop teasing me. Bellington is not in the mood to stop. He is enjoying far too much attention. Bellington has now picked up my blue-stained Abba pencil case and is walking towards the open window. All I can do is watch and sob. Bellington is now holding my pencil case out of the second floor window. He is demanding an apology from me, or he will let go of the Abba pencil case. There can't be any backing down from me. I have to stand up for myself and probably the whole of Sweden. Remembering those immortal words, 'At Waterloo, Napoleon did surrender' I was no Napoleon. I will not surrender. But now with tears and snot running down my face several of the girls are now appealing for Bellington to stop.

For a second there I think the girls are going to talk Bellington out of dropping the pencil case. He tells me to take it only for his fingers to part and poor Benny, Björn and co. to go hurtling two floors to the ground. Without looking back I run out of the classroom down the stairs and out into the carpark. Eventually I find an almost empty blue-stained Abba pencil case with pens, pencils, rubbers and all spread over the tarmac. I can't find my new fountain pen. I hate being in this new class.

Things have got a bit better during the morning. Luckily the only subject I have with Kenny Bellington in is Metalwork. History is partly good news because we (me and Tucker) are in Miss Cresswell's class. The bad news is that we now have to call her Mrs Cresswell-Farrington. I guess she wasn't going to save herself and wait until I was grown up to marry me. Mrs Cresswell-Farrington is also such a lot to write on the front of the fawn-coloured exercise book. I am sure History used to be green.

It's lunch-time so Tucker, Pincher, Spud, Noddy and I are having a kickabout just by the tennis courts. Pincher's Wembley Trophy ball dates back to primary school. I bet I have scored a hundred goals with that ball. Haystacks is the only member of the 'Local Gang' of six missing. It seems he has fallen in love over the summer with a girl from the year below and they are having dinner together. This is a surprise because Haystacks is the fattest boy in the group and quite massive. Which is why we call him Haystacks. Actually, it was Haystacks who gave himself the name after 'Giant Haystacks'. His real name is Scott Hastings.

The 'Local Gang' is only for boys, and only for boys who support a local football team. The 'Local Gang' aren't interested in girls. The only thing that matters is football. Is Haystacks going to leave the gang or are our rules going to change this year?

Pincher and Spud are always great fun. It isn't just the football chat that is interesting about them. They are just so funny together. They refuse to ever take life too seriously. You wouldn't catch them falling in 'love' like Haystacks. Both are Wolves fans and were really jealous that I got to see Wolves at Wembley last March. It was because my grandad who had a Wolves season ticket felt it was too far for him to go at his age. Pincher is really Stuart and I have known him since junior school. Our mums both taught at the same school. The nickname 'Pincher' is because when we were in the Infants he used to pinch all the girl's bottoms. He has grown out of that now. Pincher's dad has started to take him to Wolves home games this season. He has also promised to take him to Villa Park in two weeks' time when the Wolves play us.

Spud hasn't been to many Wolves games yet but his two older brothers always go. Spud pretends to be quite hard but he isn't really. He has been known to head-butt a couple of lads who really annoyed him though. Including one who'd been having a go at me. I wonder if he fancies head-butting Bellington. Spud is really Pete Hogan or to give him his full name Peter Spudnik Hogan. Although he kept his middle name secret from us all for the first year here. People think the nickname is due to his head being potato shaped but the real reason for the Spud is the middle name Spudnik. His parents apparently met the day that the Russian Spudnik Satellite was blasted into space. I am already missing being in Spud's form. We worked well together the last two years. He protected me and I helped him with his Science homework. Pete doesn't find some lessons very easy although he is far artier than me. Probably why he is so into singer Gary Numan. It seems for the new term Spud has dyed his blond hair jet black to match Gary Numan's.

Spud and I are probably the closest friends of the 'Local Gang'. We get on really well despite our differing music and football tastes. In fact the only thing we seem to really agree on is how attractive Miss Cresswell (now Mrs Cresswell-Farrington) is and Spud is devastated that he isn't in her History class this year.

While I am hoping to be a teacher when I am grown up Spud is determined to join the police force. Spud is nearly tall enough already to get into the police and his head is perfectly shaped for those helmets they wear. However the main reason Spud wants to join the police is so he gets to go to all the Wolves home games free of charge.

Oddly Spud and I have been best friends for over two years now and I have never met his parents or been to his house. He has only been to mine once.

The afternoon went quite well and even my shoes feel almost bearable as I walk home from the bus stop. I'll stop off at the corner shop to buy a 5p packet of 'Krunchi Puffs' as I didn't use the money for a drink at school. Just hope Mum doesn't notice the cheesy smell when I get home. I will just have to keep my mouth closed.

For once I am excited to get to the Express & Star newspaper before my Mum does. Just to read the report on Villa's victory over the Sky Blues. Normally I just peek at the back page to see any stories about the Villa. But today I actually go in two pages from the back to read the report. It is by the same person who had written the report on Saturday in the pink paper, Sporting Star, but as that report was written at half-time this one today actually mentions that the Villa won. It also has an up to date league table in it. So I can check my league ladders are right.

Just below the report on the win is a small story that is really good news. It says that Gary Shaw has been voted the 'Robinsons Barley Water – Young Player of The Month' for August. Well done Mr Shaw. I call him Mr. Shaw but he is only 19. Just six years older than me. I wonder if we have got any Robinsons Barley Water in the kitchen. Virginia Wade drank that when she won Wimbledon in 1977.

Time to watch Blue Peter and The Wombles before tea and then homework time. I can't believe I have three lots of homework on my first day back and four new exercise books to cover. Maybe my dad will feel sorry for me and offer to cover them for me. We aren't allowed to use wallpaper this year, it has to be that sticky clear stuff. I always end up with mine full of bubbles. Mind you, that was not as bad as when Haystacks covered his Maths book with used cling film from his sandwiches. He had a piece of black lettuce stuck to the back of it for months.

Trying to watch Blue Peter, but still don't like Simon Groome, and Sarah Greene is no Lesley Judd. Maybe I am getting too old for Blue Peter now I am a Third Year. I think I will start making a Villa scrapbook until The Wombles come on. I am going to keep all the reports of all the games this season especially the League Cup ones. I will see if Dad has thrown last Thursday's Express & Star away. I am sure somewhere in my bedroom is an empty 'Paddington Bear Scrapbook'. I can call it 'The Road to Glory' and start by sticking in that picture of Jimmy Rimmer from

'Roy's Star Team' in Roy of The Rovers. I am not cutting up any of my Villa programmes though. They are far too precious.

12:35pm Wednesday 3rd September 1980

Good to have Haystacks back with us this lunch-time. Great to have the full 'Local Gang' back together even if I have just got a nasty bang on my head from playing two-pence rugby. Pincher was a little high at his attempted conversion. The two pence piece not only cleared my thumb crossbar but struck me just above my right eye. Tucker decides that now is a good time to tell us all, that if you drop a 2p off the Empire State building, in America, and it hits someone it would kill them. He doesn't know if a half pence piece would have the same effect, but thinks you would be less likely to be hit by one as they are so small. Pincher asks how long it would take for a one pound note to drop down from the Empire State Building.

10:20am Thursday 4th September 1980

School is going so slow this week. I suppose first week back always is. Also, still seven whole weeks until next holiday. How many points will Villa have by then? At least I am in a good mood this morning, with Villa beating Leeds 3-1 at Elland Road in second leg of League Cup last night. Two more goals for Gary Shaw and one from Withey. What a partnership they are starting to form. Who needs Andy Gray? There were only 12,000 at

Elland Road. I bet Walsall get nearly that many. Still a great start to the season. Just wait until Brian Little gets fit.

My mood is even better now that Haystacks has told me we have drawn Cambridge United away in the next round. Cambridge are not even in the First Division. We beat them 4-1 in the FA Cup last season, but that was a replay at Villa Park. I was there. I remember Allan Evans scored one of the goals. We really should have won the FA Cup last season, if only Ray Stewart missed penalties. Mind you even the West Ham manager, John Lyall, didn't think it was a penalty. At least a team in claret and blue lifted the cup. West Ham used to be my second favourite team but not any more after that cheating. Second favourite is now definitely the Villa Central League team.

Thursday evening and my Shoot magazine (well Mark's and mine really) has a picture of Allan Evans on the front. That will be going in my new scrapbook. He is celebrating a goal, I think it is Gordon Cowans behind him. 'Sid' is the one Villa player who always wears long sleeves. Probably feels the cold as he's so skinny. Allan Evans always wears his Aston Villa sweatbands. Maybe I can ask for some for Christmas.

10:20am Saturday 6th September 1980

Lots of homework this weekend so I am doing it this morning instead of watching Swap Shop. History is about the end of the Romans, RE about Hindu festivals and some simple trigonometry for Maths. Maths should be easy but for some reason we have to use our old fashioned log books not our Casio calculators. Pity as it's a really sunny day so my solar powered calculator is working superbly. Decide to leave Maths and do the others first before Football Focus starts. I am a little distracted as my Shoot magazine is next to me. Instead of writing about the fall of the Roman Empire I am reading about how Liam Brady is doing at Juventus. Well, that was in Italy and the Romans were Italians.

Deliberately I skip the page on Ipswich and their great start to the season. Hopefully it won't look so great in six hours' time. Villa are playing them at Portman Road and I really think we could go top despite all their so-called 'great' players. At least all of our players are British. Ipswich had to buy two from Holland. Arnold Muhren and Frans Thijssen. I think they both know Johan Cruyff. Mind you, I might have seen him myself if Dad had taken me to the Villa v Barcelona game in 1978. Johan Cruyff scored but they still couldn't beat the Villa. Well, not at Villa Park, and who knows we might have beaten them in the Nou Camp if John Gidman hadn't got himself sent off.

I have promised my brother that I won't listen to my lucky radio today to show that I am not superstitious. I don't mind, the batteries are wearing out and I am wearing my lucky socks.

Just after half-time and Ipswich are winning despite the reporter saying Villa are dominating. One of their Dutch players (Thijssen) has scored the only goal. They shouldn't be allowed to have foreign players. I mean how will the Villa players and the referees know what the Ipswich players are saying? They could be swearing and nobody would know.

It's no good. I need my lucky radio. I go to my bedroom and put my radio faintly on but still Villa pressure without scoring. At least Wolves are losing, but the Baggies are wining well. Kevin Keegan's Southampton are also leading.

It wasn't to be. We couldn't equalise and have lost our first game of the season. Ipswich and Southampton are now two points ahead of us and for the first time this season I have no goalscorers to colour in on my Performance Wallchart. It is not going to be an easy Monday at school. At least Kenny Bellington's Liverpool didn't win.

2:53pm Wednesday 10th September 1980

On the news today there is a bit of panic. It seems Hercules, the bear from the Kleenex advert, has gone missing in Scotland. Hope he's alright. Also, apparently, war has started between Iran and Iraq. Must be confusing having two countries whose names are so similar. I suppose if they were both in the First Division that Iran would always start the season higher up than Iraq because of the alphabet. Same way as we are always ball two in the FA Cup and Arsenal are always ball one. I have always liked supporting a team whose name starts with an 'A'. Maybe that is why I like Abba as well. Big similarity that both my football team and my pop group start and end with the first letter of the alphabet. I bet Hercules is a really big bear. It can't be easy for him to hide.

Metalwork is a subject I used to enjoy until I was put in the same class as Kenny Bellington. He and his sidekick James McMullan spend all their time just messing around. My metalwork piece this term is going to be Jimmy Rimmer. Well, not a detailed sculpture of the star Villa goalkeeper, but just a stick-man model of a goalkeeper at full stretch touching the ball on to the post. So the goal posts are metal held up by metal bases, with the flying metal goalkeeper holding the ball welded against the right-hand post. I think it will look ace and I am just doing the initial sketches to get the bends in the knees and elbows right. Jimmy, is not the tallest of goalkeepers but my model will be quite long. Ron Saunders says that if Ray Clemence saves Liverpool fourteen points a season then so does Jimmy Rimmer for the Villa. Rimmer signed for us in 1977 when he replaced fitness mad John 'Budgie' Burridge. Jimmy came from Arsenal who had signed Pat Jennings and his enormous hands. Pat Jennings can hold a football in one hand. Maybe my model will be more like Pat Jennings than Jimmy Rimmer. But I will call it 'Jimmy'.

Childish Bellington is enjoying walking around with a big rubber and when people are away from their desks, or just not looking, rubbing out important parts of their sketches. I am protecting my goalkeeper sketch and have taken it with me as I go to measure the diameters of metal available. Bellington is walking closely behind me. I stop to let him pass, but at this point James

McMullan appears to my left and grabs hold of my drawing. I try to keep a tight grip but now Bellington has grabbed it as well. All three of us start pulling. Now my sketch of the 'Jimmy' model has been torn into three pieces and is totally ruined. A whole lesson's work wasted. I consider sellotaping the pieces together, but Bellington has already screwed his up and oddly started eating it. I just watch, although very tempted to push the piece I was holding into his mouth as well. I was wrong, Bellington wasn't eating it and has now taken the heavily chewed piece of paper from his mouth and placed it firmly in my blazer pocket. It is covered in Bellington saliva. I am trying to stay calm. I can't let him see how upset I am. I shall just throw the soggy chewed paper away and move on. How much saliva can one person produce?

Metalwork teacher, Mr Harpwell, is now interrogating me as to where my drawing is. I am trying to say that I didn't like it so I threw it away, but he is ranting about the importance of keeping all sketches in my portfolio. Seems that unless I have another sketch complete by the next lesson I will be in detention. I cannot allow that to happen. Detention means a letter to your parents and with the Villa playing home to the Wolves next week I don't want my dad getting a letter saying I have detention. That would surely result in no trip to Villa Park.

Spud is suggesting I tell Mr Harpwell what really happened, but I doubt any good can come of that. I was rather hoping that Spud would have been tempted to administer one of his infamous head-butts, but I guess he is still on the warning from his last one.

I suspect being expelled from school for frequent head-butting is not ideal when applying to join the police. Although, it would scare off quite a few criminals. Also, Spud has decided this year that he is very keen on Carrie Campton and is deliberately trying to show his sensitive side. I can't really tell if Carrie likes him. She does seem to snarl less when he is around. She scares me. No, I need to deal with Kenny Bellington myself. It is time to start growing up and fighting my own battles. What would Ron Saunders do?

9:38am Saturday 13th September 1980

Saturday starts with the happy news that Hercules, the bear, has been safely found. I wonder if he enjoyed his little adventure. Now I have been assuming he is a 'he' but from the pictures on the news it is difficult to tell. Although, owner Andy Robins keeps referring to Hercules as him. Obviously bears have quite small willies. Or maybe he is just a late developer like me. Perhaps he hides away in the showers too. Maybe this year my hairs will start to grow down there.

After twenty minutes of ringing I manage to get my entry of twelve goals on Guess the Goals in. I don't expect too many. Perhaps another 1-0 home win for the Villa. Surely either Shaw or Withe would grab a goal today. Villa are home to Everton while Mark and Dad have gone off to see Wolves at home to Coventry. Albion have Liverpool away. Sadly top of the table Ipswich are playing bottom of the table Crystal Palace.

For once my lucky radio is totally out of luck. Villa have lost 2-0 to Everton at home. Everton scored two goals in four minutes just before half-time. I guess dreams of being top of the league at some point this season have now totally gone. Wolves were beaten, Albion were hammered and to top it all Ipswich have gone and won again. We're not going to be anywhere near the top tonight. Guess the Goals has even added to my misery as there were thirteen goals in the end. Time to forget about the Villa and read my Roy of The Rovers. Let's see what mad little bald Hungarian manager, Viktor Boskovic, is up to in 'Hard Man'. Maybe Villa need him as well as Ron Saunders to get them back scoring goals. I don't think I will be doing my league ladders this week.

9:20am Monday 15th September 1980

Mr Walker is proving quite a popular form tutor and is also my teacher for Maths. He is nothing like I first thought and despite his uneven eyes and scruffy leather jacket is actually quite with it. During Maths, Pincher and I get him on to our favourite topic of football. We find out that Mr Walker is a Nottingham Forest fan. He has a season ticket and even went to the European Cup Final in Madrid, Real Madrid's ground, to see Forest beat Hamburg and Kevin Keegan in May. His favourite player is Martin O'Neill. It doesn't sound like Mr Walker is married. Pincher whispers that perhaps Mr Walker is gay, but I whisper back he can't be as he likes football. Anyway, who has ever heard of a gay Maths teacher, plus he likes 'The Police'. He saw them on their 'Reggatta De Blanc' tour in Newcastle a few months back.

This particular Monday morning the main talk in our form period is the school's Christmas musical production. These productions are always quite lavish and luckily with my lack of musical ability (they even made me mime playing the bugle in the Boys Brigade band) I had always avoided being part of them. This year it is to be what sounds like a Japanese opera. It's called 'The Mikado'. Apparently, according to Mr Walker, it is full of women with pale faces and knitting needles through their hair. Spud wants to be involved because he has heard that scary Carrie Campton is going to audition for one of the lead roles. So Spud is thinking of auditioning for a part called 'Pish Tush', a noble Lord. Reading through the list of parts, other male roles include some very odd names. Like Nanki-Poo and Pooh-Bah. In fact they all seem to be poo-related. Despite this Kenny Bellington says he wouldn't be seen dead in any of that "dramatic crap". So all the rest of us can breathe easy.

Mr Walker is very keen for as many of his class as possible to be part of the school's ambitious 'Mikado' production. Apparently there are opportunities to make costumes and scenery in Art classes. Also Mr Walker himself will be in charge of lighting and needs a team of lighting engineers to work with him up on the gantry. Now even though I have no idea what this entails and am not the best at heights, I like Mr Walker and think this could be a good chance to see the show for free. So I volunteer myself,

Tucker, Pincher, Noddy and Haystacks to form the lighting team. Oh, and Spud if he doesn't get a part. To my delight Mr Walker agrees straight away although he has no idea who half of these boys are.

12:40pm Wednesday 17th September 1980

Main talk at school this week is Saturday's upcoming Villa - Wolves game. Pincher and Spud both say they are going. Although Spud often says he is going to away games but never makes it. Pincher is going with his Dad and apparently he's got a ticket in the Witton Lane Stand with some of his dad's workmates who are all Villa fans. My Dad has said he will take me to the Holte End even though he will be supporting Wolves. Mark will be in the Wolves bit in the North Stand Enclosure.

Lunch time and every tournament, be it two-pence rugby or football in the playground, is Villa versus Wolves. I have to admit to being outnumbered so at one point it becomes Villa/WBA against Wolves. Amazingly Spud can do no wrong and even manages to score a header in the playground from near the half-way line. Admittedly, Haystacks went down in slow motion and did appear to be waving to his girlfriend, from the year below. At two-penny rugby, Spud manages to score a try with his first flick. Although, there is some argument as to whether he still has to push it two more times. His conversion is perfect.

In Games, the badminton doubles match with me and Noddy against Pincher and Paul Best ends up as Villa against the

Wolves. Wolves alarmingly won 11-2. Noddy might have big ears (we call him Noddy because Big Ears was a friend of Noddy's) but the shuttlecock still kept shooting past them. Even our English Literature lesson turns into a Villa v Wolves contest. The challenge is as we are reading chapter four of 'Lord of the Flies' that I would have the letters AVILLA and Spud the letters WOLVES and the first one to hear words mentioned starting with all the letters in their words would win. I thought I had an advantage with mine having two A's and two L's but Spud makes it clear I can only count each word once. The letters are quickly ticked off and I am left waiting for a word starting with 'I' and Spud one starting with 'O'. Surely Villa would finally win. But no. Kerry Mason reads 'Piggy rails on them for being irresponsible'. Both Spud and I cheer, but I quickly realise he wins with 'on'. Mrs Bruce is giving a rather puzzled and disapproving look at the pair of us.

Even at home it is Villa against Wolves and things are going no better. Mark playing me at Subbuteo destroys me and my Villa team with an 8-0 beating. I have no idea what Jimmy Rimmer was doing for the last three goals. I never did like the spring on the rod goalkeeper. I can't blame the rod for the fourth goal though. The Dennis Mortimer own goal when my hand wasn't even on Jimmy's rod. The last two years I had been school Subutteo champion yet at home Mark would always beat me. Well, he is three years older. Maybe in twenty years he will start to feel the pace and I will be fitter and younger. There was no Subutteo at school this year because the boy who organised it was sick of me winning every game and this year decided he would go home for his lunch.

The pre-Wolves v Villa battle continues as it is time to plug the old Binatone TV Master Mark 4 into the back of my black and white portable and challenge my brother to a best of three tournament. We will play a game of tennis, then a game of squash and then finally a game of football. Although all the games are pretty similar with the square ball and stick men the skill for each game varies. The Binatone is looking a little dated now and I am saving up to buy a second-hand Atari. For now I am just going to play the best I can - the pride of Aston Villa FC is at stake. I don't really think my sixteen-year-old brother saw it in quite the same light, but for me the tennis match was Tony Morley against Emlyn Hughes. The scoring isn't like tennis and instead you just get one for each time the square ball goes past the edge of the other player's side of the screen. We have to play it upstairs because the bleeps drive Mum mad. We were playing on advanced with the smaller sticks and faster ball but Tony Morley was on fire. Before Emlyn Hughes could get the pace of the game the Villa were 6-0 up. Well, he is coming to the end of his career. He wouldn't get in the Liverpool team now with Hansen and Phil Thompson. I was celebrating too early and 'Crazy Horse' under the control of Mark hit back to make it 6-4. But luckily there is no time for any more points and it is one win to the Villa. Next up is squash with the main difference being you just have to stop the ball going off the right hand side of the screen. This time I am going to give Gary Williams a go and he will be up against Willie Carr. As I won the first game my stick gets to stand in front. Definitely an advantage as you can put the other player off. Again the 'Villans' strike first and are leading 4-2. Unfortunately at this point it all goes wrong. Maybe Gary was suffering from lack of matches this season. Colin Gibson was keeping him out although the Express & Star says he might play against the Wolves. The squash game just goes from bad to worse as Mark smugly wins by 9 points to 5. So it is on to the championship decider.

The last sport on the Binatone TV Master is appropriately 'Soccer'. This time it is two against two although your two sticks move together. Both teams have a goalkeeper and a forward. The game is very quick and my reflexes will need to be at their best to give Villa victory. Obviously Jimmy in goal but who to play up front? Do I go for Peter Withe so he can head them in, or the more skilful Gary Shaw? Maybe I made a mistake picking Tony Morley for the tennis as he could have been ideal at this. I bet Tony Morley would do well on Superstars. I decide that the strength of Peter Withe is needed. Although, apparently he did once play for the other Birmingham team as well as Wolves. Villa, according to Haystacks, who knows everything, is Peter Withe's tenth club. Mark still doesn't know I am naming the players in the game but he has Paul Bradshaw and John Richards playing for him. I wasn't going to pick Andy Gray. Hopefully one day he will see the error of his ways and return to his Villa Park home.

Hopefully not at £1,500,000 this time. What a lot of money that is. It must have taken ages to count. The whole Villa team now probably didn't cost £1,500,000. I must work out how much they did cost after this game.

The 'Soccer' game starts dreadfully with Jimmy Rimmer conceding four goals in less than a minute. Peter Withe did score a great goal off the top left corner of his stick but the final score of 8-1 is an embarrassment. Just hope it isn't going to be a sign for Saturday. If Villa lose by more than two goals I am not going to school on Monday. Perhaps I should start showing signs of feeling ill now. No, that would never work as Dad might say I was too ill to go on Saturday. Oh, the pressures of being a West Midland football fan.

1:03pm Friday 19th September 1980

Final lunchtime before the big game and I have managed to sneak my 'Jimmy', electronic football game, into school. So Pincher, Noddy, Tucker and I have found an unused classroom to play it in. We have clipped on the plastic yellow footlights in each of the corners of the red stands and put on the team name boards on each end. First game was me against Pincher so my end said 'Aston Villa' and Pincher had 'Wolves' his end. Spud did comment that both names seem to be in Wolves colours. At least my seven players all have blue rings around their claret lights. We have to explain several times to Tucker how the game works. How you have to secretly select the number of the player you are passing to and if the defender guesses that number they win the ball. Then if an attacker clicks the shoot button then the defender has to click the S/G, shoot button, or it is a goal. I love the way the player's lights flash in sequence when they score and it plays 'When the Saints go marching in'. Pincher is trying to be clever and shoot with his number 4, he said it was George Berry, but as it does sometimes if you try a long range shot, it gives a penalty to me. Supreme penalty taker 'Sid' Cowans steps up, I press number 2 and the 'Jimmy' game plays "When the Saints go marching in'. 1-0 to the claret and blue. Pincher is soon back on the attack and yet again decides to shoot with George Berry. This time though I don't press S/G to move Jimmy Rimmer and the ref doesn't give a penalty. So George Berry scores a rare goal (in the right end) and the Wolves are level. At this point we have some unwanted visitors.

Kenny Bellington and his sidekick burst into the classroom and without saying anything Bellington takes one of the plastic floodlight pylons and snaps it in half. Tucker protests, but this just encourages the demented thug. Bellington then proceeds to put the 'Aston Villa' team name board in his pocket before rigorously pushing the 'Jimmy' game off the table and walking out. Bellington has stolen Aston Villa. The battery compartment is cracked as well and it looks as if it might need some serious repairs. We aren't really supposed to be in the classroom and I shouldn't have brought 'Jimmy' from home so there is no one that we can really complain to. It is probably just good that Spud wasn't here or it might really have kicked off. Spud is busy auditioning for 'The Mikado'. We had all had to promise not to go and watch him as he was going to try to sing a solo. Pincher agrees to call the match a draw, but Tucker is still trying to work out how George Berry had scored.

7:14am Saturday 20th September 1980

Finally, today is match day. The big local derby; Aston Villa against Wolverhampton Wanderers. I am awake really early but then I didn't sleep much. Far too excited and nervous. For the Villa lads it might be just another game but for me it is everything. Lose and it will be horrible coming back in the car with Wolves-supporting Dad and brother even before I have to go to school on Monday. Surely Ron Saunders can stop our losing run. He always ends his programme notes asking for 110% from his players but today he needs them to give at least 120%. It is going to be a long morning. Dad says we are leaving at 12.45. I'm worried that might be too late and try to get him to leave at 12.30. You never know with the M6 traffic. Dad says he's cooking us gammon and chips for 12 o'clock. Not sure I am going to be able to eat. There's just too much at stake. Anyway, I've always been a slow eater. Wonder what time Ken McNaught and Allan Evans have their lunch? I expect they're big eaters. Hopefully they will have the Wolves forwards for breakfast. Worryingly I have never seen the Villa beat the Wolves at Villa Park. It still hurts to think about the 3-1 defeat in March. Especially as Wolves played so many reserves players. Never did like Norman Bell.

Trying to make the long wait until midday go quicker so I'm listing the cost of each Villa player who has played this season to see if it comes to as much as the price we sold Andy Gray for.

We have used just fourteen players. Williams and Deacy played in the opening game and Geddis has been the substitute. This is the list then: Rimmer, Swain, Gibson, Williams, Deacy, Evans, McNaught, Mortimer, Bremner, Shaw, Withe, Cowans, Morley, and Geddis.

Now, I know that Shaw, Gibson and Williams all came through the youth team so they didn't cost any money. They were all in the youth team that reached the 1978 FA Youth Cup Final. It said so in my programme from last year's FA Youth Cup Final. When we beat Manchester City 3-1 before losing 1-0 at Maine Road to win the cup on aggregate. I wonder how many of last year's winning youth team will end up in the first team like Shaw, Gibson and Williams. I bet Ray Walker makes it he looks quality, Mark Walters is quick and I like Paul Birch as well, even though he is so little.

So no money for Shaw, Gibson or Williams and I know Eamonn Deacy came over from Ireland for a trial. Oh, and of course Gordon 'Sid' Cowans has been with the Villa since he was 15. It said that in Shoot last year. 'Sid' played in both the replays in the 1977 League Cup win against Everton. Five players down and we still haven't spent a penny. We spent £500,000 on Peter Withe, he's our record buy, the previous highest being £300,000 for David Geddis from Ipswich Town. So I'll add that on. With the £200,000 we gave Burnley for Tony Morley, summer before last, makes a cool one million pounds. I am sure we also paid £200,000 for big Ken McNaught after he played against us in the League Cup Final. That leaves Jimmy Rimmer, Allan Evans, Des Bremner and Captain Dennis Mortimer. Maybe I can find out more in my Football 79 sticker album. The one that I got with Shoot with Cyrille Regis and Bob Latchford on the front. I never did complete the 1980 album. I was just missing the Arsenal shiny team badge, Trevor Brooking and an 'Andy Anderson and Jackie Campbell' sticker from Partick Thistle. I'd have paid for the extra ones but I am saving up to buy an Atari console with Space Invaders.

It took a little researching including looking in Mark's 1979-80 Rothman's Football Year Book but eventually I have the prices I need. It seems Jimmy Rimmer cost £70,000, Kenny Swain £100,000 from Chelsea and Dennis Mortimer cost £175,000. That makes £1,545,000, good job I am in top set at Maths. Still missing Des Bremner and Allan Evans though. Have to guess at around £45,000 for Allan Evans from Dunfermline. He was apparently signed by Ron Saunders as an understudy for Andy Gray as he was a centre forward in Scotland. Ron Saunders seems to like changing forwards to defenders as Kenny Swain was a winger at Chelsea. Oh, found the Des Bremner fee in the season preview from the Express & Star. He came from Hibernian, in Scotland,

and was £275,000. So that makes a grand total of £1,875,000. I have totalled this up inside the back cover of my Homework Diary, but in pencil so I can rub it out. If I can just find a rubber. Well, Mr Walker will understand. I bet 'Cloughie' spent more than £1,875,000 on his Forest team. Well, they paid Birmingham £1,000,000 for Trevor Francis. Ron Saunders is cleverer though, not only did he get £1,500,000 selling Andy Gray, but also £500,000 for John Deehan to the Albion and £750,000 for one of my favourite players, John Gidman. So Ron Saunders has made a big profit. I'm sure the Chairman (Harry Kartz) is pleased with Ron's transfer dealings. We'll have to wait to see if they were good dealings. At least they have helped pay for the new stand. The days of 1977, with Gray, Little and Deehan were so good. Just hope Brian Little recovers from his injury soon. It doesn't look good. At least Alex Cropley is back playing for the reserves.

Dad lets us watch Football Focus on Grandstand while eating our gammon and chips on trays. Mum isn't happy with this and eats hers in the kitchen. She says she's praying for a draw. Apparently Football Focus's Bob Wilson used to play in goal for Arsenal before Jimmy Rimmer. No mention yet of the Villa - Wolves game and it's really time we were going. I've got my Villa rosette ready but won't pin it on until I am in the ground. Mum's made some strawberry yogurt using her new yogurt maker, but we haven't got time to eat it. Just as well, as despite the lumps of strawberries I really don't like the yogurt from the yogurt maker. The Braun yogurt maker is a square plastic thing and contains eight little plastic cups. You have to pour some milky liquid into the cups, add some form of fruit (if we're lucky), plug the box in, and eventually the cups contain what Mum calls yogurt. It isn't like you get from the mobile shop, this yogurt is yucky. It tastes sour and tangy and with whatever fruit is added into the mix it tastes horrible. I am not really a fan of yogurt anyway, but this stuff is just sickly. Good job we have to go. Mum gives us all an orange-flavoured United biscuit bar for half-time. I am not going to eat mine if we are losing.

We walk around the outside of Villa Park to see Mark into the new impressive North Stand. So different to the old Witton Lane. It even has a roof. I'm still not sure how that big roof stays up with only the end walls, no pillars. There are quite a few Wolves fans all in their orange. No sign of Pincher and his dad. A long line of police are now stopping us from walking towards the Holte End. Dad politely asks one of them if they can let us through, they ignore him and we have to walk all the way back around the ground.

I guess next time I see Mark we will probably both be in different moods. For some reason I am suddenly not feeling confident. If we had being playing them two weeks ago it would have been different. However after losing to both Ipswich and Everton it doesn't look so good. Even worse now that I have just heard two Villa fans saying that Gary Shaw definitely isn't playing. Instead David Geddis is going to play his first game of the season. Well, I suppose he is blonde like Gary Shaw. Ron could have chosen Terry Donovan, he's scored four in just four reserve games. Mind you Geddis has played in the FA Cup Final. He made the Ipswich winner for Roger Osbourne against Arsenal in 1978. Surely playing against Wolves won't frighten Geddis. He only scored three goals last season and Gary Shaw has already scored five this season.

As we walk back around to the Holte End, past the fantastic-looking Trinity Road entrance, it's great to see everyone wearing claret and blue. I love the smell of the hot dogs, the shouts from the programme sellers and the chatter of the Villa fans. It feels so magical. To think next season, the 1981/82 season, I will have my own season ticket here at Villa Park. I can see people at the turnstiles with their white season ticket books out, ready to tear out the ticket from the book that matches the number above the turnstile. Today is '21'. Probably alphabetically, Wolves is number 21 in the teams Villa play. Hope when I have a season ticket I don't pull the wrong ticket out. A Juvenile Season Ticket this year is £14 which is good value for 21 games. It's only the league games though.

As we won last game I came to against Leeds I am determined to do the same things. This includes going to the same programme seller just on the corner of the Holte End at the Trinity Road side. Dad's not impressed because there's quite a queue and he thinks there would be less of a queue inside. Still he finds me 35p for a programme. Typical, it has Gary Shaw on the front. The one player who won't be playing today. Great picture though, of him controlling the ball on his head yet still having clean hair. Such concentration in his face. I wonder if the Villa Photographer, Terry Weir, took that one. Haystacks says he used to live next-door to Terry Weir's uncle. But then Haystacks does claim to know everyone. He even said his sister went to school with Wayne Clarke and that she has met his elder brother Allan Clarke several times. The Clarke family did come from Willenhall so I guess it makes sense. Andy Gray, not surprisingly, is not mentioned in the programme. Luckily he's out injured today. Which Mark says means Norman Bell is back to torment the Villa.

The Holte End is starting to fill up, we manage to find the same crash barrier as against Leeds. Surprisingly I see a couple of lads in front with Wolves scarves. The stewards shouldn't allow that. Didn't they see the big metal claret and blue sign saying 'HOME SUPPORTERS ONLY'? Still an hour to kick-off and the groundsman is painting the white lines on the pitch towards the Witton Lane Stand. Looking down at the impressive new stand opposite, the North Stand, it's so modern. The claret seats can still be seen and the light blue ones which make up the AV logo. I wonder if you pay more to sit in a light blue seat. This new stand dominates the view, it's at least twice as high as the old Witton Lane Stand one on its left. I like the Witton Lane Stand and all the advertising boards along it. There's a new one this season for 'ASH'. 'ASH' apparently stands for 'Action on Smoking and Health'. Kenny Bellington says he smokes twenty a day. Hope none of the Villa players smoke. I am sure Mr Saunders wouldn't allow that. The slogan on the advertising board is 'KICK SMOKING – AND SCORE'. I suppose that means stop smoking and you will be better at football. The Witton Lane Stand, like the opposite Trinity Road Stand, still has old wooden seats. Trinity Road Stand is definitely the best-looking one. It has fantastic pillars and the curved blue balcony has claret trim. It is more like something you would find at the theatre. That's where all the important directors sit and the press people. I wonder what time Harry Kartz gets to his seat. He probably has his dinner inside first. Apparently in the Executive Boxes they serve food and drinks. Proper food not just pies. Chairman Harry Kartz nearly lost his job last year. Two of the directors including the former chairman (Doug Ellis) tried to gain control, but Harry Kartz and Ron Bendall fought them off. Not sure who agreed to the sale of Andy Gray.

The Wolves fans are now starting to fill terracing at the bottom of the North Stand, but I can't see Mark from this end of the ground. Hope the Villa fans in the seats above him don't throw things down on the Wolves supporters. Just glad I am in the 'Home' end this time. The Holte End is building up too. I have tried to read my programme, but too nervous. The next ninety minutes really do mean everything.

It says on the front of the programme that 'Bradford & Bingley Building Society' is sponsoring the game. Why doesn't my building society - 'The Staffordshire' - do things like that? Perhaps I should ask my grandad if I can move to the 'Bradford &

Bingley'. I must read Ron Saunders team notes at least. He's not happy with the performance against Everton, but generally thinks we are playing sparkling football. He's confident that we can win today as long as the players give 110% effort and we the supporters back them. Ron, you can count on my vocal support. Although, I won't sing any naughty words to any of the songs as my dad would probably make me leave the ground. Lots of pictures from the Everton defeat in the programme. I didn't know Everton had 'Hafina' on the front of their shirts. I thought it was only Liverpool and Coventry who had shirt sponsors. You wouldn't catch Villa having some company's name on the front of their magnificent claret shirts. Just their famous round badge on the left side and the small Umbro logo on the right. That's real class.

It says in the programme that Noele Gordon from Crossroads, who's a big Villa fan, will be presenting a specially equipped minibus to a handicapped children's association from Sutton Coldfield. Hope it doesn't ruin the turf. Never watched an episode of Crossroads in my life. I always run out the room when the theme tune starts. My grandad always has to watch it when he stays with us. Lots in the programme about the new 'Aston Villa Sports and Leisure Centre'. Apparently, David Coleman from Sportsnight was at the opening. It has six squash courts and 'Team Fiat' one of the country's top basketball teams are going to start playing there. Maybe they need to become my basketball team. I can have the Villa for the football, Somerset for cricket and Team Fiat for basketball.

I will have to read about Tony Morley later as I have to clap the Villa players as they come to warm up in front of us. There is Peter Withe, Colin Gibson and Des Bremner. The Wolves fans are cheering now because a couple of Wolves players have come out. Think one of them is Rafael Villazan, their Uruguayan defender. Don't know much about him, but at least he has the word 'Villa' in his name. Pity it is a 'Z' in his surname not 'F'. Be great if his name was Rafael Villafan. The other Wolves one looks like Dave Thomas. He's played for England, as have Wolves players John Richards and Emlyn Hughes. The Villa only have one England cap and that is for Jimmy Rimmer, long before he joined us.

Time to kick-off is going so slowly, but the seats in the top of the North Stand are starting to fill up. I can't see many light blue seats now. The Villa players are all back in the changing rooms probably hearing Ron's last-minute tactics. Hopefully telling Tony Morley to take on Derek Parkin because he's old. And Jimmy please don't let Norman Bell score.

At long last it's 2.50 and out comes the Wolves team. They go to the end where Mark is and lots of gold coloured tickertape is thrown around from the crowd. Some of the Villa fans boo but I'd better not. My dad gives them a little applause, but nobody finds this unduly odd. Now here come the mighty Aston Villa, running on to the pitch led by Dennis Mortimer with substitute

Eamonn Deacy following on at the back in his tracksuit. Just hope nobody gets injured. I wonder who would go in goal if Rimmer got injured. Maybe big Allan Evans would do well. Surely Deacy wouldn't go in goal.

The booing returns as the referee and his linesman run on. They must get bored of wearing all black and being booed. Looking at the back of my programme I see in the 'Officials' section that the referee is P.G. Reeves, from Leicester. At least he didn't have far to come. The linesman with the yellow flag is from Gloucester and the other one with the red flag is from Burton-on-Trent. I am sure Uncle Jacob lives in Burton. He probably knows the linesman. Apparently, ref Mr. Reeves used to play for Leicester City but now he is a Sales Director for a hosiery company. According to my dad that means he sells tights.

Looks like our Dennis has won the toss and Villa will be kicking towards to Holte End in the second-half. The way they like it. Hopefully we will be winning by then. I wish Gary Shaw and not David Geddis was wearing No.8 today. Wow, that was incredible! Gordon Cowans just chipped the practice ball from inside the penalty area straight into the bag that kit man, John Paul, was holding open on the sideline right by the dugout. I have never seen such skill. The kit man did not move the bag at all and the ball went in without touching the sides. Did anybody else see that amazing piece of genius?

The waiting is finally over as John Richards kicks off for the Wolves. Come on the Villa.

Villa have started very brightly and Gordon Cowans has played a brilliant long ball into the feet of Tony Morley. Morley's advancing down the wing, pulls the ball across. It's a GOAL! I am jumping in celebration. No idea how the ball ended up in the net. It never reached David Geddis, must have been an own goal. The whole Holte End is bouncing. What a great start. It isn't even 3.05! My Dad is clapping while shaking his head. Bloke behind says it was an Emlyn Hughes own goal. But what a ball by 'Sid' Cowans. He is so much better than Glenn 'tight shorts' Hoddle. Surely the Villa can now score a few goals today. I am looking forward to Monday at school already.

Half-time and it's still only 1-0. Despite a number of good Villa chances. I think if Gary Shaw was playing, it would be more than just one. Jimmy Rimmer hasn't had to make a save. I could have played in goal for Villa in that half. But still Wolves are only one goal behind. It will be a very nervous second-half.

The half-time scores are being clipped on. Game A is 0-0; back of my programme says that is Birmingham v West Brom. Walsall are at Fulham and game Z, but they haven't put that score on yet. In fact half of the scores aren't on yet. I bet at a lot of grounds we are Game 'A' today and it will read 1-0. The voucher on back of my programme is number '5' today. It says, "VILLA VOUCHERS ARE VALUABLE, SAVE THEM". But I am not going to cut up my Villa programme. I put them all safe in the drawer under my bed. Some people I notice have crossed Gary Shaw's name out on the Villa line-up on the back of their programme and written Dave Geddis. How can they vandalise their precious Aston Villa matchday magazine? The voucher team picture shows nineteen players. The ones who haven't played yet this season are Terry Donavan, Nigel Spink, the reserve goalkeeper (made his only appearance for the first team at Forest last Boxing Day), fit again Alex Cropley, super Brian Little and very ginger-haired Brendon Ormsby. Coach Roy MacLaren is in the Villa tracksuit on the right and Physio Jim Williams the other side. Of course, the main man Ron Saunders is in the middle of the front row. I bet Ron is now telling them off now for not scoring more goals in the first-half.

Second-half is starting and Wolves are bringing on Wayne Clarke and looks as if Norman Bell has gone off. Villa are continuing to attack, but the Holte End seem subdued. Wolves are on the attack and it looks like Allan Evans and Kenny Swain have got in a bit of a tangle. No. 11 for Wolves (Mel Eves) manages to get the ball past Jimmy. I don't believe it. All this play and we are drawing and Wolves players have even scored both goals. I can just see Spud's face on Monday. Surely we can't lose to the Wolves again.

Less than eight minutes to go now. Free kick to Villa right in front of us. A chance for 'Sid' Cowans to float one in. Maybe Allan Evans can get his head on it, or Peter Withe. Come on, Villa, we need a goal. Your Holte End expects. Fantastic ball in by Gordon Cowans... surely... Yes. Yes. Yes. David Geddis with a great header. Bradshaw just watched it sail into the bottom corner.

Great goal. What a delivery from Cowans. Even my dad is celebrating that one. That must be the best goal I have seen close up. Now surely we can hang on.

Waiting by the Trinity Road gates for my brother to return. I am delighted but obviously will try not to gloat too much as I know Mark will be feeling miserable. But I am absolutely buzzing. It might only have been 2-1 but this Villa team are looking good. Just maybe this year they could win a cup or get back into the UEFA Cup. Although, if they win the FA Cup they will be in the Cup Winners Cup. Maybe I am getting carried away.

Back in the car and Dad for some reason has Radio Two on instead of Radio Birmingham. He says he likes the theme tune for Sports Report. Mark is quiet. The 'mind your car' lad seems really pleased that Dad has given him two ten- pence pieces. I think Dad's just relieved that his window hadn't been smashed like the three we had seen on the walk back.

We're all silent during the classified results. Seems Mr Walker will be pleased as Forest have beaten Leicester 5-0. The baggies have only drawn at Birmingham. Blooming Ipswich have won again and Everton have hit five at Crystal Palace. Palace are rubbish this season. Looking at the table in my programme I am trying to work out our new league position based on the radio scores. Of all the teams who started on seven points this morning only Everton and Villa have won. So we will go at least three places up. In fact four because Arsenal on eight points have lost. I think we will be 6th but Ipswich will be three points clear at the top. They are going to walk away with the title this year. Not surprising as they have got eleven internationals. Saying that though, if Villa had beaten Ipswich two weeks ago, instead of narrowly losing, we would both have eleven points now. I thought it best not to say in the car how low down today's results leave the Wolves in the table.

10:00 Monday 22nd September 1980

Registration is rather pleasant this morning. Bellington is missing. Hopefully he's off ill. If I am lucky something which takes weeks to recover from. Mr Walker is wearing his Nottingham Forest tie and describing to us in detail the Forest goals from Saturday. It's all very light hearted and even the unexpected locker check cannot dampen the mood. Mind you, Mr Walker is more laid back than the other teachers and even turned a blind eye to 'The Blue Lagoon' poster in Stephen Hayes' locker where Brooke Shields only has her boobs covered by her long hair. Apart from Marie Parker's locker all the girls' lockers were so much tidier than the boys' even though they tended to have more stuff. Not counting Paul Hampton's locker which was the neatest of all the lockers and everything was sorted by colour and then piled by shape, with the smallest item of that colour being on top.

Just as Mr Walker was getting to my row of lockers Bellington turns up. So much for a happy week. Bellington grabs my locker key from my hand and savagely kicks it under the lockers. I just watch as it flies off across the floor passing under several rows of lockers before I lose sight of it. I have no idea where it has landed. I am stuck with a locker I can't open for inspection. I try to explain that I must have dropped the key, but it's obvious that Mr Walker is suspicious that I am hiding something. I don't know what he thinks is in my locker, but he says that unless I can show him by tomorrow the inside of my locker that he will have to report it to the Head of Year.

That's the bell sounding for first period. So no more time for locker checks. There hadn't been time to check Kenny Bellington's. With the knees of my school trousers on the dusty floor I begin looking under the rows of lockers for my small key. Suddenly the day gets better, Grace Taylor, a quiet but pretty girl, holds her hand out to me and passes me a locker key. She smiles but then just turns and walks off. That smile reminds me so much of the girl on the horse on holiday. Surely that wasn't Grace Taylor, was it? The horse riding girl seemed more bouncy. Although, I have never seen Grace without her fastened blazer on. That blazer could hide any type of chest. I have never spoken a word to Grace either and thinking about it I can't really recall her speaking. Yet that smile just was so warm. What was this key she had given me? Is it her locker key, a spare locker key, or has she found my locker key? Best way to find out is to try the key in my lock. Great, it works. What just happened then?

Lunchtime is great, the whole gang are together, even Haystacks. Apparently his new second-year girlfriend is having netball training on a Monday lunchtime now, she's been picked for the school team. It is great that only my team (Villa) won at the weekend. Noddy and Tucker had gone to Walsall together, only to see them lose to Rotherham United. Although Tucker, to my delight, is much happier trying to wind up Pincher and Spud about losing to the Villa. Haystacks seems happy with Albion's draw at the Bluenoses.

Even though Villa are now 6th and his Baggies only 11th Haystacks is claiming they will finish above the Villa. He says they have better players. Haystacks is insisting that Bryan Robson is better than any Villa midfielder. I think this is wrong, but as Robson plays for England it is difficult to argue. Haystacks also considers Derek Statham and Brendan Batson better fullbacks than Kenny Swain and Colin Gibson. Statham's played for the England Under-21s, even though he is already 21, and Brendan Batson's in the 'England B' team. Neither the Villa full-backs can match that. Haystacks does concede that Evans and McNaught would probably give John Wile and Alistair Robertson a close match. Especially as John Wile is 33 now. He is old enough to be our dad. I tried to fight for the Villa midfield, but Remi Moses and Gary Owen are both regulars for the England Under-21s. Mind you, so is Gordon Cowans. It is always difficult to argue against Haystacks because he knows so many football facts. It's good he's back part of the 'Local Gang' lunchtime debates. I have missed him. I have to agree that Cyrille Regis is potentially a better player than Peter Withe. Even though I don't think Regis has been quite the same player since Laurie Cunningham left to join Real Madrid last year. Thank goodness Cunningham isn't still at the Albion. Haystacks takes the opportunity again to remind us all how he once saw the Albion win 5-3 at Man Untied and what a great goal Cyrille Regis scored that day. Noddy's pretend yawn doesn't go unnoticed and Haystacks' enormous left forearm sends Noddy flying.

Spud suggests that despite their defeat on Saturday Wolves are still the best team in the Midlands. His main argument is that they are the current holders of the League Cup. Fair point I suppose. Villa need to win a cup. Tomorrow's the next round of League Cup so hopefully we can beat Cambridge and take a step closer to glory. Haystacks picks up the stunned Noddy, whose big left ear is now rather red.

Still Haystacks is praising his Albion players. He's bizarrely claiming that Ally Brown is better than Gary Shaw. This is my chance to quote that Gary Shaw is the current 'Robinsons Barley Water Young Player of the Month'. At least all of us agree that Jimmy Rimmer is a better keeper than Tony Godden, although Pincher does suggest that Paul Bradshaw is better than them both.

The argument of which local team is the best is getting pretty heated. Obviously Noddy and Tucker accept it isn't Walsall. Haystacks decides to ask both Noddy and Tucker to choose who they think is the best team. A touch unfair, really, as Haystacks is bigger than the two of them combined. Not surprisingly, both wimps decide it is Haystacks' blue and white striped lot. They are both wrong. Villa are the best and Ron Saunders is a better manager than Ron Atkinson any day. I have to defend my team. So I suggest a bet on which of the three teams will finish highest at the end of the season. I am rather shocked when Haystacks says we should all put a one pound note in. That is much more than I was thinking. But I have to back my team. Spud and Pincher will both put 50p in so it will be a pound for each team. It doesn't seem fair that Tucker and Noddy aren't involved. So Haystacks thinks we should include Walsall, but take their final position in the Third Division. Noddy is not convinced but has agreed that he will put in 30p and Tucker will pay 70p as Tucker gets more pocket money than him. So that will make £4 altogether. Quite a large amount for the winner. Pincher insists we write it all down. He wants to clarify what happens if Walsall finish in the same position as the top team in the First Division. Spud thinks it should go to who has the most points followed by highest goal difference. Haystacks points out that Walsall play four more games in the Third Division. So I suggest that if level on positions we take the highest average points per game as the winner. Tucker questions which average this is: Mean, Mode or Median. Apparently he has all three buttons on his new scientific Casio calculator. We decide that this is all getting too difficult and if Walsall did end up in the joint top place we would just split the money between the Walsall fans and the other team. For some reason Spud thinks I should be in charge of all the money and that everyone should pay it to me by the end of September. I am more than happy with this because I could put it in my

Staffordshire Building Society account for eight months and get about 30p interest. So even if Villa didn't finish highest I will still only be 70p down.

Mr Walker comes into the room and asks what we are discussing. We don't mention the bet but tell him that we are trying to decide who the best Midlands team are. His face lights up and he quickly says, "No competition". Just as I thought he was going to agree it is the mighty Aston Villa he says, "The current European Champions, Brian Clough's Nottingham Forest". We all tell him they aren't a proper Midlands team, but he won't have it. I suppose the fact they are currently second in the league doesn't help our argument either. There is no way Mr Foster is joining our bet. If Villa had Brian Clough and Peter Taylor in charge we would probably be second in the league. But it is nice to have a teacher who really follows football. Even if he does always correct Noddy when he calls them 'Notts Forest'.

The main reason Mr Walker had been looking for us is to tell us that we had all been accepted on 'The Mikado' Lighting Team. Well, all of us except Spud who will be starring on the stage. Then Spud tells us that he hadn't got one of the main parts. Instead he is going to be in the onstage choir. Noddy bursts out laughing saying he has heard the onstage choir are all wearing girly red silky dressing gowns. Spud seems happy to wear a girly red silky dressing gown because Carrie Campton will be on the stage with him. Although Carrie Campton won't be in the choir she is far too important.

Mr Walker tells us that next week he will show us the 'Lighting Galley'. He hopes we don't mind heights and climbing up a small metal ladder. I just hope Haystacks fits up a small metal ladder.

7:07pm Tuesday 23rd September 1980

Today went well and we even got to act out some pretend football violence in Drama. I played a St. John's Ambulance man. One of the girls groups did a romance at a disco. Grace Taylor was dancing very nicely at the back. She can certainly swing her hips. I am sure she looked at me at one part as well. Maybe I should try to talk to her at some point. No idea about what. I don't expect, being a girl, she likes football. She doesn't seem to have any real friends. Seems a bit of a loner. Mind you some of the girls in 3FO can be horrible. They are really mean to some of the other girls. Several of them won't talk to Jemma Jones because she hasn't got her ears pierced. I wonder if Miss Cresswell, I mean Mrs Cresswell-Farrington now, has her ears pierced. I will check in History tomorrow. She doesn't seem to smell the same now she's married. I suppose she doesn't have to try to attract men any more. Maybe Mr Cresswell-Farrington doesn't let her smell as nice when she is outside the house in case other men fancy his wife. If I ever get married I will make sure my wife doesn't change because we're married. Not sure if I would like her to be a Villa fan or not. It would be nice to go to the games together, but she might be offended by all the rude words. You don't get many girls at football. Mind you, no one's language is as bad as Shirley Ashcroft's. She was sent to instant detention last week for what she said to the dinner lady who only gave her seven chips.

Slightly nervous about the League Cup tie tonight at Second Division Cambridge United. They were only elected to the league in 1970, when according to Haystacks they replaced Bradford Park Avenue. Cambridge have done really well since to reach the Second Division. Mainly because they had the now Albion manager Ron Atkinson in charge. Cambridge finished 8th last season, but they lost to Shrewsbury Town on Saturday so probably a good time to play them. Only one game in this round, unless there's a replay. Wolves, the holders, played Cambridge over two legs in the last round and surprisingly lost to them. Villa won't lose though. This is our season a win the League Cup. We won the first ever League Cup against Rotherham in 1961, so it makes sense we will win it 20 years later in 1981. At least the Wolves beating Forest last year means that we still hold the record for most League Cup wins. We are the greatest cup team as we have also have won the FA Cup more times than anybody else. I am so proud to support such a fantastic club.

Oddly when I turn on Radio Birmingham at 7:30, after I'd finished writing my English essay about life in the year 2000, there is just music. Oh no, seems they aren't covering football tonight. I can't believe it, they haven't got a reporter at the Abbey Stadium. I should have checked earlier. I am scanning right across the medium wave, but no football on any of the channels. Well, one sounded like it could have been football but it was in Welsh and a very weak signal.

A great idea has just come to me. My parents have just had a new portable colour telly in their bedroom. It came with a remote control so you don't have to press the buttons on the side when you are feeling lazy. Mum doesn't trust the remote though so still gets out of bed and presses the buttons. Best of all you get Ceefax on it. You don't just watch Ceefax flick through when no other programmes are on, but proper Ceefax. You can choose which pages you actually want to see. I asked Dad if I can use the TV in their bedroom to check the Villa scores and although he wasn't keen, a few tears seems to have done the trick. I can watch their TV but I have to stop by 9:30.

The colour portable TV seems to take even longer than usual to start up and I decide to keep it on BBC1 as I don't know how ITV's Oracle works and where they keep the football pages. Ceefax Sport Grandad has shown me is on number 300 and Football is always on 302. I press the 'TEXT' button and then 3-0-2 to go to the football index. There to my delight it says 303 'League Cup Scores'. So I click to 3-0-3. What amazing technology. There are 3 pages for the League Cup scores. Cambridge United against Aston Villa is on the second page but it seems to take an eternity to go through the pages. After five minutes of play all the games seem to still be goalless, although Mark did warn me that the scores aren't updated that quickly. The pages seem to change about every thirty seconds. So it should be back to the Villa page at 19:39:20. Other games tonight include Mr. Walker's Forest at Bury and an East Anglia derby between Ipswich and Norwich. Wouldn't it be great if Bobby Robson's Ipswich get knocked out? Birmingham are at home to Blackburn Rovers and Liverpool are hosting Swindon. I am not even sure who is playing for the Villa. The Express & Star suggested they would be unchanged from the team that beat Wolves as Gary Shaw is still not fit. Anyway, David Geddis deserves another go after scoring that great header.

Oh a goal, Ceefax is great. Who needs a lucky radio? It reads Cambridge 0 Aston Villa 1, and beneath says Tony Morley. We are on our way to Wembley, perhaps we can score quite a few goals tonight. I stamp my feet on the bedroom floor with delight, but nobody seems to hear me, or they are just ignoring my triumphant celebration.

Ten minutes, then fifteen minutes of Ceefax watching go by. I even tried clicking away for short times to other pages. I even flicked on to the news page and read about a CND rally at RAF Greenham Common. Tucker had mentioned something about that today. Apparently his Aunty Carol has gone there to protest about the use of nuclear bombs. She's a little strange, wears really long skirts and she doesn't eat chicken. I suppose we should all stand up for peace. More important things to think about now, so I flick back to page 303. It eventually comes to page two of three. It is still 1-0 to the Villa. I expect it is all Villa though and the next goal won't be long. I missed a couple of goals at Bury it seems. Forest are suddenly winning 3-0. Perhaps we will draw them in the fourth round.

It is now two minutes past eight. I think that Ceefax has made a mistake. The page with the Villa match on states that there have been two more goals. One in the 6th minute and one in the 17th. What had taken them so long? Surely it must be wrong. The score reads Cambridge 2 Aston Villa 1. Goals from Tom Finney and Spriggs. I thought Tom Finney had retired years ago. I am sure my grandad talks about him in some final years ago. How can we be losing to Cambridge? Hopefully there have been more goals since or Ceefax has got it wrong.

Now it is nearly twenty past eight and most games now have HT to the right of them which I think means half-time. Liverpool and Forest are both certainly going through. Looks like Villa are the only First Division team losing. Ipswich Norwich is all First Division but they are drawing. The Villa game now has HT by it. Still forty five minutes to turn it round. If we don't win then we should manage a draw. I will get Dad to take me to the replay next week. Then we can thrash them like we did in the FA Cup replay last season.

Ceefax is so slow but time does seem to be going surprisingly fast. All the other games keep having goals. Forest have now scored six and Liverpool five. But still it says Cambridge 2 Aston Villa 1. Maybe it is difficult to get in contact with Cambridge, that's why the goals in first-half took so long to appear. Probably Ceefax has much better links to Anfield. Come on Villa, give us a goal.

9:05pm and still no change in the Cambridge - Villa score. I have the score and all the scorers from all the other twelve games now embedded in my brain. Forest are seven up, but still the Aston Villa name is followed by 1. It is 9:10pm now, so injury time has probably started. An FT appears after Ipswich 1 Norwich 1. That'll be a difficult replay for Ipswich. But I won't care about the League Cup unless we score. Birmingham have beaten Blackburn Rovers, West Ham have won at Charlton Athletic and even Notts County have walloped QPR. I don't want an FT by the Villa game yet. Watford have beaten Sheffield Wednesday. They obviously don't play well on a Tuesday. Like the Villa we are a team that usually plays on a Wednesday. 7-0 final score for Forest and 5-0 at the end for Liverpool. Still the Villa game goes on. I check my lucky radio again but still BBC Radio Birmingham is playing blooming old music. Barnsley have won, Coventry have won and Manchester City have gone through. No shocks apart from the one that might happen at Cambridge. Bristol Rovers 0 Portsmouth 0. The only game without a FT is Cambridge v Aston Villa. It is now 9:27. They must have finished now.

I am waiting on page 303 on Ceefax to click back round to the second page. Oh no, my worst nightmare has come true. FT is now at the end of our game. Final score 2-1. We are out of the League Cup. I can't believe it. My eyes are filling up with tears. I bravely manage to hold them back for a short while. I switch off my parent's telly and go to my bedroom closing the door behind me. I shall just get into bed and if anybody comes up pretend to be asleep. This is horrible, I really thought this was our year. I don't want to go to school tomorrow.

9:28am Wednesday 24th September 1980

How is it I had to follow last night's game on Ceefax, yet this morning everyone knows Villa lost to a Second Division team? Even the bus driver seemed to give me a knowing look. Mr Walker even made mention to it when he took the register. Changing my surname to Cambridge. He also mentioned seven whenever possible. Asking for 'SEVEN volunteers' or telling us there were, 'SEVEN minutes to the bell'. I have to accept that despite Villa's good start to the season we are still miles behind teams like Forest and Liverpool.

At lunchtime Pincher and Spud take it in turns to wind me up about our embarrassing cup exit. I had only had two days to gloat over beating the Wolves and now this happens. Tucker and Noddy also joined in with making fun of the Villa. Just hope Albion get knocked out tonight to Everton. Eventually the conversation changes when Tucker announces that his Aunty Carol got arrested at the CND Rally. Apparently, she had done something disgusting with a policeman's helmet. I do think Tucker's exaggerating when he suggests she could get ten years in prison though. Paul Waterhouse's mum stole four coats from

C&A and she only got a fine last winter. It must run in the family because Paul Waterhouse himself got caught pinching sweets from Woolworths in Willenhall.

In Metalwork I have reached the point where I'm bending the metal rod to form the shape of the goal. I have got all my sizes worked out. Just need to heat the rod first and then I can bend it using the vice. Bellington has written 'Cambridge rules' over the back of my Homework Diary, but I'm not rising to his bait. He has actually written 'Camebredge rules', but I best not comment on his poor spelling. Instead I focus on bending my metal goalposts. Hammering gently trying to achieve a 90-degree angle. The problem is that I am too aware that Bellington is in the vicinity along with sidekick McMullan. They are just waiting for an opportunity to strike. I try to keep my guard up and make sure I am always in sight of Metalwork teacher, Mr Harpwell. Unfortunately Mr Harpwell has become deep in conversation with one of the girls who is making a hanger for her jewellery. Bellington and McMullan have spotted this and are coming over. I probably should be protesting more as Bellington takes my bent metal rod out of the vice. I can't work out what he has planned. How can I know what somebody who can't spell 'Cambridge' has planned for me? Bellington holds my hands out and James McMullan passes me my model. Well, not really passes. He pushes the very hot bent corner against the palm of my hand. Quickly I drop the rod and Bellington lets go of me. Mr Harpwell turns round, sees the disturbance and is marching towards us. Now I'm apologising to Mr Harpwell for dropping my metal rod. Very quickly I'm walking over to the sink and running the coldest water possible on to my burnt palm. The burn isn't too bad and hopefully my Boys Brigade First Aid training has helped to prevent a blister, but it is really painful.

The rest of the day isn't going well. Holding my pen in my hand is very uncomfortable with my burn and I generally feel totally miserable.

It is raining heavily as I walk from the bus. By the time I reach home I am completely soaked. I can feel the rain running down the inside of my charcoal grey trousers and into my socks. Even my pants are drenched. I try ringing the bell, but the house looks oddly empty. My mum should be in but for some reason she isn't. Something is wrong!

Mrs Manford, from next-door, comes out and calls me in to her house. She is a lovely lady but not who I want to see now when I am soaking wet. Mrs Manford says my parents have had to take my grandpa to hospital. That's my dad's dad, as we call my mum's dad Grandad to save confusion. With her arm around me Mrs Manford is telling me there is nothing to worry about. It doesn't really seem like that. How long will they be and how long will I have to sit in these wet clothes? Mrs Manford offers me a bath and hot drink and says I can borrow one of her daughter's tops. I just accept the hot cup of tea.

Villa are away at Crystal Palace today. Gary Shaw's back for David Geddis but a number of players have been suffering with a stomach bug. I was hoping they could beat the bottom team quite easy but doesn't look as if it will be that way with this bug.

We have all been to see Grandpa in hospital and he says he is doing well and hopes to be back home soon. He chatted to me about the Villa and to Mark about the Wolves. He seemed the healthiest person on the ward. We finally got home at 4:10. I protested about going but Dad said it was important to Grandpa. Villa are still goalless at Palace and the Wolves are losing to table-topping Ipswich. Albion have just taken the lead against Southampton. Surely Albion can't beat Southampton? It's certainly time to get my lucky radio on and see if it can find Villa a winner.

That's the goal horn. It signals another goal at Molineux and yet another Ipswich goal. Can anyone stop them? Liverpool seem the only team capable, they have now scored four against Brighton. Still no Villa goal; obviously that bug isn't helping.

Five minutes left in all the games. Looks like Albion are going to hang on and we will have to settle for a draw. Oh wait, another goal horn. Probably another Ipswich goal. No, it is at Selhurst Park. Come on Villa, please don't be losing. It sounds quite noisy there, probably a Palace goal. No, it's 1-0 to the VILLA!!! Goal scored by the Birmingham-born Gary Shaw. I fall off my bed in celebration landing on an unsuspecting Action Man. What a great time to score.

With my Roy of The Rovers comic half read I am entering today's 1-0 away victory on to my chart and colouring in another square for Gary Shaw in the goal scoring section. That is his sixth goal this season. Villa are now 4th in the league and heading for Europe after eight games. Nottingham Forest lost at Arsenal so we are now above Mr Walker's team. We are level on points with the two Merseyside teams, but they both have superior goal differences. Everton won 5-0 at Coventry today. McBride and Latchford both scored two. It seems that my former Villa hero, John Gidman, was yet again the Everton star player. Graeme Souness scored twice for Liverpool. All three of us though are four points behind Ipswich Town. They beat Wolves 2-0 with Alan Brazil and Paul Mariner scoring. Wolves are now in 19th place so only a place above the relegation zone. Albion might have won but they are still only 10th, although only two points behind us. Walsall are 14th in the Third Division. So if the season finished now I would be winning all the money.

3:17pm Sunday 28th September 1980

With the Villa winning at least I can enjoy Sunday without dreading Monday morning at school. After finishing my History and English homework there is still ten minutes until Match of the Day starts at 4:55. It is still odd seeing Jimmy Hill on a Sunday afternoon. He looks far more casually dressed on a Sunday afternoon. Jimmy Hill's pointed beard looks extra neat today on that famous chin. Grandad always says you could get pickles from a jar with that chin. The main game today is the Manchester derby. Still no Villa on this season. We are not even on the opening credits although there is a scene from a semi-final at Villa Park. Still a great goal at start from Norwich's Justin Fashanu. I like the policeman with the binoculars bit as well.

Wolves against Ipswich is the third match, but Mark doesn't seem very keen on watching it. The lower league game is Portsmouth against Fulham. In the Manchester United - Manchester City game City have just equalised from a Steve Daley corner. Still cannot understand how Wolves got so much money for him. I suppose if they hadn't then they wouldn't have been able to afford Andy Gray. Then probably wouldn't have won the League Cup. I think Andy Gray and Gary Shaw would make a fantastic partnership especially with Tony Morley supplying the crosses. But Peter Withe is doing well, so maybe it was all for the best. Steve Coppell is playing well for Manchester United. He scored their first goal. Maybe Ron Saunders could buy Steve Coppell and play him instead of Des Bremner. There must still be some money left from all the selling.

Match of the Day has finished so I am in my bedroom and going to listen to the Top 40 on Radio 1. They should have reached about number twenty by now. I need to retune to Radio 2 on the FM as Radio 1 always moves on a Sunday night.

Apparently FM is in stereo and Medium Wave isn't but my radio only has one speaker so there isn't much difference.

We are on number seventeen on the chart countdown. It is Sheena Easton's '9 to 5'. The singer who was featured in that TV programme, The Big Time. The one hosted by Ester Rantzen from That's Life. They were trying to find a pop star and found a Scottish lady, Sheena Easton. '9 to 5' though was apparently also sung by Dolly Parton, but Tony Blackburn says this is a different song. It starts 'My baby takes the early morning train'.

David Bowie is at fifteen with 'Ashes to Ashes'. What's that all about? I wonder if I have missed the Abba song. I am cutting out the report on yesterday's game from the Sunday People to put in my Villa scrapbook and some pictures I found in Football Monthly as they count down the chart. Mum will be pleased Cliff Richard is in the chart at number twelve with 'Dreamin'. She likes him because he is a good Christian boy.

The newspaper is saying that because of the Villa bug yesterday Ron Saunders gave the players a drop of brandy before the game. Bet they enjoyed that. At least it kept them going right to the end to score the winner.

Sheena Easton is number nine, as well, with 'Modern Girl'. Obviously a lot of people watched The Big Time. Will Kelly Marie's 'Feels like I am in Love' still be number one? The Sunday People seems to be obsessed with Prince Charles taking a young woman on the Royal Yacht Britannia. She's called Diana Spencer, apparently a Lady and related to Barbara Cartland who writes the books Grandma likes. Surely she is too young for Prince Charles. She's only 19! We always joke that Noddy is related to Prince Charles because of his enormous ears. Imagine a man who had both Prince Charles's ears and Jimmy Hill's chin? I suppose if you also give him Barry Manilow's nose then you really would have a monster. 'Prince Jimmy Manilow' could be a character in Doctor Who. Maybe I could give him a Kevin Keegan perm.

The new 'Disco' song is now number eight. 'She is D, delirious. She is I, incredible. She is S, superficial....' Not really sure what 'Superficial' means. I think Grace Taylor is pretty 'incredible' but not sure if she is 'Delirious'. I think that is some kind of sickness bug. I have been thinking more about Grace Taylor lately. Definitely need to aim to say 'hello' to her next week. Maybe I am ready for a girlfriend. As long as she doesn't interfere with my Villa supporting. The Villa boys need my full focus this season if they are going to qualify for the UEFA Cup.

Wolves might be going out of the UEFA Cup on Wednesday. They are playing the second leg against PSV Eindhoven, from Holland, and are trailing 3-1 from first game. Spud is confident though and says they will win 2-0 and go through on the 'Away Goals' rule. Mark and Dad are both going on Wednesday but Dad's moaning because it isn't covered by their season tickets. Does that mean I will have to pay for my own European tickets next season if the Villa do finish in the top six? Mind you, depending who wins the FA Cup and League Cup there could be more places. Although, Arsenal finished 4th last year and because Forest won the European Cup and Wolves won the League Cup for some reason they didn't qualify for Europe. I don't really understand why, Haystacks did try to explain it to me. So this season only Wolves, Manchester united and Ipswich are in the UEFA Cup. West Ham are in the Cup winners Cup with Liverpool and Forest in the European Cup. Mind you Arsenal only have themselves to blame for missing out. They had two chances but lost in the Cup Winners Cup Final to Valencia, on penalties, and then let Trevor Brooking score a headed goal against them in the FA Cup Final. West Ham a Second Division team and they beat both Arsenal in the Final and us cheatingly in the Quarter Final.

Number five is 'Madness' and 'Baggy Trousers'. I quite like that song. If I was musical at all the saxophone is an instrument I would like to play. Musical ability in my family stopped firmly with Mark. Hence my bugle miming in the BB band. I suspect Grace Taylor is quite musical because she goes out of Chemistry every other Tuesday morning for a clarinet lesson with the appropriately named woodwind teacher, Mr Blower.

Kelly Marie is no longer number one, she is down to number four. Maybe Randy Crawford who was number two, with that flying away song, will be number one this week.

I am looking at next week's fixtures in the 'Pools' section of the paper to try to see where the Villa could be if they beat Sunderland at home next Saturday. Liverpool are at Man City so maybe they won't win that. Everton have a hard game against

Southampton, but they're at home. Ipswich are at home to Leeds so I can't see them losing that. I write my predicted scores by each of the games. Although my 4-0 to the Villa is perhaps a touch optimistic. I'll put Albion down to beat Crystal Palace as everybody seems to. Wolves have Birmingham at home and I am predicting a 1-1 draw there.

'The Police' are the new number one. I didn't even know they had a new song, but 'Don't stand so close to me' is straight in at number one. Mr Walker will be pleased. Not sure myself if I like it but sounds very 'Police' like.

I have managed to get Dad to let me watch The Professionals tonight even though it is Sunday night. I told him everyone at school watches it. Doyle has just found out that the woman he is going to marry is wanted by CI5 for drug smuggling. Plenty of shooting which Dad thinks is excessive. Doyle says, "Cowley's got a slack mouth!" But the best line is probably when Bodie is sniffing the air and says, "Have you bought a cat" then says "Oh, it's your aftershave!"

End of September Top of Division One			
1.	Ipswich Town	Pl: 8 Po: 15	+13
2.	Liverpool	Pl: 8 Po: 11	+11
3.	Everton	Pl: 8 Po: 11	+9
4.	Aston Villa	Pl: 8 Po: 11	+2
5.	Forest	Pl: 8 Po: 10	+9
6.	Sunderland	Pl: 8 Po: 10	+8

Villa September League Results	
6th Ipswich Town (a)	0-1 Lost
13th Everton (h)	0-2 Lost
20th Wolves (h)	2-1 Won (Hughes (og), Geddis)
27th Crystal Palace (a)	1-0 Won (Shaw)

Chapter Three (October)

Just watching the highlights of Wolves beating PSV on Sports Night, far too tired really but as Mum said I could stay up and watch it then that is what I am doing. I know the score because Mark returned quite dejectedly. Wolves only managed to win 1-0 so they have gone out 3-2. Mel Eves scored just after half-time, but Wolves couldn't score that vital second goal that would have put them through. Not quite sure if I wanted them to get through or not. I suppose I wouldn't have minded. Spud deserves some good luck at the moment. He has had a bad week. Firstly, he was demoted to the offstage choir for 'The Mikado' and then Carrie Campton started going out with Ben Robinson because he is black and she thought it was cool to have a black boyfriend. Ben Robinson is really nice, if a bit of a swot. Spud did not take the news well but is determined to get Carrie to notice him. He having his dyed jet black hair highlighted at the weekend to make more of an impression.

All change with the football managers. Terry Venables is no longer Crystal Palace manager and now he manages QPR. So Tommy Docherty ('The Doc'), who once managed the Villa, has been sacked at QPR. Grandad always claims that Tommy

Docherty says he has had more clubs than golfer Jack Nicholas. Well, he needs to find another one now. Another of 'The Docs' famous quotes was, "Villa have amazing support. If you hung eleven Villa shirts on a washing line five thousand fans would turn up to watch them!" Grandad also remembers Tommy Docherty when he took over the Villa and promised to get them out of the Second Division. Apparently, next year they were relegated to the Third Division.

Man City have finally sacked Malcolm Allison as well. That will teach him to spend so much money on Wolves players.

10:45am Thursday 2nd October 1980

Maths has finished and Mr Walker's taking us lighting lads into the school's Theatre Hall. Really it is just a big hall where there is a stage, but it is labelled as 'Theatre Hall'. All big events that aren't done in the Sports Hall take place here. Always better when we are in here as we have chairs instead of having to sit on our bottoms on the hard cold concrete floor. This is the first time I have ever gone behind the impressive red curtains. Tucker, Pincher, Noddy, Haystacks and I follow Mr Walker, in his old much-worn brown leather jacket. Still not sure if Mr Walker is cool, or just very scruffy. He points to a metal ladder in the corner behind the stage. It is attached to the wall with a curved metal guard around it. It isn't just Haystacks who is worried he will not be thin enough to get up this now. I don't mind heights, but climbing this ladder reminds me too much of some of my worst

PE nightmares. At least it isn't a rope ladder and I hopefully won't be burning my inner thighs this time. Tucker is keen and quickly sprints up the ladder. Next up goes Noddy who is a little slower. He was probably making sure he protected his ears. I am going to follow Pincher up with Haystacks bringing up the rear, hopefully. Pincher is doing well until his locker key on a chain comes out of his pocket and bangs me right on the top of my head. I try not to show it, but that was a hefty blow. Just hope I don't suffer any long-term brain damage.

We're all on the gantry now. High up, overlooking the empty stage. It's even higher than I had expected. We can nearly touch the ceiling. Mr Walker is excitedly showing us all the mounted spotlights. There are twelve, all pointing at different places on the stage. Suddenly I begin to think that this lighting work might not be quite as easy as I had anticipated. Perhaps not quite the giggle I had signed up for. There are several signs saying 'Silence'. I can't remember the last time Tucker was silent. Tucker is even now trying to explain to us how the lights work even though Mr Walker has not said a word. Tucker is nearly believable, but I don't think having a large pole and gently pushing each one individually seems likely. Pincher has found two control-boards though that look like one of those mixing desks that Pop stars use. Each board has six sliders that go from 0 to 10. Mr Walker seems excited to find that Pincher has discovered what he calls the 'Piano Board'. Oh dear, no one said musical instruments were involved. Mr Walker explains how each of the lights would stay in a set position and this 'state of the art' console would decide if the light was off or on. Ten being fully on and 0 being fully off. Sometimes apparently we would have to have it on but not on full brightness. It was now that Mr Walker start to lose us. He's suddenly referring to 'Auto-transformer dimmers'. Haystacks is complaining about feeling sick. I think he has been looking down too much or maybe that third plate of roly-poly pudding at lunchtime has caught up with him. Mr Walker continues his detailed talk anyway and to me it is actually starting to make sense. It seems that all the spotlights have a plastic slide in front of them to tint the light. These are called gels and are either steel blue (odd as steel isn't blue) or straw yellow. We will be following the script and bringing sets of steel blue and sets of straw yellow on at the times marked in the script. Noddy is looking confused, but before he can ask Mr Walker for clarification, Haystacks is very sick. I am not sure it is lucky or not, but he is sick over the galley on to the stage below. At least nobody is walking underneath. Probably wouldn't have gone down well during a real performance. Mr Walker is pretty cool and just tells us all that if anything major happens like that on the night just turn all the slides to 0 and it is called a 'blackout'. Pincher suggests we call it a 'sickover' in future. Haystacks is a very funny colour.

4:34pm Saturday 4th October 1980

What a great afternoon. My lucky radio is working overtime. Villa have just scored a fourth goal at home to Sunderland. Allan Evans scored the first and the fourth. Tony Morley and Gary Shaw have also scored.

4-0, what a final score. It sounded like Villa could have scored lots more, but it is still our biggest win of the season. Today my radio has been lucky for all the West Midland teams. Wolves, Albion and Walsall all winning. Seven goals in the Walsall game. Wish I had been at the Villa today. At least it is on Match of the Day tomorrow afternoon. Maybe if I ask Grandad he will record it for me on his new video recorder. We are supposed to be having the same model, but Dad still hasn't got round to buying it. Grandad's is a VHS one, although Pincher says Betamax are much better. Grandad's can record at LP which means a 180 minute tape can record 360 minutes of telly. A whole night of programmes. It does go black and white if you fast forward or pause it on LP though. Perhaps I can put together a tape of every time Villa are on telly this season. Either on Match of the Day or Star Soccer. I think they should rename it 'Match of Yesterday' now it is on a Sunday.

Mr Walker will be pleased, Nottingham against Manchester United is on Star Soccer. Hugh Johns is the commentator. Mr Walker won't be so happy that Forest lost though. We are still 4th in the league but at least our goal difference has improved. Six wins out of nine games this season and only blooming Ipswich have won more. If only we had beaten them. At least I am not a Manchester City fan. All that money Malcolm Allison has spent in the last two years and they still haven't won a game.

3:09pm Sunday 5th October 1980

Sunday afternoons are perfect. Reading all about the Villa win in the pink paper and The Sunday People, lying on the living room floor after a very yummy Sunday lunch. I had an extra two Yorkshire puddings with my beef. I do like having Grandad here on a Sunday afternoon. Not just because he brings the papers. It is great to chat to him about the football and the cricket. The John Player Sunday League season has finished now, that was always good to watch together. Especially as this season my team Somerset fought for the title with Grandad's team (Warwickshire). Mind you I only really follow Somerset because Ian Botham plays for them. I would probably be a Warwickshire fan too otherwise. Not sure when I started following Ian Botham, but my previous favourite England player was Tony Grieg. I like players who bat and bowl so they are always involved. During the summer holidays I spent a lot of time at Grandad's watching the England Test matches. Tucker and Spud are both anti-cricket and think it is the most boring game especially Test cricket. But it fascinates me. Even though five of the six tests, against the West Indies, this summer did end in draws. Well, it did rain a lot. I don't think being England captain is really helping Beefy (Botham). It seems ages since he scored a century. Perhaps playing football for Scunthorpe isn't helping either. At least they play in claret and blue. It would be great if we drew Scunthorpe in the FA Cup and Ian Botham actually played at Villa Park. Mind you he will probably be off captaining England in the West Indies. That isn't going to be easy. I wouldn't want to face Garner, Holding, Roberts and Marshall. If Peter Willey goes on tour we might get that great quote again, "The Batsman's Holding, The Bowler's Willey".

Another reason for liking Somerset is because they have the world's best batsman playing for them, Viv Richards. When I play cricket with Mark I try to copy Viv's batting style by leaning on my bat. Although, sometimes I do a Mike Gatting where I stand straighter and keep raising my bat and continually striking my feet. When we play French Cricket in the back garden though my style is more Chris Tavaré. Then I can stay in a long time without the ball striking my legs.

Time at Grandad's watching cricket is special. Not only due to his exceptional tea making, with his whistling kettle. Grandad makes me feel so important. I was only seven when Nan died and to be honest I don't remember her ever being well. Mum says she spoilt me and Mark, but it seems a very long time ago. Grandad is great and he makes me laugh. He's my mum's dad and she was an only child. I think deep down Grandad probably wanted a son as he is very technically minded. Apparently, he did buy Mum a train set when she was a little girl, but she never really took to it.

Over the past couple of years I have enjoyed two special full days at Grandad's house in Bilston watching Somerset in the Gillette Cup Finals. That's the sixty-over one that's played at Lord's. In 1978 Somerset lost to Sussex, but last year we beat Northamptonshire. Viv Richards scored 117 and Joel Garner got six wickets. It was close though, until Allan Lamb was out. It was so good being just me and Grandad, especially with the way he has the sound from his posh telly coming out of the same speakers as his radio tuner. It is like it is in stereo.

I always love the smell of my Grandad's house. It smells of him with a hint of Lifebuoy soap. His kitchen is tiny, but he has a pantry and a coal shed. His greatest pride, apart from his VHS video recorder, is his garden. It goes back forever and has two lawns. Mark and I still play football on the top lawn with garden canes each end for goal posts. It's the ideal size for one against one cup finals and the grass is probably better than Wembley's. We do have to be careful not to knock the petals off Grandad's impressive roses. Sometimes apples might fall on our heads while we're playing. This means they are ready for picking from the best apple tree I have ever known. Every other year we spend a day picking all these apples. Filling the tin bath, buckets and baskets with the thousands of apples that keep us in pies and crumbles for the rest of the year. Although my favourite fruit in Grandad's garden is always his rhubarb. There is nothing better than eating a stick of Grandad's rhubarb with a pot of sugar. The combined sour and sweet taste is just perfect. As is my Grandad. Especially as he had set his timer on his video to record Match of the Day today. He has even apparently found me a special tape that he is going to use just for recording Villa football on for me. Mark, of course, has a tape as well, as Grandad always treats us equally. I was delighted to hear that Grandad had set the record up using the LP speed so we could get lots on the tape. Just hope he has set the timer right. Maybe we should have taken him back to his house to check. He says he set it to start five minutes before and end ten minutes after just in case it was running late. Just need Dad to get on with buying our video recorder so I can watch these recordings and maybe record some myself.

Five o'clock now and time for Mum to leave the room as Grandad, Dad, Mark and me da-da along to the famous Match of the Day theme tune. Is there a better theme tune? To my annoyance Villa aren't the main match. For some reason that is Middlesbrough against Norwich. At least with Boro' winning 6-1 there are plenty of goals. In fact with Villa scoring four that means the two games will have eleven goals between them. That doesn't happen very often. There is also Bournemouth against Scunthorpe from the Fourth Division. Not sure how many goals are in that game or if Ian Botham played. Back in March it was against Bournemouth that Botham made his footballing debut as centre-half. I remember Scunthorpe were trailing 3-1 when he came on and it ended up 3-3. Ian Botham nearly scored the winner right at the end.

John Motson is commentating on the first game. He's definitely my favourite commentator. John Platt is back in goal for Boro' and the player with the funny name Bosco Jankovic is playing. Captain Tony McAndrew has scored really early on, according to 'Motty' on his 200th appearance, and John Motson is always right. He is the Haystacks of the BBC. The Middlesbrough red Adidas shirt is just like one of those Mum bought me from Sportsco. I like Adidas tee-shirts, but think Umbro is the best kit maker. The England Admiral one is very good too. The new England top is great, with the big blue and red stripes across the top. Just above the Three Lions badge. I am sure Gary Shaw and Gordon Cowans would look perfect in one of those England tops.

An own goal from Norwich defender Clive Woods makes it 4-0. 'Motty' said it was an own goal straight away and the slow-motion replay, with the 'R' on the screen, confirmed he was right. Just checked in 'The Sunday People' and I see Middlesbrough are now 11th and Norwich are 19th. John Fashanu scores at the right end. Incredibly his tenth goal of the season and I thought Gary Shaw was doing well. Australian Craig Johnson has now scored the fifth. Come on, must be time for the Villa soon. A great goal from Bosco Jankovic. John Motson sums up by saying it was an old fashioned football score when games used to have lots of goals.

Now to see the Villa spank Sunderland. Mark decides he doesn't want to watch this high quality performance. Barry Davies is the commentator this time. What a great goal! Allan Evans with a fantastic half volley. You can tell he used to be a forward. Another good ball in by Tony Morley after Dennis Mortimer has found him. Evans raises his two fists with his Villa sweat bands on his wrists. Grandad and Dad both agree on what a good goal that was. Wish I had been in the Holte End yesterday. Tony Morley somehow scores number two with a long shot that seemed to fool the slow Sunderland goalkeeper, but it is all Villa. Match of the Day haven't shown a single Sunderland attack. Will we see Jimmy Rimmer at all? Morley hits the bar and even substitute Eamonn Deacy is getting forward. Barry Davies keeps mentioning the fact that Peter Withe is still to score at Villa Park. He comes close quite a few times. Once he is past the keeper but the Sunderland defender on the line keeps the ball out. Aston Villa are ripping them to pieces. Even Dad is impressed. Middlesbrough might have scored six but they didn't dominate like this. Good save from another Allan Evans chance. He could have had a hat-trick. Amazing skills by Gordon Cowans in the penalty box. He lays it off to Gary Shaw - 3-0. Sunderland goalkeeper maybe should have saved the miss-hit shot, but great Villa move. What a player 'Sid' Cowans is. Hope Ron Greenwood is watching. If 'Sid' had played against Italy in the European Championships then we probably wouldn't have lost and been knocked out. He is still only 21. So I am sure a long England career is ahead of him. A Cowans cross from a short corner and Allan Evans scores with a header. That is all four then. It should have been more like ten. I can hear the Villa crowd chanting 'We are going to win the League'. Despite his Wolves allegiances my grandad sings along, although his false teeth don't seem to join in. Maybe we have got a chance to win it, but there are so many other good teams with lots more experienced players. Teams like Liverpool, Forest, Ipswich, Manchester United and even the Albion. The Villa have won a few cups in the last thirty years, but we have not been champions since 1910. Grandad was only three then. It is a long time ago. We have had two World Wars and England have even won the World Cup since then. The most important thing is this Villa team is just getting better and better. Apart from Jimmy Rimmer they are all under 30 and can play together for at least the next four years. Peter Withe is 29 but still seems quite fit for his age. Must be a chance that before I leave school Aston Villa could win the First Division title. This year though I will happily settle for winning the FA Cup for an 8th time.

9:20am Tuesday 7th October 1980

French teacher Miss Tully has joined us in our form period with Mr Walker. The two of them are getting on quite well it seems. Miss Tully can be quite intimidating, especially when she is teaching French, but Mr Walker seems to have got her giggling. The morning has started well, because when Grace Taylor walked past my desk she had smiled at me. I took this as a good sign and even managed to say, "Hello". She nodded back and smiled even more. She always moves very elegantly and has nice teeth.

Mr Walker explains why Miss Tully is here. It seems she is here to advertise a five-day trip the school are organising to France in January next year. There are 30 places on the trip to a French city called Saint Malo, which is in Brittany. I guess Brittany is like a county. Mr Walker appears to be volunteering himself to go on the trip to help. Miss Tully is surprised by this but says she will see what she can do. I have never been outside of England. Well, apart from Scotland. Oh and Wales. With my poor French ability this probably isn't for me, but it might be worth thinking about. Miss Tully gives us all letters to take home and emphasises it will be the pupils who send the forms back first with the £10 deposit that will get the limited places. Bellington announces that you won't find him eating snail legs. Mr Walker hesitates then seems to decide not to correct Bellington. I am just relieved that Bellington isn't considering the trip. My brother went to Paris a few years ago so I think my parents would pay for me to go. I overhear Grace Taylor talking to Michelle Pearson, she's saying she'd like to go as she wants to do French at O-Level next year. So maybe I should go. Will have to check which Villa games I would miss, as I don't think my lucky radio will work in France.

Lunchtime and Spud is quite excited about the French trip. He says Carrie Campton has already put her form in as Miss Tully told her own form class first. Spud is also very cheerful because Ben Robinson has dumped Carrie. It seems he didn't like her family when he went around for tea on Monday. Spud has also been moved into the top Maths set today. Really great news to have Spud join me in the top set. He worked so hard copying all my answers and yet making it look like his own calculations. It would be good to spend five days in France with Spud. He'd keep me safe from any violent French students. Apparently we have to spend a day in a real French school. Maybe both Grace Taylor and Carrie Campton can come and the four of us can have a 'double date'. What is double in French? Tucker, who is in top French set, claims it is 'deux fois'. Noddy confirms this is correct after checking his chewed up pocket English to French dictionary. Tucker reminds us that he is so good at French because his grandad was based in France during the Second World War. To this Pincher and Spud burst into song singing the theme to 'Dad's Army'. 'Who do you think you are kidding Mr Hitler...? '

9:00am Wednesday 8th October 1980

The 702 is late again. It is 8:55 already. I have my Saint Malo trip form and deposit to hand in. Just hope I am not too late. My parents convinced me I should go. Obviously they will be glad of a few days without me. I have only been away from them twice. First time was when I stayed over at Pincher's then the other time was Boys Brigade Camp. Then Mark was with me. If I get a place I will be missing the Villa playing Coventry away. But we always beat Coventry so they can manage without me and my radio for one match.

When I finally get into school Bellington has decided to sit in my usual seat. The only available seat is next to him. I hesitate, but Mr Walker tells me to get a move on. So I sit by Kenny Bellington. I am polite and say 'Hello' to Kenny. He grunts back.

Despite my best attempts to give Mr Walker my trip form and money he tells me I need to take it to Miss Tully's office at break time. I soon realised that putting the envelope on my desk was a mistake because Bellington thought it would be amusing to hide it from me when I looked to see if anybody else had brought their form in. I could tell straight away he had taken it, but could not obviously see where he was hiding it. My protests were met with a telling off from Mr Walker. He commented on how first of all I arrive late and then I misbehave. Totally unfair. I mean it isn't my fault if the 'School Bus' is always late. Then I saw that Bellington was sitting on my brown envelope. I tried to yank it from underneath him but it ripped.

Mr Walker, who's obviously in a bad news, shouted, "That's it! One more whisper from you and you are in detention".

How unfair! I am the innocent party here. Bellington hands me his part of the ripped envelope which now contained a ripped form and a ripped cheque from my dad. How am I going to explain to Dad that I need a new cheque and I am probably too late for the trip anyway? I decide it is easiest just to forget it and tell my parents that all the places had gone. Kenny Bellington seems to be finding this all very funny. He will get his comeuppance one day. Perhaps I should get Spud to head-butt him.

As we are walking out of Mr Walker's classroom I am tapped on the back, it is Grace Taylor. To my delight she wants a word. Obviously I am doing something right. But it isn't a long chat. Grace, with her smiling face and lovely shape, asks to me to meet her at 12:10 in the Science section in the Library. Wow, what is happening here? She even touched my right arm as she left.

History with Mrs Cresswell-Farrington and looking at what the Romans have given us. Richard Fox shouts out, "Up Pompeii" and the class laugh. I am miles away though. Partly at Old Trafford for tonight's game, but mostly on my lunchtime 'date' with Grace Taylor. I glance over to Grace and she is stroking her dangly earlobe. They are very pure and unpierced. Her short brown hair means I could see her smooth neck above the top of the collar of her blue blouse. There is a mole-like spot just underneath her chin, but it does not distract from her beauty. What are her plans for our lunchtime meeting? Grace never says a lot and I don't even think I have ever heard her speak in a lesson. There's so much I want to find out about Grace Taylor. But maybe I need to focus more on the Villa tonight.

Results last night didn't go well. Liverpool beating Middlesbrough 4-2. Bosco Jankovic scored again, but Terry McDermott scored two for Liverpool after Kenny Dalglish had scored their first. I think Liverpool must still be favourites for the league, again. We can't compete with a midfield of Graeme

Souness, Ray Kennedy, Terry McDermott and little Sammy Lee. Liverpool have won the last two titles so I guess if they win it again they will get to get to keep the trophy. They won it in both 1976 and 1977 as well. In fact only teams managed by Brian Clough have won the League apart from Liverpool since 1974. Liverpool even won it in 1973. No wonder there are so many glory-hunting Liverpool fans, like Bellington, at school. Liverpool manager Bob Paisley has won even more than Brain Clough and he didn't even manage anywhere else first. Haystacks says Paisley is from the 'Anfield Boot Room'. Not really sure what this means but it seems it all goes back to former manager Bill Shankley who started the Liverpool dominance. Shankley had the famous quote about how football is more important than life and death.

Everton also won last night so the pressure is really on the Villa. Everton won 3-1 at Brighton. Wolves lost 4-2 at Southampton and Southampton didn't even have Kevin Keegan playing for them. Former Villa captain Chris Nicholl scored though.

Ipswich aren't playing tonight in the league, they have to replay their league cup tie with Norwich. If Liverpool can score four past Boro and Boro scored six past Norwich then how many could Ipswich score tonight?

It is 12:05 and I am in the Library waiting for Grace. I got here early to make sure the Science section was empty. I had to tell a couple of First Years to move out. They had been checking out some of the interesting pictures in that Human Biology book.

The school Library is quite large and stays open until 4pm. It is quite state-of-the-art as well. There is a new Acorn BBC computer but you have to be in the 'Computer Club' to use it. James Lopez did give me and Pincher a demo once but it looked very complicated and you have to know the exact commands. Also the green colour of the writing gave me a headache.

As I pretend to read a Physics book about radio frequency I am tapped on the back by Grace's delicate finger. We smile at each other and it is a little awkward. This is all very new for me. Yes, I had been kissed on the swing-boats by Jenny Perry in the 4th year at Junior School but nothing else since. I was very taken back when Grace then handed me a £10 note. Not quite what I had expected. What was I supposed to do with it? Grace smiled again, but this time revealing a brace on the top row of her teeth. I hadn't noticed that before.

Grace then told me, "It's the deposit for your French trip. Please take it. I want you to".

Then Grace turns and walks away. I hadn't had the chance to say a single word. A girl I have never really spoken to has just given me TEN POUNDS. Enough to buy every Villa programme this season. My Dad could fill his car up with four-star petrol for that. Although he still hasn't recovered from when petrol went to a pound a gallon last year. He came home that night and said he wasn't going to use his car anymore. Of course, now it is £1.40 a gallon. According to Pincher this is why his dad says it was a mistake to elect a woman Prime Minister.

Eating my tuna sandwiches next to Tucker I am telling him about the incident in the Library. Trying to ask him not to tell the others, but knowing that was not going to happen. I did however keep the identity of the pretty lady from him. Although, this just resulted in him going through the names of all the girls in the year. Interestingly all but Grace Taylor. Tucker seemed to suggest that the girl had probably wanted a kiss at least in return. He didn't seem to follow my thinking process about how I couldn't accept the money. Even though it was in my pocket. I am getting fed up of tuna sandwiches, I've had them every day for the last two weeks? Probably shouldn't have told my Mum I wanted a change from ham.

Noddy has now joined Tucker and me at the table and straight away Tucker is filling in Noddy on how I was propositioned in the Science section of the Library. Noddy asked if I had seen the naked lady picture in the large 'Human Biology' book there.

Surprisingly, Noddy was quite supportive of my predicament. When he wants to he can be quite clever. Noddy suggests I should pay the money in but then look to pay the mystery 'girl' the money back as soon as possible. He recommends I destroy the cheque and don't tell my dad as he will probably never notice it was never cashed. Tucker asked about the form and Noddy quickly explained that Spud wasn't able to go so we could use his form and copy my dad's signature. I was disappointed Spud wasn't going, but it seemed his parents thought it was too expensive. I was unsure about forging my dad's signature but Noddy said he often copied his parents' signatures and he would happily do it. The idea is appealing, I do want to go. Also I have got over £20 saved in a tin in my bedroom for buying an Atari. So I could give Grace the money back and then everyone would be happy.

Ten minutes later and I have given my French trip form and deposit to Miss Tully. She seems very pleased I am going and taking French so seriously. She told me I was the 30th child to pay the deposit, so the trip was now full.

On the trip next January there will be myself, Tucker, Noddy, Pincher and Haystacks so it should be fun. Just a big pity Spud isn't coming. There is better news for both Spud and me later in the afternoon when it is announced that he will be moving into our 3FO form class. It seems that our year was being reduced from six form classes to five while work was being completed on the new Science block so each class was getting an extra four or five children. Spud is really pleased that we will again be sitting together. I am delighted. It was like a late winner for the Villa. Spud was my best friend and also having him next to me would be a good deterrent for Bellington's bullying. The only downside was that Kenny Bellington's little friend, James McMullan, is also joining our class. A number of 3FO sighed when his name was read out on the new list. I don't care that Bellington has got his little friend with him now, as I have got my big friend and he has got a bigger forehead.

It wasn't the Wednesday night I was planning. My parents have taken me to Grandad's. Reason it seems is that Grandpa is not well, again, so my parents have gone to my dad's parents' house. They didn't tell me much but an extra evening with my grandad, as Mark is out, is quite welcome. We can listen to the Villa game together on the radio.

My grandad has decided that we will listen to the first-half reports and maybe goals on BRMB with Tony Butler and then put Radio 2's 'Midweek Sports Special' on for second-half commentary live from Old Trafford. It isn't my lucky radio but in stereo the second-half will sound like we are there.

I am sitting on Grandad's two-seater plastic settee, with a speaker each side of me, as the reporter announces Old Trafford line-ups. No Colin Gibson, so it's Eamonn Deacy at left back. The other ten players are the familiar ten. Grandad asks for my prediction and I confidently go 2-1 for the Villa, with goals from Shaw and Withe. Grandad is more cautious, though, and suggests it might be a high scoring draw. He reckons Dave Sexton has got quite a good team there, with Gordon McQueen, Sammy McIlroy, Steve Coppell, Lou Macari and Joe Jordan. Allan Evans will keep toothless Joe Jordan at bay and super Tony Morley is as good as Steve Coppell. I am optimistic. Especially as I don't rate United's goalkeeper Gary Bailey.

Manchester United might have been good in the late 50s and 60s with players like George Best and Bobby Charlton but they haven't started this season very well. They have already been knocked out of the League Cup by Coventry and the UEFA Cup by a team from Poland who I can't even pronounce, Widzew Lodz. Anyway, Villa owe Man United one, as when Ron Saunders got us promotion in 1975 United pipped us to the Second Division title. Then in 1977, when we were on to win both cups, Manchester United knocked us out of the FA Cup quarter-final. Mind you, Grandad tells me about how Villa beat them in the 1957 final despite us being underdogs. He does add it might have been different if the United goalkeeper, Wood, hadn't been unconscious with a broken cheekbone. No substitutes in those days. Wood even came back on for the second-half and played as an outfield player. It wasn't a foul by Peter McFarland though. Grandad says you were allowed to charge into the goalkeeper in those days. I bet Peter Withe would have loved to have been playing then.

A great start again for the claret and blue, or even the whites as they are tonight. Peter Withe has scored after quarter of an hour. It sounds like an exciting game. Suddenly I can hear the radio even better because the noise of the video tape going round under Grandad's telly has stopped, his timed recording of Coronation Street has finished. Tony Butler is getting very excited on the radio. Still no goals in the Albion - Coventry game.

Nearly 40 minutes of the football have gone and Grandad has gone to put the kettle on ready for our half-time cuppa. The Villa are still winning. I spoke too early. There has been a goal at Old Trafford. No goal horn on BRMB. Manchester United had a penalty and Sammy McIlroy equalised. But before the reporter hands back to the studio there are loud cheers. More bad news, Steve Coppell has just scored to put flaming United in front. Grandad is a touch hard of hearing and when he returns it is obvious that he hasn't heard either goal.

The second halfs have started. We are now tuned into the BBC Radio 2 commentary of the game. The commentator is Peter Jones. He does seem Manchester United-biased. Compared to Tony Butler, he also sounds frightfully posh as well.

Villa are starting to press again. I think Ron must have given them a good telling off at half-time.

Grandad shouts, "Come on the Villa", but probably just for my benefit as I am feeling quite miserable at the moment. Why didn't I leave me lucky radio on quietly in my bedroom before I left? Mum and Dad did march me to the car quite quickly. They didn't even ask me if I had any homework. Luckily I haven't got any due in tomorrow morning. My Maths needs to be done for the afternoon but I can quickly do that at lunch time as it is quite straightforward. PENALTY!!!

Aston Villa with a chance to equalise. It is Gordon Cowans against Gary Bailey. 'Sid' will score he always does. 2-2 and you can hear the Villa fans cheering. Grandad's neighbours can probably hear me cheering as I fall off the shiny settee. The commentator seems to be concentrating on how disappointing United are this season, instead of how well the Villa are doing. Sounds like we could get a winner now.

Flipping Sammy McIlroy has scored again, just two minutes after we got back level. Looks like we are heading for our third defeat of the season. Well, fourth if you include Cambridge in the League Cup.

Albion are suddenly winning at home to Coventry as well. They will be level on points with us if scores stay the same. Albion still have to score three more goals to overtake us though. Unless, of course, Manchester United score three more. Surely we can't lose 6-2. If so I shall keep a very low profile at school tomorrow.

Mum and Dad have arrived at Grandad's looking extra serious. My dad's face is very grey. I have noticed that he is starting to look older. I suppose he is 43 now. He was 30 when I was born. While still listening to Peter Jones's commentating I ask them if everything is alright. It clearly isn't but Mum reassures me that there is nothing to worry about.

With the Villa still a goal down we drive back home. I wanted to stay at Grandad's until the end of the game, but it was obvious Mum just wanted to get home. For some reason my dad's car radio is playing up (even though it's a new car) and we just can't get any reception on Medium Wave. So I can't hear if there are any more goals.

It is now 9:10, as soon as the car pulls into the drive, I race to the door and press my finger firmly on the bell. Mark answers, but before he can see what the emergency is, I run up the stairs to my little bedroom and turn on my radio. The final whistle has just blown and very quickly they start talking through all the goals. But what was the score? They get to 3-2 and the second McIlroy goal. Then, to my delight, they describe a Gary Shaw equaliser. Super Gary Shaw. That was it, a cracker of a game had finished 3-3. We had, thanks to my lucky radio, got a draw at Old Trafford and we remain ahead of Haystack's Albion.

I am drifting off to sleep, but still have my radio on to hear that Forest have drawn at Sunderland and Ipswich have won their League Cup replay. Paul Mariner scored two more and the reporter was almost purring about Ipswich and how many trophies they could win this season. I don't mind if they win the League Cup and the UEFA Cup, as long as they leave the FA Cup for us. Still don't think they should be allowed to have all those Dutch players, or that Spurs should have the two Argentinians. Surely Ricky Villa should be forced to play for Aston Villa because of his name. I wonder if there are any other players in the First Division who have the name of another club. It is funny enough that Mike England manages Wales.

10:48am Friday 10th October 1980

Mrs Burton is off ill today so our Games lesson is for once mixed genders. It makes a change playing with the girls, especially as Grace Taylor is in the group. We are in the Sports Hall playing volleyball. It is the first time we have played and no one including 'Yeller' Yates (PE teacher) seems quite sure what the rules are. Carrie Campton is trying to explain the rules to Mr Yates. Apparently, we need to be in teams of six. That works out well, as there are 24 of us. Surprisingly Mr Yates selects me as one of the four team captains. Kenny Bellington is another captain. So at least I won't be on his side. More good news when 'Yeller' Yates shouts out that there will be no need for team colours, as each team will be either side of the net. This is good because as there are four teams I was thinking he was going to make one team be 'skins' and they would have to take their tops off. I hate getting my chubby nipples out in public. Mind you, I suppose as there are girls as well we probably aren't allowed to play 'skins'. The twenty children who aren't captains are now standing along the wall of the sports Hall. The wall where you could still see splatters of blood from when Tucker crashed his head against it in the Second Year. This is my chance to pick Grace Taylor in my team, but it isn't going to be easy. If I pick her too early it'll be obvious I fancy her. Wow, I fancy Grace Taylor. Where did that come from?

Bellington chooses his little mate James McMullan as his first pick, predictably. The two girl captains both pick popular tall girls. So I play safe and pick Spud. A tall friend who had played in goal for the school football team, ideal. Second pick and I really want to pick Grace. I am looking at Grace and she looks so lovely. It is the first time I have seen her in her white PE top close up. With her pleated navy blue gym skirt she looks quite grown-up. That girl I saw on holiday, on the horse, must have been Grace's double. I will pick Grace as my third pick and then nobody will guess why.

My team serving first against Bellington's team. I still can't believe what just happened. Why did Kenny Bellington pick my Grace Taylor with his second pick? There was still fourteen others left including volleyball expert Carrie Campton. So why choose Grace? I mean she isn't extra tall or particularly sporty. At least I was now stood opposite her across the net. Hopefully she would have to jump a bit and I would get to see her well-proportioned chest move. I wonder if she wears a sports bra or her normal bra. As I am studying the voluptuous beauty in front, the ball strikes me firmly in the face. I think Bellington struck it at me deliberately. Spud reacts fastest and manages to return it over the net before it bounces. Bounce also is what Grace's breasts appear be to doing as she jumps up and smashes the ball back over my team's side. She is obviously more sporting than I had thought, although my vision is blurred. Thanks to Grace Taylor's shot we are now a point down. A further six points from the hands of Miss Taylor follow. She is an expert and is the main reason that Kenny Bellington's team are totally destroying us. It isn't just my face that is hurting now but my pride. At the end of the annihilation my only comfort is that Grace comes over to check I am not in too much pain. Before I can convey the full extent of pain my nose is causing, she is pulled away from our team by captain Bellington.

Spud was our star player of the tournament. After winning our next two games our team had to sit and watch the last game. If Bellington's team wins then they win the tournament. If they lose though both of our teams will have won two games. Not sure what happens then. Hope it isn't a play-off match because I am shattered. You should wear gloves for this game. My knuckles are bleeding. My shin is also throbbing from where Bellington gave me an almighty kick as he walked past me on his way to the court. Spud tried to get me to tell 'Yeller' Yates, but I wasn't going to risk any further punishment. Spud is quite happy, because Carrie Campton is sitting down beside him (very close), grumbling about how Mr Yates is not following the rules right. I just can't see what Spud sees in her. She scares me.

Match point now to Bellington's lot. Thanks to another great shot by the delightful Grace Taylor. That's it, game over. Lesson over. I wonder if I can try and dodge having a shower by claiming I have a verruca. The last thing I want today is Bellington and his cronies making fun of my lack of pubes. His looks like a chimney sweeps brush.

3:36pm Saturday 11th October 1980

Madness, Saturday afternoon, the Villa are playing in the big Second City derby at St. Andrews and I am eating a chicken drumstick at my cousin's wedding. Why do people insist on getting married in the football season? I mean it isn't even summertime. Just hope we are winning. My dad hasn't even got his car here so I can't nip out to the radio. I am not very confident either. Blues haven't lost at home since last December. Twenty games ago. Surely we can go home soon. How much longer do these weddings go on for? We have been here for over two hours. At least the bride seems to have dried out after getting wet in that downpour. Mark says he got some good black white pictures of the couple holding that clear umbrella outside of the Church. So many relatives that I don't know all commenting on how I have grown. Why can't they tell me something I don't know, like the Villa score? Grandpa doesn't look well, but he at least he made it. I think he is losing weight. Perhaps Grandma has put him on a diet. He is sitting down a lot as well. He's probably as bored as I am. Think I will go and ask him if he saw Eddie Charlton win on Pot Black last night. I know he loves Pot Black. One of the reasons he gives for not getting a colour telly is because he claims he can follow the snooker better in black and white.

I don't believe this, finally at nearly 9:00 we are home and pathetically I still don't know the Villa score. Dad has suggested that instead of looking on Ceefax I wait and watch the game on Star Soccer in an hour, without knowing the score. I suppose I have waited this long so I might as well wait another 60 minutes.

For the first time this season the Midland's top team are on Star Soccer. They couldn't not have the region's biggest derby on. Gary Newbon introduces the show. Come on get on with it. He's mentioning the Wolves - Norwich game coming up and how Wolves are hoping to sign Peter Reid next week. Still Newbon is going on. Now, about the Forest game and their signing top Dutch player Johan Neeskens. If they go to a break before the game I will scream.

Finally it is over to Hugh Johns. This is madness. I am nervous about a game that finished five hours ago. Did they really have to mention that Birmingham have beaten us five times in the last eight games?

The Birmingham line-up looks quite impressive. Both Frank Worthington and Archie Gemmill are playing. As well as Colin Todd and Alan Curbishley. They have an unusually good team. If they could only win away they might be near the top with us. Birmingham aren't a very cool team, nobody follows them at school. The Blues hate the Villa probably more than we hate them. Albion hate us as well. I am not really sure why. Perhaps they are just jealous.

Eamonn Deacy still playing in place of Colin Gibson, so Gary Williams is on the bench. The Blues fans look very cross and there seems to be terracing all around. Even right down the side of the pitch. At least the caging should keep them from getting on the pitch. Hugh Johns says that Gary Shaw will play for England Under-21s in Romania in the week. Hope he doesn't get injured. Gordon Cowans is in that squad as well, but probably won't play as he has been called up to the full squad. He deserves a full England cap.

This isn't what I had hoped. It is all Birmingham City. Flipping Frank Worthington is running the show. Oh, Blues must score, no, thank goodness, Ken McNaught somehow hooked the ball off the goal-line. Villa need to just defend. I would take a draw. The clock at the end where Villa fans are says 25 minutes gone. Great save again from Jimmy Rimmer, Kevin Dillon nearly scored. Fifth corner now for Birmingham and Villa have only had the one. It is just endless Birmingham attacking. Mark gleefully suggests we are going to get a pasting. Maybe wearing blue shorts with our claret shirts is unlucky. Ooh, Eamon Deacy has won us a corner. McNaught does well from Mortimer's corner. What's happening? Has the referee given a penalty? YES he has! Mark can't believe it, but I think the slow motion replay shows it was handball.

Second time in a week for Gordon Cowans from the spot. He turns, runs and strokes the ball to the keeper's right. Another perfect 'Sid' kick. 1-0 to the Villa. I can hear the Villa supporters telling the City fans the score now. The commentator says it is against the run of play and Mark agrees, but who cares.

Great move, with Bremner and Shaw putting the galloping bearded Mortimer through on goal. Here comes number two. NO!! Keeper, Whelan, came out well. Half-time and a chance to drink my Hot Chocolate from my Villa mug as they go to the adverts. But not before they remind us again about Birmingham's unbeaten home record. Wish I knew the score so that I can relax.

Dennis Mortimer shoots well, but it goes wide after it hits a Birmingham leg. How can that not be a corner? Villa are doing better this half though. I think we might have won.

Mark Dennis plays a good ball in. Oh dear that looks a messy challenge by Eamonn Deacy. Another penalty. Given away like he did at Leeds. Looks very harsh. I think the referee was just trying to even it up because he gave us that handball. The same way that there was one for each side on Wednesday night. Come on Jimmy Rimmer it is time you saved one this season. Dad thinks Rimmer will save it. Oh, he nearly saved it. He went the right way, but Worthington hit it right in the corner.

I suppose a draw wouldn't be a disaster, but I guess the Blues fans will really roar them on now. Go Gary Shaw! So close to a winner. Villa getting on top. I feel really nervous. I have one sock on and one off. Tony Morley just wide. Hugh Johns says, "Villa building up a whirlwind pace".

Another chance for Gary Shaw, but somehow off the line by Mark Dennis. Fantastic dribbling by Tony Morley. Great shot by Allan Evans. That was so close to a winner. Time is running out though. The replay showed that it just brushed the top left corner of the goal frame.

Ken McNaught gives away a silly free-kick in a dangerous place. Frank Worthington and Archie Gemmill are over it. Mark announces that this is where they score the winner. I didn't know he knew the score. Delicate chip in by Worthington, but Villa keep it out. Good job the other Blues players are not as good as Frank Worthington. He is far too good for them.

Only about five minutes left now so it looks like Mark was wrong and it was a draw. What a GOAL!! How did he do that? Cruyff would have been proud of that. If it had been on Match of the Day it would have been 'Goal of the Month'. Gary Shaw was trying to control it and Allan Evans just shrivelled and caught it on the half volley, as he was falling, with his left foot. It flew in. The Villa fans are going crazy. Ken McNaught is hugging his fellow defender. Amazing goal. Absolutely amazing.

Villa are keeping the ball now, time nearly up. Kenny Swain rolls it back to Jimmy Rimmer who picks it up and clutches it to his chest. He finally kicks it up field making sure he doesn't do anything silly, like taking too many step. Come on ref, blow your whistle. A chance for Birmingham. Ainscow's shot is going to loop in. No, great save by Jimmy. He just got a finger to it. Bremner and McNaught then work really hard to stop Kevin Dillon getting another shot in. Tackles are certainly flying in. There will be some sore shins tomorrow. A great tackle by Eamonn Deacy and he feeds Tony Morley. That's it. It's all over. Another superb win for the Villa. First time Birmingham have lost at home for twenty games. What a brilliant performance.

Allan Evans is being interviewed by Nick Owen and says it is the best goal he has ever scored. I wish my hair was that curly. He is wearing a pale pink tie which isn't even pulled right up. Our Headmistress, Miss Thatcher, would never stand for a pupil wearing their tie that low. I wonder how long it is. Kevin Sullivan was given detention last week because his tie didn't even reach his belly button. Mind you he was wearing white socks as well.

Gary Newbon is talking about Villa's league position now. We are 3rd and only 2 points behind Ipswich who it seems drew today. We have gone above Everton, but we are still only a point clear of West Brom. They must have won again.

Nick Owen is now interviewing Ron Saunders. That's rare. Ron looks very smart, but as usual doesn't smile. He is asked about our chances of winning the league. I suppose we have got a chance now. Ron reiterates what he said at the start of the season, that he would know where they were going after twelve games and they have only played eleven so far.

That certainly was a fantastic win. Gary Newbon is now asking expert Jimmy Greaves what he thinks of the Villa. That is some moustache Jimmy has got. Grandad always goes on about what a great player Jimmy Greaves was. Apparently he was dropped for the World Cup Final though for Geoff Hurst. The one who scored the hat-trick. That was 1966. About nine months before I was born. I wonder if my dad was celebrating that night. Jimmy Greaves believes that the Villa are the worst sort of team to play against. He says they are always up at you. Every time you get past one player another Villa player appears.

5:02pm Monday 13th October 1980

School went really slowly today. Great having Spud in same form as me though. Bellington seems to keep his distance more. Only problem with him today was he put a big blob of black paint on one of my sketches in Metalwork. My flying goalkeeper model is coming along well. I should have it finished in two weeks.

John Craven's Newsround is talking about a speech that the Prime Minister made at the weekend. Mrs Thatcher said, "The Lady is not for turning" I think she was talking about herself.

People, it seems, are blaming her for the fact there are no jobs and nobody has any money. The Conservatives don't seem to be doing very well. I don't think they will get my vote in five years' time. Although, maybe the Villa perform better under a Conservative government. So if Villa do win the League this year perhaps I will vote for them. I wonder who was in power the last time we won the league in 1910. Football news next. Perhaps they will mention the Villa. No, it is all about Allan Clarke being the new Leeds manager.

Looking through our red Britannica Encyclopaedias trying to find out who was Prime Minister in 1910. Probably book with 'P' in for Prime Minister is best. This is a great set of twenty volumes of encyclopaedia and I am always using them for my homework. Guess I am lucky to have them. They fit so nicely as well on that shelf in my parents G-Plan furniture unit. Not sure why they call it G-Plan as it isn't in a G shape. That can't be right. No Prime Minister listing. Instead it goes 'Primate' (all about monkeys) straight to Prime Numbers. So if I want to know who was Prime Minister in 1910 I will have to go to the Library at some point. I can't be bothered. Primates are more interesting than politicians anyway.

1:22pm Wednesday 15th October 1980

Haystacks is having girl problems; for some reason he thinks talking it over with Pincher, Noddy and me will help. The problem appears to be that his girlfriend (Georgina) wants him to go to a party with her next Saturday afternoon, but his uncle has offered to take him to see Albion play at Forest. Surely there is no contest and girlfriend, Georgina Ramsey, will fully understand that football comes first. I mean there are only 42 league games a season. If you allow for possible cup games and replays that is only about 50. So that still leaves another 315 days in the year for seeing girlfriends. Even if you allow 15 more days for European matches and 5 for internationals that still leaves 295. Yet my cousin still got married on the day the Villa played at Birmingham. If I ever do get to go on a date with Grace Taylor I will make it clear that it isn't on a football day. Dates can be on Sundays, Mondays, Thursdays or Fridays as football isn't played on those days. Unless it is Boxing Day, of course. Friday is a good day for dates, as long as It's A Knock Out isn't on, but that finished for this series last week. Kettering won so they get to represent Great Britain in the Jeux Sans Frontières. My grandma loves the new large form 'Drunkards'. She reckons it reminds her of quite a few men she used to know on a Friday night.

Haystacks seems to think he should go to the party with Georgina Ramsey. Noddy is not convinced. The chance to visit the home of the European Champions and see Brian Clough is much more appealing. I pointed out that Albion are fifth and Forest sixth so it should be an exciting game. A draw would be the best outcome for the Villa. It's only now that Haystacks tells us that it is actually his girlfriend's own party. She will be thirteen and her birthday is next Saturday. Normally he would go to the

Albion, but his mum says he should go to the party. Worse still, Georgina Ramsey says that if he doesn't go, she will snog Karl Slater from her class instead. It is obvious that Haystacks is very fond of Georgina Ramsey and is not keen on the idea of her snogging Karl Slater. At least Haystacks has had a kiss this year.

9:24pm Friday 17th October 1980

News tonight is full of the Queen visiting the Pope in the Vatican. She is the first British Monarch ever to do this. Pictures of her being welcomed by Pope John Paul II, who I always think looks just like Ron Greenwood, the England manager. A big fuss it seems is being made over the Queen's outfit. Unusually she is wearing black and a veil. They are calling it spectacular but it looks a bit odd to me. The Pope is also in black and wearing a little pink hat. I forget what they are called but we have mentioned them in R.E.

9:33am Saturday 18th October 1980

Today is a monumental day. It is the day the Stadler family finally join the technical revolution and we get a video. Dad went to 'Tyler's' this morning and got the exact same Panasonic one as Grandad has got. Not only do we have a new VHS video we also have a new large telly, with teletext and a remote control that somehow works both the video and the TV. The whole thing also comes on a stand with wheels on it. Real 'state-of-the-art'. Mr Manford from next-door has come round to have a look at it. He banged on the wall first. We have this great system with next-door, where if anyone bangs on the wall three times the other house has to pick up the phone. Because we are on a 'party line' we can then talk to each other and Dad says it doesn't cost us anything. Dad is showing Mr Manford how you can set it to record any programme on any of the three channels over the next fourteen days. If it is like the automatic timer on the oven then Mum will still come home and check it has turned itself on.

Our new video is much better than Tucker's, you can set it to record more than one channel. It has also got a great feature that Grandad uses, called OTR. If you press this button once it will record whatever is on the channel the video is currently on for thirty minutes. So no need to spend time setting the time record. It is even cleverer because press the red OTR button again and it makes it a whole hour. I think you can press it a maximum of four times making an amazing 120 minutes.

Dad is now demonstrating how you could record 'Swap Shop' whilst watching 'Tiswas'. Mr Manford seems more interested in what Sally James is doing with a bucket of water. My favourite part of our new TV and video is on the remote control. There at the top is a brilliant button. It is the AV button. The video plays on the channel called simply AV. Sadly AV doesn't stand for Aston Villa but I can pretend. When Grandad brings the tape with Villa matches on tomorrow I can press the AV button and watch them. See us beat Sunderland and Birmingham all over again.

I can't believe that Haystacks talked me and Tucker into coming with him to a 13th birthday party. Especially on a Saturday afternoon. I guess that is what real friends do. At least I have my lucky radio with me. I have promised to keep Haystacks instantly up to date with any goals in the Forest - Albion game. The party is actually a disco in the Short Heath Methodist Church Hall. I used to come to BB (Boys Brigade) here. They have tried to blackout the afternoon sunlight so you can see the flashing disco lights. It isn't really working because Georgina Ramsey's dad keeps opening the curtains to see what the lads outside are up to. The lads outside are trying to hide their bottle of cider from Georgina Ramsey's dad. Haystacks seems to be spending all of his time being polite to Georgina Ramsey's mum. Georgina Ramsey's mum is quite attractive, she looks like Ria, from Butterflies. The one that drives the red mini with the Union Jack on the roof.

Tucker and I are sitting just by the entrance to the Church Hall. Tucker is watching carefully for when the cling film comes off the sausages on sticks. I am listening to the radio. Colin Gibson is back for the Villa. So no penalties conceded by Deacy today. Villa are at home to Tottenham Hotspur. Apart from Aston Villa I think Tottenham Hotspur is the best name in the division. Spurs have started the season a little slow and are mid-table. Today only one of their Argentinians is playing, the aptly named Ricky Villa. They have the former Villa defender Gordon Smith in their team who I never liked. He used to score too many own goals. Hopefully he will score one today. A chance for

Gordon Cowans and Glenn Hoddle both to show why they should be England's No. 10 not Terry McDermott. If 'Sid' had been playing on Wednesday night England wouldn't have lost in Romania in that World Cup qualifier. Up front Tottenham have a strike force to match Withe and Shaw in Garth Crooks and Steve Archibald. Crooks is one of the fastest players around.

The disco is going slowly. All the girls are on one side of the room and about six boys, from Georgina Ramsey's class, are at the other side of the Hall. The DJ is certainly trying to get them dancing but even 'D.I.S.C.O.' is failing to interest them. 'Summer Nights' from Grease has probably been his only success so far. He needs to play Abba's 'Dancing Queen', that even gets my grandma dancing and she has a dodgy hip.

Even out of the house my lucky radio is not letting me down. Two goals either side of half-time by Tony Morley have put Villa in control and as the buffet food is finally unwrapped Peter Withe makes it 3-0. Haystacks really needs a bigger paper plate as he piles on so much food; including four sausage rolls, five cheese and pineapples, three egg and cress sandwiches and tons of crisps. At least it is helping take his mind off the Albion losing 2-1 at Forest.

It was only Albion who have let the West Midlands down today. Villa, Wolves, Walsall and even Birmingham have all won.

The news for the Villa just keeps getting better. The Merseyside derby has ended 2-2 and Ipswich have only managed to draw at home to Manchester United. This means we are the only winners from this morning's top five. I can't wait to see the league table tonight. We will be second. Level on points with Ipswich, so kind of joint top. Pity they have a better goal difference and have played a game less. So what does Ron Saunders think of our chances of winning the league now that we have played twelve games?

Now the football is over I can join Tucker and Haystacks for the only dance I can do all the way through, 'The Birdie Song'. Haystacks manages a new twist to the dance by continuing to carry a plateful of food whilst dancing.

The familiar sound of the last dance of the disco 'True' by 'Spandau Ballet' starts to play so I walk to the door. Standing there are Tucker and Haystacks both scuffing huge slices of Georgina Ramsey's very pink 'Barbie' birthday cake. Looking back in the Hall I can see only one couple dancing to the slow song. Dancing cheek to cheek are Haystack's Georgina Ramsey and Karl Slater. I don't think Haystacks has noticed.

8:07pm Tuesday 21st October 1980

I am finding it difficult to concentrate on my Tuesday night Music homework because my dad has agreed to take me tomorrow night to the Villa - Brighton game. Even though I have been nagging him since Saturday and done a mammoth tidying up session on my bedroom I hadn't really expected a 'yes'. This will (hopefully) be the game when Villa go top of the league. Thanks to the UEFA Cup, Ipswich aren't playing a midweek league

match. So a draw and we will be top. Villa top of the league and I
will be there in the Holte End to celebrate it. Only promise I have
to keep is to have all my homework done. That includes making a
big start on this music project 'Twenty Years of Pop'. I should
really have started it two weeks ago, but it didn't seem as
important as the other subjects.

For our 'Twenty Years of Pop' work we have had to choose
four groups who have influenced Pop Music over the last two
decades and produce a scrapbook-style project on them.
Obviously I am including Abba and I think, as it covers the 60s, it
must have The Beatles in. My brother is quite a Beatles fan and
has all their records and quite a few books about them. Who were
that other group that was around the same time? The one that the
guy with really big lips used to be in. I recall seeing him in the
Sunday People so I'll check if I can find it. It was Mick Jagger and
his group used to be called 'Rolling Stones'. I am not sure if they
are still together. I need a fourth group to go with Abba. Beatles
and Rolling Stones. I think I am going to go for Queen. Maybe it
might bring the Villa luck as one of Queen's songs is called 'We
are the Champions'. Who knows what might happen next May. I
can dream.

Nearly ten o'clock and I have made a really good start on
my Music project. I have written four pages on The Beatles thanks
to Mark's books and magazines. Loads of interesting facts about
them, like they once had all five top singles spots in America, and
that their first album was recorded in a day. They're not even still

together yet everyone knows the names of John, Paul, Ringo and George. They certainly changed though from nice clean shaven lads to hairy scruffy blokes. I suppose fame does that to you. Probably with all their money now they don't have to try too hard to attract the women. I wonder if Grace Taylor likes The Beatles.

The Abba pages are looking super. Pity I had to cut the photographs of Anni-Frid out of my Abba book. You can definitely see her nipples under that tight top. I have written quite a lot about their Eurovision song contest win in Brighton. I hope Abba don't break up, like The Beatles did. Perhaps if they keep going they will be even bigger than The Beatles. They are cleverer, as English isn't even their first language. I am sure John Lennon couldn't write a song in Swedish however talented he might be.

7:10pm Wednesday 22nd October 1980

Just twenty minutes until kick-off, as I stand reading the page on full-back Colin Gibson in the programme. It calls him, 'among the most promising left-backs in the country'. I would agree with that. He is still only twenty yet he has played over fifty times for Villa. Good to see he is playing tonight. The line-ups on the back of the programme though are confusing as playing number three for Brighton is Gary Williams. Not our Gary Williams though, but the Brighton one. Apparently Colin Gibson is a very good at golf and has a handicap of eight, which sounds impressive. Ray Matts in the 'Press View' section is surprised that

Scotland manager, Jock Stein, is not picking Allan Evans. That makes two of us Ray.

I am showing Dad the page in the programme about reduced season tickets. A Juvenile standing one is now only £9.50. That doesn't include the cup games like the seating ones do, but there are still thirteen home league games left. It also says it guarantees you an FA Cup Final ticket if Villa get there. Dad says I am still too young to go on my own and that I have to wait until next season. I suppose I can't complain, he has brought me to see us hopefully go top of the league. Although Brighton will not be the easiest team to score against. Their centre-halves Steve Foster and Mark Lawrenson have been receiving some rave reviews. We must give John Gregory a big welcome back to Villa Park. He always played well for us. He played in every outfield position for Villa. He wore every shirt from number two to number eleven. I bet not many players have done that.

Here come the Villa players. There are quite few empty seats and Brighton haven't brought that many. I thought it would be a full house today. Villa look confident. I am feeling confident too. We will soon be top of the league. Bloke behind is moaning loudly about Brighton's manager Alan Mullery. His complaint is that Mullery has followed through with his threat. I am not sure quite what the threat was, but it seems to be due to the fact that Brighton have 'British Caledonian Airways' printed on their shirts. I question this with Dad and he informs me that sponsored shirts mean the game can't be shown on TV. I am not sure if it was planned to be on Midweek Sports Special or just the goals, if there are any, won't be shown on the news. The Brighton centre-half looks enormous with his big fuzzy hair. That must be Steve Foster. He has so much hair that he has to wear a headband. I am sure Ron Saunders wouldn't let a Villa player wear a girl's headband. Mind you Bjorn Borg seems to do quite well wearing his. Even though I always support Jimmy Connors at Wimbledon. Well, I can't see John Lloyd ever winning Wimbledon for England. Hopefully his wife Chris Evert will count as English soon.

Twenty minutes gone and Villa are looking nervous, but not playing too bad. Could do with a goal really. It feels so cold tonight. Time for my Villa gloves I think. Perhaps they will bring us a goal. A draw does put us top by a point, but Ipswich will have two games in hand. It was a good result for the Villa, Albion drawing at Everton last night. Liverpool are playing at Aberdeen (from Scotland) in the European Cup tonight so they can't catch us. Don't know how Aberdeen won the Scottish Premier last season. My Scottish team Rangers only finished 5th. Steve Archibald it seemed scored all their goals, which is why Spurs bought him. Aberdeen manager, Alex Ferguson, is also highly thought of according to my sticker album. Why do they call their top league in Scotland 'Premier' and not 'First Division'? How odd is that. First is first and nothing can be higher than first. We're more sensible in England.

Come on Villa. Even with my gloves on my hands are really cold. I need a goal to warm them up. Nearly half an hour gone. I don't believe it, Brighton have gone and scored. They have hardly had an attack. I have never seen the Villa lose a league game with my dad. It's former Villa player John Gregory who has scored. Blimey, I really thought this would be an easy win tonight.

Half-time now and I am having to queue in the horrible toilets for a wee. There must be five people lining up in front of me to use the big trough. It is so horrible and smelly. Probably won't be able to go with all the other men in the line watching. If I can't go I wonder how long I should stand there trying. Most of the men seem to be standing there for about twenty seconds. At least the gentlemen are moaning less now Dennis Mortimer has made it 1-1. The captain's first goal of the season. No, I can't go. I will have to paddle out through the pee on the floor and try to survive until full-time without going.

Peter Withe is through on goal. He must score. He has. YES!!! Two minutes into the second-half and we are winning. We can start singing 'We are top of the league'. Just waiting for somebody else in the Holte to start it off. I don't think they would listen to a cold 13-year-old boy who really needs the loo.

They're all scoring now. Des Bremner has scored a rare goal after a neat passing move with Gary Shaw. Now we are all singing 'we are top of the league' and Villa are on fire. 'We are going to win the League, we are going to win the League. And now you're going to believe us…'

Gary Shaw to Tony Morley and back to Shaw. It's four! Villa have scored four goals in twenty minutes and destroyed Brighton. How many more can we score in the final half an hour?

Oh, I needed that. The game has finished, Villa have won 4-1, we are top of the league and I have the trough in the Gents to myself. I even have time to move the discarded ping pong ball along the urinal with the flow of my wee. I must remember not to drink a cup of tea before I next come to an Aston Villa game. What a great night. I can't wait to fill in the league position on 'My Teams League Performance 1980-81 Chart'. The graph will have gone to the far left and No. 1. To myself I am singing the words from the Villa 1975 League Cup song. I have the single at home. 'We're going up, we're going up, we're going right up to the top. We are the boys of claret and blue. We'll win this game especially for you. Villa the Villans that's our name. So sing this song along with us'. Those words, from the early days of the Ron Saunders Villa era, have never been as true as they are today.

Walking back through the grounds of Aston Hall, lit by the superb AV floodlights I can't help thinking that this is perhaps just as good as life can get. The look of sheer joy on all the faces around. This is real happiness. Whatever happens the rest of this season we will always have this moment. The day that my beloved Aston Villa were top of the 92 clubs in England.

Using the results from Teletext I update my 'Shoot League Ladder'. Proudly placing the claret and blue Aston Villa tab at the very top. Above Ipswich, Liverpool and the other nineteen teams.

The Villa now have 20 points from 13 games. 9 wins, 2 draws and 2 defeats. Both Manchester clubs and Mr Walker's Forest had also won tonight. Manchester City's 3-1 win at home to Tottenham is their first win of the season. Maybe new manager John Bond might keep them up. He had been at Norwich since 1973. Interestingly, he replaced Ron Saunders there. I bet he didn't enjoy losing to Ron's Villa in the 1975 League Cup Final.

10:40am Thursday 23rd October 1980

School is great today. I am still basking in the glory of being top of the league. Even Bellington 'accidentally' trapping my left arm with my locker door did not dampen my mood. Grace Taylor smiled at me again and I got an 'A' in English. For my story about the haunted grandfather clock that always strikes at twenty past two at night, when the door mysteriously opens.

Spud has decided that he is going to finally ask Carrie Campton out. He is asking me for my advice where to take her on a 'real' date. Not sure why he thinks I have knowledge of dating, but I know that girls quite enjoy going to the cinema. The ABC Cinema in Walsall is also quite easy to get to on the 341 bus. The main film showing at the moment is still Close Encounters of the Third Kind. My brother has seen it and says it's really good. I think that if Carrie says yes to Spud then I shall be as brave and ask Grace Taylor out. Surely with the Villa top of the league at the moment this is my time.

It is proving difficult to concentrate on my Pop Project about the music of Lennon and McCartney with last night's game still in my head. I am supposed to be doing my homework but keep stopping to watch every news item on every channel for any mention of our table-topping. I even watch Nationwide. Man behind last night was right though. The Brighton shirt sponsors has meant a total TV blackout of this historic event, The Villa were mentioned right at the end of Midlands Today, but most news seems to be about IRA prisoners refusing to eat. Mrs Thatcher says we won't give in to the hunger strikers though. Expect if they were suddenly given a nice Sunday dinner with a giant Yorkshire pudding they would soon stop their hunger strike.

I need to get writing more of my music project. I haven't even started the Queen and Freddie Mercury bit yet. I will have to spend time on it during half-term. Must make sure I cut out the league table and report from tonight's Express & Star, after Mum has finished reading it.

2:30pm Friday 24th October 1980

Last but one lesson of the half-term is Games. I will be a sixth of the way through the Third Year in just two hours. We're in the Sports Hall playing 5-a-side football, actually five v six, as there is an odd number. My team has the five and unluckily we are skins. That's the main reason I volunteered to go in goal. The goalkeepers are allowed to keep their tops on. I do enjoy playing in goal and flinging myself around. Unfortunately I bruise very easy and will look like I have fallen down several flights of stairs in the morning. Spud is on my team and playing in the middle of the defence. He isn't in the best of moods because Carrie Campton turned down the idea of the date at the cinema. It turns out she'd seen 'Close Encounters of the Third Kind' twice already. Once with Brian Dobbins and then again with Keith Bentley. She certainly gets through the boys does Carrie. Surely it must be Spud's turn soon. Spud is taking his frustrations out on the other team's forwards. He has just given away his sixth foul. 'Yeller' Yates says one more and Spud is back in the changing rooms.

One minute left in our 5-a-side game and we are winning 3-2. I probably should have saved that second goal, but I was thinking about the Villa playing Keegan's Southampton tomorrow at the Dell. I did produce a fantastic save earlier, though, when Bellington was clean through against me. He still managed to give me a whack in my back with his elbow, when Mr Yates wasn't looking. Victory will be so much sweeter as it is against a team with Bellington in. He didn't even know Villa were top of the league yesterday. He thought it was flipping Liverpool.

Ouch! I felt that whack from here. Spud has just totally flattened Bellington. Even Kenny Burns would have been ashamed of that foul. Mr Yates is sending Spud off and ordering him to go and get changed. Yates has also decided, for some bizarre reason, it is a penalty despite it being on the half-way line. He's rewriting the laws of Association football. This penalty will almost certainly be the last kick of the game. So if I save it we win.

I am determined to save this for Spud. The ref should have been more understanding of his broken heart.

Looks like Paul Best is going to take the penalty. No, wait! Bellington has pushed him out of the way and is going to take it himself. Bellington stares at me and mouths something that I suspect is very offensive. I think he is telling me what he is going to do to me if I don't let this in. There is no way he is intimidating me. This is football. I can't possibly not try my best. It is a game of honour. I am going to save this penalty however hard he belts it, whatever the consequences might be. I am doing this for Spud, for our team and to show Bellington he doesn't scare me. Even though I am petrified of him.

Wow, I have done it. Somehow I got my left hand in the way of an absolute cannonball Bellington shot. He gave it an almighty kick and I was going the wrong way, but somehow managed to just move my left hand to the ball as I was diving to my right. Yes, the force pushed my left hand right back, my wrist took the entire force of the impact, but I saved it. We have won. Like 'The Villa' our team are winners. Take that Bellington you bully. No one messes with Jonathan Stadler.

I am now in absolute agony with my left wrist. Maybe I have seriously hurt it. Goalkeepers are tough though and should never show that they are in pain. I bet Jimmy Rimmer would play on even if his whole arm was dropping off. I am trying to keep my very painful injury quiet. It's my left hand so at least I will be able to write in the last lesson, which is History. It is unbearably painful. Maybe I should tell somebody. No, I don't want Bellington to know as he would probably just give it a hard pull. Hope I haven't dislocated my wrist. I can't grip my thumb and fingers together at all. The save was worth it though.

2:10pm Saturday 25th October 1980

Saturday afternoon and stuck in Casualty at 'The Royal Hospital'. My arm is very painful and swelled up alarmingly in the night. We have been here over three hours. Two different doctors have vigorously twisted my wrist to confirm what I already knew. That it blooming hurts. I screamed out the second time just to emphasise how painful it is. Now I am waiting to go to X-ray. The Villa kick-off at Southampton in just 48 minutes. My own fault really I should have agreed with my parents to come last night, but it did seem a little easier. Today though it is really hurting and even Allan Evans would struggle to play in this much pain. It might be impressive to have a broken arm and have it in plaster, but I would much rather it not be broken and for me to be back home in time for, at the very least, the second-half.

You would have expected them to have the radio on in fracture clinic. The X-ray has revealed that I have broken the bone in my arm called the 'Ulna'. So I am now sitting here as the nurse puts it in very cold wet plaster. Pity next week is half-term as I could have asked Grace Taylor to sign it. Not sure if I should tell Bellington that it was caused by him. At least I saved the penalty. Why are they so slow? It must be half-time by now. I guess I will have to get used to wearing my digital watch on my right hand for a few weeks. It never feels right on that wrist though. Just my luck to break my left arm. If it had been my right I might have got out of doing my homework. That is so horrible and slimy. At least it doesn't feel quite as painful now. Doctor said it was a 'clean' break so it should heal well. Slightly worried that he said 'should'. The plaster is going around my thumb now. That is really going to stop me doing things.

In the car on way home and frantically waiting for Radio Birmingham to tell me the Villa score. Game would have finished half an hour ago. My plastered arm is already starting to itch. Come on, what about the Villa? They are currently talking about a poor performance by the Wolves at Leicester. It finished 2-0 to Leicester City. Wolves 7th defeat of the season, apparently. Now, they are purring about Albion. Ron Atkinson's team beat Middlesbrough 3-0. But what about the Villa? Are we still top of the league? I don't believe it now they are talking about Walsall winning at Chesterfield. I must have missed the Villa talk. Dad puts Radio 2 on instead. Ipswich have won at Sunderland so if we have lost Ipswich are top. Finally they are going back to the Dell for a report. Southampton 1. Come on Villa, please have scored at least one. Aston Villa 2. YES!!! It has been a good day after all. I mistakenly clap my hands together and the scream could probably be heard by all the cars on the road.

Tony Morley and Peter Withe had scored for AVFC (Aston Villa Football Club) and Moran got the Southampton goal. Glad to see Kevin Keegan couldn't get past the Villa defence. He might have been 'European Footballer of the Year' (1978 and 1979), but he is no match for Allan Evans and Ken McNaught. What a team we have. 1. Rimmer, 2. Swain, 3. Gibson, 4. Evans, 5. McNaught, 6. Mortimer, 7. Bremner, 8. Shaw, 9. Withe, 10. Cowans and 11. Morley. A real team who all give the 110% that Ron Saunders expects. I like it that unlike many other teams, our No. 4 is a defender. Wolves' No. 4 plays in midfield and their No. 6 is a defender. Then our forwards are No. 8 and No. 9. Wolves and others have their strikers as No. 9 and No. 10. Ten to me should be team's midfield playmaker. The Gordon Cowans, Glenn Hoddle or Trevor Brooking. Mind you Liverpool play No. 7 as a forward. First Keegan and now Dalglish.

Updating my League Ladders with one hand is proving difficult. At least top three in the First Division have stayed the same. Forest are up to 4th. It is going to be so difficult for the Villa up against two teams who have won the European Cup in the last few years and Ipswich who just keep winning. But in the last eight games we have taken fifteen. We only dropped that one at Manchester United. Man U are now 5th and the Albion 6th. What a top six that is and the Villa are top of all of them. Pity Ipswich have two games in hand. They haven't lost all season and they are still in both the League Cup and the UEFA Cup. They will take some stopping.

Wolves are down to 17th place now. I bet Andy Gray is having second thoughts now. Manchester City are finally off the bottom. They won again. That means Crystal Palace are now bottom. In the Second Division Notts County are top. Mr Walker won't like that. He claims that there is only really one team in Nottingham. Haystacks reminded him that Notts County are the oldest club in England. They were one of the original twelve teams in the league when it first started. Of course, so were the Villa, Albion and Wolves. Teams like Spurs, Liverpool, Arsenal and Manchester United are all much younger, so they aren't proper teams. Sad to think that we won the league six times in the first 21 seasons but haven't won it since. Maybe 1981 will be win number seven to match our FA Cup wins. Or maybe we can win the double, like we did in 1897, and make it FA Cup win number eight. It would be a long time before anybody could catch up eight cup wins.

Walsall did well to beat Chesterfield as they are top of the Third Division. Walsall are in 15th place so only Albion I think have any chance of stopping my super Villa from being the highest placed of the West Midland teams. Hopefully I will win the money in May, but a trophy for Villa is far more important.

3:09pm Thursday 30th October 1980

What a frustrating week it has been with my lack of mobility. School holiday and I can't even ride my chopper bike, due to my plastered arm. At least, as a teacher, Mum has been off and been able to help with quite a few jobs. Hadn't expected getting my trousers on to be such a difficult task. At least I can still play Subbuteo even if I did break the crossbar with my plaster-cast as I went to take a shot with Tony Morley.

5:32pm Friday 31st October 1980

Halloween tonight which means only five days to Bonfire Night. I must start making a guy ready for 'Penny for a Guy'. I think it should be five pence for a guy these days with inflation. The old man at number nine usually saves all his half pennies in a jar ready to give to the kids with the best guy. Maybe my plastered arm might encourage people to be more generous. I really need to get more money for my Atari fund.

As I push a knitting needle down my cast to reach an annoying itch I am watching Harold Lloyd on the telly. It still seems odd watching a black and white programme on our new high spec. TV. I am bored. Wish I was going to see the Villa at home to Leicester tomorrow. Dad is going with Mark to watch Wolves at home to Sunderland so no chance of him taking his wounded son to Villa Park. Anyway, Mum would worry about me knocking my arm. I might not be allowed through the turnstiles with it as they might think it is a weapon. Perhaps on Monday I can accidently bang Bellington over the head with my plaster. It really is rock hard. Probably harder than Spud's head. What shall I tell them at school happened to my arm?

Lofty is funny on It Ain't Half Hot Mum. He and the Sergeant Major just don't get on. I wonder if the people who play them, Windsor Davies and Don Estelle do in real life. June from

'Terry and June' is in this episode for some reason. Mum says her name is really June Whitfield, so she really is called June. She has been in some 'Carry On' films as well. I don't think she was in Carry On Camping though. The one when Barbara Windsor's top flew off. Next time it is on I must record it on our video. Then I can try to pause it just as the top pops off. Carry on Screaming is my favourite of the 'Carry On' films. June Whitfield seems to be getting very close to Captain Ashwood. She is planning to spend the night with him in the Jungle.

End of October Top of Division One		
1.	Aston Villa	Pl: 14 Po: 22	+14
2.	Ipswich Town	Pl: 12 Po: 20	+15
3.	Liverpool	Pl: 13 Po: 18	+16
4.	Forest	Pl: 14 Po: 18	+11
5.	Man United	Pl: 14 Po: 18	+11
6.	West Brom	Pl: 14 Po: 18	+6

Villa October League Results		
4th Sunderland (h)	4-0 Won (Evans 2, Morley, Shaw)
8th Man United (a)	3-3 Draw (Withe, Cowans (pen), Shaw)
11th Birmingham City (a)	2-1 Won (Cowans (pen), Evans)
18th Tottenham (h)	3-0 Won (Morley 2, Withe)
22nd Brighton (h)	4-1 Won (Mortimer, Withe, Bremner, Shaw)
25th Southampton (a)	2-1 Won (Morley, Withe)

Chapter Four (November)

It'd be great if we could still be top of the league at the end of November. We have to play Leicester, Albion, Norwich, Leeds, Liverpool and Arsenal this month. Some tricky games, especially at Anfield and The Hawthorns. If we can get nine points from those six games I will be happy. My plaster cast has to stay on for another four weeks, so most of November.

Runner Seb Coe is on Multi Coloured Swap Shop. He's talking about how he won his gold medal in Moscow. He didn't mention that the Americans weren't there. I like Seb Coe. I was supporting him against Steve Ovett in the summer. It was good that they both won an Olympic gold medal, but odd that they each won the race the other was favourite for. I don't expect it'll be as easy at the next Olympics. It's in America, so I don't think the Americans will boycott that one. Perhaps the Russians will get revenge and do the boycotting. Mind you, Pincher doesn't think the world will last until 1984, he thinks somebody will blow us up with a nuclear bomb. I hope they wait until the end of the football season. At school next year we have to read George Orwell's book '1984', apparently it is all about the future. It was written about 30 years ago. Somebody should write a book now about the year 2000. I will be 33 then.

Seb Coe was a bit boring so watching Tiswas now. Noddy was in the Tiswas cage once. He even met 'The Phantom Flan Flinger'. According to Noddy 'Tiswas' stands for 'Today is Saturday Watch and Smile'. Saturdays are definitely the best day of the week, with all the footie. Chris Tarrant is wearing an enormous yellow dickie-bow with black spots.

Terry McCann from Minder is on Tiswas, oddly dressed in a school uniform. He is competing in a quiz against the girls from 'Legs and Co.'. They certainly have very impressive long legs. The one at the back reminds me of Mrs Cresswell-Farrington. I do like their long white boots. The question is, "What is the capital of Wales?" How easy is that? They are even giving the Minder chap three options: Cardiff, Harry Secombe's vest, or Scotland. I think he needs Arthur Daley to help him.

Part Two of Doctor Who episode 'Full Circle' starts soon. I'm going to quickly nip up and fill in my 'My Team's League Performance' chart, while Basil Brush is talking to some bloke called Frankie Vaughan. Mum says he is one of my grandad's favourite singers. Great to see that line on the league position graph being flat below the No. 1. It really was a fantastic win today (Leicester at home). Two goals and another clean sheet. That is five straight wins. I can't wait to watch us on Star Soccer tonight. See what Jimmy Greaves thinks of the Gary Shaw and Gordon Cowans goals. Sounded like it was all Villa on the radio.

That was Shaw's 8th league goal. He is two ahead of Withe, and Tony Morley has scored five. So between them the three have scored 19 goals in just 15 league games. I'm really pleased Albion managed to get a draw at Ipswich, even if it was goalless. It means we are now three points clear at the top and finally have a better goal difference than Ipswich. When do Ipswich play their two games in hand? Bet Mr Walker will enjoy his Saturday night with Forest going above Liverpool into third place.

Despite my broken arm it's a happy house with both Villa and Wolves winning and Mum is happy because Juliet Bravo is on this evening. I love Saturday afternoon teas. Tonight we are having scotch pancakes and ham sandwiches. The ham is on real crusty bread, the kind that gets stuck in your teeth.

Still not a fan of Tom Baker as Doctor Who, but I do like his new lady companion Romana and of course K9. I keep forgetting Romana is a Time Lord as well, also from Galifry. I am a little confused with what E-Space is. How long's the Doctor's scarf? The 'Marshman' is hardly frightening. The costume might have a good mask, but the suit is very unconvincing. I could make a better costume than that, even with my broken arm. Wow, Doctor Who has ended, with the 'Tardis' leaving Dr Who, Romana and poor K9 behind fighting a giant insect.

Wish it wasn't so long until Star Soccer. I expect it takes a long time getting the film back from Villa Park and then editing to get the best bits. That must be a fun job to do. I wonder what qualifications you need.

The Generation Game is rubbish now it's Larry Grayson and not Bruce Forsyth. Mum likes Isla St. Clair, but I think she is too Scottish. My favourite bit is still the conveyor belt at the end. I manage to remember all but one of the items which is better than they do.

Juliet Bravo is on in the background, as I read about a blunder by Charlie Carter that gives Stambridge City a shock League Cup lead against Roy Race's Melchester Rovers. It hasn't helped that Roy has just sold two of his players to Rovers' bitter rivals Melboro. Mum is engrossed in Juliet Bravo; from what I can work out there's a gang of counterfeiters causing problems on Jean Darblay's patch. Not sure why it is called Juliet Bravo when nobody has that name in the programme. I ask Dad who says it is something to do with JB being her radio handle. Seems J on the radio is Juliet and B is Bravo. Would make more sense if her initials weren't JD. Shouldn't it be Juliet Delta?

Good to have the Two Ronnies back. The new series of sketches called 'The Worm that Turns' looks like it'll be funny. The woman who plays Mrs Bott in Just William has turned up in it. Mum says her name is Diana Dors, which sounds familiar. The year is 2012 (way in the future) and Britain is in the grip of a new regime. It's being run completely by woman thanks to the Germaine Greer uprising of 1984. 'Big Ben' has been renamed 'Big Brenda'. Men are scared. Even the 'Union Jack' has now been called the 'Union Jill'. Dad seems to quite taken with the new police force of women, marching in tight leather shorts. Diana

Dors is saying, "No men will again be allowed to wear trousers. They must be kept in frocks".

Leicester City in white shirts are having more of the ball than I expected. As usual Hugh Johns is commentating. I've pressed the OTR button on our new video recorder. Gary Williams is playing now. He is wearing twelve so must have come on for somebody. Gary Shaw's just wide with his shot. Villa are on top and attacking towards their favourite Holte End in the second-half. Commentator keeps saying how sticky the pitch is getting. Great control by Cowans to Kenny Swain. Peter Withe rises and heads the ball down for Gary Shaw. You can see the rain coming down as Hugh Johns says, "A beautiful goal. Those two strikers seem to know each other so well". The Villa fans are singing 'Liverpool you're not champions any more'. Maybe a little too early. I certainly wouldn't write Bob Paisley's team off just yet. Gary Williams must have replaced Colin Gibson and Williams is playing very well. Another fantastic goal. Again Peter Withe heads the ball down, but this time to Gordon Cowans. Peter Withe is certainly winning everything in the air. A great signing from Ron Saunders. Allan Evans hits the post. That should have been 3-0. But a superb win and another good recording on my Villa videotape.

9:07am Monday 3rd November 1980

Walking into form 3FO, late again due to the 702, there are gasps as my classmates see my plastered arm in a sling. Many of the class seem genuinely concerned for me. Bellington says I'm just pretending. I'm relieved when Mr Walker refuses to let Bellington test if it really is broken. Perhaps I am being a little dishonest by not saying how I really hurt it. But I am doing the school a favour by not saying it happened during a lesson. Just think of all the forms they would have to complete and the questions Mr Yates would face. Of course, I have to say something. The question of how I had broken my arm, coming from all corners of the room. I have prepared myself for this and have the story very clearly planned. I tell everybody who asks (and some that don't) that I broke it rock climbing. I had slipped from quite a height and landed on my arm. Perhaps I should go on about how I heard the snap. I have lots of details ready, like that we went to the Lake District for a few days, but nobody seems interested in the technicalities. Instead the class, especially the girls, all just want to write on my plaster cast. I hadn't let anybody write on it yet because I didn't know what Headmistress Miss Thatcher's rules are on plaster cast graffiti. A few weeks back she gave Tucker detention for having 'The Fonz' written on his sports bag in permanent marker. It wasn't even Noddy who had done it, but his little brother James.

Frances Coulton is the first to write her name on my plaster cast. She has somehow found a bright pink marker pen. Mr Walker is trying to tell them to be careful with my arm, but they're not taking much notice. Five girls have now signed it, but I have no idea exactly what Beverley Cartwright has written. Spud is now doing a very artistic drawing of a wolf on my cast. Bellington has just pushed a drawing pin into my plaster. Mr Walker is not impressed and has ordered him to remove it. Ouch!! Bellington pressed it in further before pulling it out. He's drawn blood. I see he's put the pin on my chair now, I am not falling for that trick.

My plaster cast is now plastered with all sorts of things written by the class. I even let Kenny Bellington write 'Kenny Woz Here', I didn't really have a choice. Julie Duggan is now in the middle of writing in big letters on my sling. Julie is the only girl Villa fan I know, she's decided that my sling needs some claret and blue writing on it. I say claret, but it is just a dark red pen. This angle is actually quite a painful position to have my injured arm in. Mr Walker is starting to look concerned at the amount of colour now on my plaster and sling.

Finally, just in time for the bell, Julie Duggan has finished. My sling now dynamically reads 'ASTON VILLA ARE THE GREATEST. Julie did originally miss an 'E' out but Mr Walker helped her to correct it. I don't think I've ever been so popular. The only disappointment is that Grace Taylor has not signed my cast. I don't know why but she stayed at the back.

As I am leaving the form room, Mr Walker calls me over and asks me to stay behind. Oh, dear what have I done? After the others have left, Mr Walker asks me how long my arm would be in a cast for. I tell him about four more weeks. The reason he's concerned is that we were going to start rehearsing the lighting for 'The Mikado' at the end of November. He's just seeing if he needs to ask somebody else. I reassure him that I will be fit and ready for action by then.

As I am hurrying to catch Spud up for our first lesson, I find Grace Taylor waiting just outside for me. This is certainly a bonus. She's asking if it was very painful when it happened. Difficult to know what to say, but I smile and nod. Unexpectedly she touches me on my shoulder. This is going well, but I need to take the initiative. Perfect chance to ask Grace if she'll sign my cast. She is very keen and says that she has been waiting to. I pull the sling away from my plaster cast to reveal a small area that is still white. Unfortunately turning my arm to reveal this white patch is incredibly painful, but I bravely don't let it show. Hope I haven't re-broken it. Grace has written something on it now in yellow, I'm unable to see precisely what. I will have to try and look in the mirror in the boy's toilets at break.

Some days don't get much better than this. Villa are top of the league, I have found out that Grace Taylor put a kiss after her name on my plaster and now Tucker is suggesting we go the Albion - Villa game on Saturday. Spud's disputing it is a kiss and unfairly claiming it's 'T' for Taylor instead. Just because his love-life is going so badly.

Tucker might be a Walsall fan but he's always wanted to go to a First Division game. He reckons that we can get his dad to drop us in Darlaston, by the Asda, then we can get the 79 bus to The Hawthorns. I am not sure if my dad will let me go to a game without any adults, but maybe if he thinks Tucker's dad is taking us, then it might be different. I mean it isn't really a lie.

6:10pm Wednesday 5th November 1980

I can't believe I am sitting here on Bonfire night covering my plaster cast with white plimsoll polish. All the writing is taking some removing. This must be the fourth coat and I can still see Frances Coulton's name. I'm leaving 'Grace x' until the very last minute. Wow, that was an impressive rocket. I think it came from Scott Johnson's garden. Dad says we are going to light our fireworks in about half an hour. He has just nailed a Catherine Wheel to the fence and put a milk bottle out for the rocket. Hopefully I'll have finished covering my plaster by then. I can't believe the way Miss Thatcher reacted when she saw my arm. I think she was most horrified by Julie Duggan's Villa message on the sling. It seems Miss Thatcher is allowed to have her purple-rinsed hair, but an injured lad can't have his plaster signed. Maybe I was lucky she was in a good mood and just gave me a day to have it painted over, instead of giving me an instant detention. This is hard work though. Perhaps I would be better off with emulsion out of the shed. Pity I haven't got a purple wig to put on the guy before he goes on the bonfire. It is quite ironic that new sketch on the Two Ronnies. The one about women being in charge and the men all suffering. I mean, we already have a woman monarch, a woman Prime Minister and a woman Headmistress. My world is already ruled by women. I wonder if I will ever see a male on the throne or a real man at No. 10 again in my life. Maybe men have had their day. Probably end up with a female England Manager at some point, or worse still a woman presenting Match of the Day.

9:15pm Thursday 6th November 1980

Amazingly, in America a Hollywood actor has been elected President. His name is Ronald Reagan, but I don't think I have seen any of his films. The clips of them on the news were all in black and white. Oddly, even though he has won the election, he doesn't take over from Jimmy Carter until early next year. Apparently Reagan at 69 is the oldest ever elected president. I wonder if he can still collect his pension whilst he is president. It's probably paid straight into his bank account instead of him having to queue at the Post Office.

9:33am Friday 7th November 1980

Spud is being great this week, helping me cope with only having one fit arm. He has carried my books, helped me put my coat on and just been brilliant. Unlike Bellington who has just seen it as a chance to do even more things to me. He tied my shoelaces together and when I tried to reach down to untie them one handed he pushed me over. Today hasn't been a good day. Half the girls in my form are refusing to talk to me after I whitewashed my plaster. They think I am a chicken to give into Miss Thatcher. I am sure they'd all have done the same. Well, except for Frances Coulton maybe. Frances is quite a rebel. She regularly wears makeup at school and a very short skirt. She reminds me of Trisha Yates off Grange Hill.

Haystacks has decided he isn't coming with Tucker and me to Saturday's game. It seems that instead of seeing his beloved Albion lose to the mighty Villa he is going to watch his 2nd Year girlfriend, Georgina Ramsey, play netball for the school team. Perhaps I should have told him that she snogged Karl Slater. I have managed to persuade Tucker to support the Villa on Saturday. This could have been influenced by my offer to buy him a programme. My parents have agreed that I can go as long as Tucker's Dad takes us and brings us back. I am not sure if they think Tucker's Dad is going to the game or not, but I definitely never said he was.

11:59am Saturday 8th November 1980

Swap Shop has finished and I am sitting on my Villa jumper waiting for Tucker's dad to arrive. I wasn't really sure if I should wear my Villa jumper, but my coat will cover it up on the 79. I have a feeling the bus will be full of West Brom fans. I have two lots of bus fare safe as well as my £1-50 entrance money and 70p for two programmes. Dad very generously gave me £2 for admission money and some food, despite me already having my November pocket money. I feel bad now for not mentioning that we are going on our own. Actually, I am suddenly feeling quite apprehensive. Not only have I never been to a game without my dad or big brother, but I have never ever been to the Albion. We'll have to ask the bus driver to tell us when we reach the ground.

Tucker's dad has pipped his horn and it's time to go. Oddly though, there's somebody already sitting in the backseat of the Ford Cortina. It's Tucker's annoying ten-year-old brother Sammy. Obviously he has come along for the ride. Sammy says he will be supporting the Villa. That is interesting. I am starting to think he is coming as well. Perhaps Tucker's dad is going to come with us after all. I think I will be happy if he does, as I am a little scared. I really don't want to end up in any fights with my bad arm. West Bromwich Albion fans usually seem quite friendly, but I suspect there are a few fights at these local derbies. Haystacks always tells me how much the Albion hate the Villa.

It is official, Sammy's coming with us and Tucker has been told by his Dad that he has to look after his little brother. So we are now waiting in the rain for the 79 bus. I don't think anybody else in the queue is going to the game. Most of them seem to be going to the Asda. Sammy is keen to find out why my arm's in plaster. He doesn't seem to be buying my rock climbing story. He is far too smart and thinks I would have damaged more than just my wrist if I had fallen that far.

On the bus and there are a few Albion fans on the top deck, including a couple of skinheads who look especially hard. Tucker and I are being deliberately quiet, but Sammy is shouting "Villa" at the top of his voice. Surely they won't hit a poor invalid with a plastered left arm. Tucker has just discreetly put his glasses on. At least we will know when we have to get off because of the number of blue and white scarfs. Not a single claret and blue one to be seen. Hope we win but it might be a very difficult journey back if we do thrash the Baggies.

It's obvious where to get off because the road is just packed with men and lads in blue and white. Where are the Villa fans? I can hear them chanting, but I can't see them. I have never seen so many policemen. I expect they are all keen to volunteer for football duty today and the chance to see the terrific 'table-topping' Aston Villa.

Tucker has now spotted the noisy Villa fans. They are amassed the other side of the line of police. Tucker has shot off and seems to have left me in charge of his irritating little brother. Sammy is smashing his fist against his hand and looking quite threatening for a midget. He seems ready to thump any passing Albion fan. What happened to 'friendly rivalry'? I had only just discovered, as we were getting off the bus, that Sammy has never been to a real football game. He hasn't even been to see Walsall with Tucker at Fellows Park.

The police, with their riot shields, make us walk right to the end of their line to get past them. I did show them my plastered arm, but they wouldn't let us through. I considered telling them that I had a 'Blue Peter' badge, but thought better of it. Sammy is now holding on to my plastered arm as we try to make it to where the Villa fans are queuing to get in. Haystacks had told us that the

'Away' fans would be in the 'Smethwick End'. I am surprised that The Hawthorns seems so small in comparison to Villa Park. This is the first time I have seen it and it lacks the majestic nature of Villa Park. Maybe I am just being biased. It did smell like a proper football ground though. You can smell the Bovril, hot dogs and cigarette smoke.

There must be 5,000 Villa fans here. All queuing outside to get in just four turnstiles. Just hope we all get in. I am having my doubts that this was such a good idea, but the Villa fans are all singing away. There really does seem to be a belief that we might possibly have a chance of winning the league. I still think Liverpool and Ipswich will probably finish above us. Maybe we can beat the 4th place we managed in the 1977 League Cup winning season. We managed 51 points that season. That's only 27 more points than we've got now and there are 27 games still to play. So if we draw every game we will match that record.

Here come the mounted police. I always find police horses so frightening. They're massive and just charge at you. I must make sure Sammy doesn't get clobbered by one of their enormous hind legs. The horses are now just ramming into us. They don't seem to realise that we are just children. This is definitely the scariest thing I have known. Meeting Miss Thatcher in the corridor with your top button undone isn't even as scary as this.

That's disgusting. Two Villa fans weeing against the wall by the turnstile. There is no need for that, even if they had been waiting here for over an hour. The offending urinaters are rather startled as they are whacked on the back of the legs by a mounted policeman.

At this rate we will struggle to get in for kick-off. They need to open more turnstiles. Wish the police wouldn't keep pushing us. Can't they see my left arm is in a sling? Great, and now it is raining. The Villa players had better win for us. The wind is so cold. I can't believe Tucker hasn't brought a coat. I am freezing in all my layers. It must look odd though with one arm inside my jacket. I must look like the Irish waiter from Robin's Nest. I remember that Haystacks always goes on about The Hawthorns being the highest ground of all the 92 in the football league. Not sure if that is true because we haven't had to climb up anywhere to get here. But it's one of the coldest. At least we are finally reaching the turnstile.

Inside, Sammy is loudly joining in with all the Villa songs. The Villa fans are just crammed in. Surely everyone won't get in. I'm very worried about my arm. There are no crush barriers free so we just stand half way up behind the goal. I don't know how Sammy is going to see. Tucker says, "It isn't like this at Walsall".

The ground looks absolutely jam packed. Albion only usually get around 22,000, but there must be 35,000 here today. I think that's what the ground holds, but this Away End I think holds considerably less than there is in here now. I can hardly breathe and I am sure Sammy's feet can't be touching the ground.

Here come the Albion players. We all boo. Bryan Robson and Cyrille Regis are both clapping the West Brom fans. Albion have three black players in Batson, Regis and Remi Moses. Moses has the biggest afro I have ever seen. Here come the Villa. Little Sammy is going wild. I don't know what he will do when we score. Gary Williams is playing, so Colin Gibson must still be injured.

The rain is absolutely pouring down and the pitch is getting very muddy. Come on Villa, start attacking more. It's an even game, but not really much happening. These local derby games can be so tight. I think it's a disadvantage for the Villa having to play so many of them. We have fourteen to play this season. A third of our league matches. The close ones being Wolves, Albion, Birmingham and Coventry. Then the slightly further ones are Nottingham Forest, Leicester City and Stoke City. Next season we could have Notts County and Derby County as well. I suppose we shouldn't complain though as we have already beaten Coventry, Wolves, Birmingham and Leicester. Eight points from four games. We really are the 'Kings of the Midlands'. Just need to score against the Baggies now. A good save by Jimmy Rimmer. That was difficult with the wet pitch.

Back standing on the packed 79 bus trying to keep my arm from getting bashed. Albion fans seem quite happy with their draw. It wasn't a very good game though and perhaps not surprising there weren't any goals. I shall be glad to get home and dry out. Not sure how Ipswich did but at least we'll still be top with our point. Even if they have won at Southampton.

Dad hasn't asked if Tucker's dad came with us to the game, so I haven't mentioned it. Mum is just delighted I kept my plaster cast dry. I am just writing down today's scores off Ceefax in my parents' room before having a bath to warm me up, with a plastic bag over my cast. Ipswich drew 3-3 at Southampton. They are obviously not as good as us, we won there. Liverpool and Forest was also a draw, which means no change at the top. So not a bad day. Seems everyone has drawn today as Wolves finished 2-2 at Tottenham. Only team in the top six who didn't draw were Arsenal. They beat Alan Clarke's Leeds 5-0 at Elland Road. Former Wolves player Alan Sunderland, who scored that dramatic Arsenal winner in the 1979 Cup Final, scored and John Hollins got two.

4:44pm Sunday 9th November 1980

Three generations of us are watching the Villa on Match of the Day. Grandad keeps joking that Villa might score this time. The BBC have been unlucky with their choice of games. I expect Liverpool v Forest and Villa v West Brom sounded very appealing. They weren't to know they would both end up without any goals. At least Alan Parry has three goals in the Second Division match between West Ham and Grimsby. Surely West Ham must go up this season. They are far too good for the Second Division.

What a scruffy bloke. The Labour Party have selected a new leader to take on Maggie. What sort of name is Michael Foot? It reminds me of the rhyme we said at junior school about Kings. 'A King is a ruler, a ruler is a foot and a foot is smelly'. I don't think my feet are particularly smelly. Noddy's feet are really smelly. Whenever he takes his shoes off everyone leaves the room.

12:50pm Wednesday 12th November 1980

It's lunchtime and I am sat by the netball court talking to Haystacks. He is regretting the fact he didn't go to Saturday's match. Apparently the netball tournament was rained off which is why they're playing now. Georgina Ramsey isn't bad, despite her lack of height. I am struggling to follow the rules of netball though. It seems you can't keep the ball for more than three seconds and oddly where you are on the pitch is decided by what position you are. A throw-in seems quite similar to football though. As in it goes to the team who didn't touch it last. Our school team seem to be losing, but I am not quite sure how many points you get for a goal. Haystacks is explaining that Georgina Ramsey is wearing a WA because she is Wing Attack. Apparently this is like Tony Morley, or Peter Barnes. The only difference is that she isn't allowed to score. I bet Tony Morley wouldn't be happy if Ron Saunders told him he wasn't allowed to score.

Haystacks is talking about his feelings for Georgina Ramsey and how difficult having a girlfriend is. He's explaining how he had thought boys and girls were quite similar, but now he knows they aren't. His other problem is that although they are both now thirteen Georgina is still in the year below. I think he is looking for some advice. Other boys with young girlfriends would be made fun of but nobody makes fun of Haystacks. I think I am going to tell him about Grace Taylor and how I like her. But I am not going to mention her name. I will just say that there is this girl I like.

Rather surprisingly when I am telling Haystacks about the girl he replies, 'Yes, I know Grace Taylor, who has the clarinet lessons'.

It seems my secret isn't quite as secret as I thought. Haystacks it seems is very astute and has seen all the looks I give Grace. And I thought I was being discreet. The Villa might be top of the league, but Haystacks has just crushed all the joy out of me. He might as well have sat on me. He could have been gentler with me, than to just blurt it out like that, "You do know she is seeing Kenny Bellington don't you?" Haystacks said. Surely he's mistaken. Grace Taylor would never look once at Bellington. That comment just didn't make sense. Haystacks, the marvel of football knowledge must've got this wrong.

Haystacks goes on to explain that he has seen them out together three times in the last fortnight. Apparently quite near to where Bellington lives. But she put 'Grace X' on my arm.

It was a lack of planning on my part. My lucky radio needs new batteries, the Villa are away at Norwich and I have no spare ones. This really is turning into a rubbish Wednesday. Now I have dropped the knitting needle (that I was using to scratch my arm) down the inside of my cast and got it stuck. Dad and Mum are at the Asda and have promised to bring me some batteries back. I just hope they don't forget. They're taking their time. Surely Asda is closed by now. Mark says that they have to pop into Grandma and Grandpa's on the way back, as Grandpa isn't very well again.

Writing more John Lennon stuff for my music project, with my mum's small radio on in the dining room. John Lennon really was into peace. It seems him and his wife Yoko - odd name - once stayed in bed for two weeks. I wish Bellington would stay in bed for two weeks.

Yesterday's results were nearly perfect, with Ipswich finally losing. They lost 1-0 at Brighton. Obviously all the games they are playing is starting to catch up with them. With getting knocked out by Birmingham in the League Cup they haven't won now for four games. Forest lost as well last night. Sadly, Liverpool beat Coventry, but if we win tonight we will be five points clear at the top. Just can't believe I have no batteries for my lucky radio. It is the only one that takes those big chunky ones.

Only two games on *Radio Birmingham* tonight. The other one is Wolves at Manchester United. There goes the goal horn. It's at Carrow Road. Just as I expected, we are losing. Graham Paddon has scored. Sounds like poor defending. At least with Ipswich losing last night we'll still have a good lead. You would have thought Norwich would have let Villa win just to annoy their neighbours.

Half-time and Wolves are still goalless. Villa are still losing and according to the reporter it could have been more than one. Finally I hear my parents' car pull up. I race out to help carry the shopping in. There's bags of it. No idea which one has the batteries in. My parents look very serious tonight. I suppose shopping at the Asda isn't much fun.

Great, at the top of a bag with tins of peaches, a tin of pears and strawberry flavoured Crusher are the batteries. Good old Dad didn't forget. The Villa can soon turn this game around now. I know that my radio can't really affect how the Villa play, but it makes me feel more confident. I can see Mark shaking his head as I fiddle with putting the new batteries in.

About half an hour left in the games and finally a second goal horn. It came in stereo; as well as my radio in the dining room my Dad and Mark have the tuner on in the front room. Was it Old Trafford this time, or Carrow Road again? It's a second goal in East Anglia. Superb news. A Villa equaliser and it is the blonde bombshell Gary Shaw yet again. I wonder if he celebrated more this time than when I saw him just puff out his cheeks after scoring against Leicester on Star Soccer. According to reporter, Tim Russon, this goal today was from a Peter Withe cross. Blimey, was Peter Withe playing Wing Attack?

After 9pm, so time to put my homework away. Although I haven't actually written many words since kick-off at 7:30. Looks like both games will finish draws. I'll take that. They are moaning on the radio that the average wage for a First Division footballer is now £500 a week. That is certainly a job worth doing. But if the Villa win the League they will deserve their £500 a week. I do remember an article in the Sporting Star though, saying Ron Saunders has got the Villa players a very good bonus deal when they win games and they're in the top three. If I was on £500 a week and a good win bonus I am sure I would celebrate more than just puffing my cheeks out.

Sounds like there is a winning goal at Norwich. Thank you lucky radio. It's another Gary Shaw one. This time a Peter Withe shot is saved and Shaw struck home the rebound. We're winning. What a season. Who cares if Bellington is going out with Grace Taylor? There are much more important things in life. That's Gary Shaw's eleventh goal of the season and we aren't even half way through November.

Oh no, another goal horn. Please let it be the Wolves game. I don't care who has scored. It's the fourth goal in the Villa match. For some reason I am putting my hands over my ears. Bashing myself in the face with my plaster as I do so. Double good news. Firstly, it is Allan Evans who has headed in Gary Shaw's cross for 3-1 and secondly, the needle has finally come out of my cast.

What a great set of midweek results. Mark was quite pleased with 0-0 draw at United, Ipswich losing yesterday and the Villa winning 3-1 tonight. I will have to cut the league table out of the paper tomorrow, we are now five points clear of both Ipswich and Liverpool. Ipswich have still only played fifteen games, but even if they win their two extra games it still keeps them a point behind. Also when we play them again this season it'll be at Villa Park. 'Oh now you are gonna believe us, we're gonna win the League...' Next season, when I have my first season ticket, I could be witnessing Villa playing in the European Cup. Perhaps I could see Laurie Cunningham's Real Madrid or Karl-Heinz Rummenigge's Bayern Munich at Villa Park. No idea who is currently winning the leagues in Spain and Germany. I will have to check in next Monday's Daily Express. They have the European scores in there usually.

If we win the League, or the FA Cup, we will get to play at Wembley in the Charity Shield. I wonder if my season ticket will give me a voucher for that.

1:20pm Friday 14th November 1980

Mr Walker seems to be acting out climbing stairs. No idea why, but Spud and I need to get this question right, or we'll be trailing with one round to go. The question Chemistry teacher Mr Fairclough has asked is, "Which World Champion Formula One racing driver was killed in a plane crash?" All the ones I know, Niki Lauda and James Hunt, are very much still alive. Spud has no idea, but he did do well with the Welsh rugby players in the last round. Obviously Mr Walker is giving us a clue and he is definitely climbing. I think he would really like 3FO to win the 'Question of

Sport Cup'. I don't expect Emlyn Hughes or Gareth Edwards would know the answer to this on the TV programme. David Coleman might give them a clue. No we are going to have to say we don't know. Mr Walker is now shaking his head and it has gone over to the other team. The other team is 3TY, Mrs Tyson's class. Their two contestants are Felicity Mason, who captains the netball team and Haystacks. Typical Haystacks gets a bonus point by saying, "Graham Hill". Obviously Mr Walker was miming climbing a hill. I have never heard of him.

The quick-fire question round now. Why are there no Villa questions? I can't believe Felicity Mason was quickest to answer "Stoke" first to the question, 'Who did Brian Clough sign Peter Shilton from?' I did manage to name David Gower's county though and Spud got the one about 'Robin Cousins' winning a gold at the Winter Olympics. How did Haystacks know it was Bobby George that Eric Bristow beat? Haystacks is in full flow now, that's four on the trot he has got. For a big lad he strikes that chime bar very quickly. Mind you it helped having a question about Albion's Derek Statham.

I am sitting by Grace Taylor, as we watch Felicity Mason and Haystacks taking on 3GA in the 'Question of Sport Cup Final'. We had come third out all the classes, but Mason and Haystacks were unstoppable. I think 3GA would surrender now if they could. Quite pleased that Grace decided to put her chair right next to mine. In fact the chairs are touching. Lucky chairs. She compliments me on my sporting knowledge, but I'm not in the mood for polite chat. How can she be going out with that thick thug?

My arm is definitely starting to have more movement. Hopefully next Friday I will be able to get this heavy plaster cast off. It seems ages since I saved that Bellington penalty. I have noticed that Ipswich have failed to win a game in all the time I've had my arm in plaster though. Hopefully that will continue today when they entertain Leicester City. We are at home to Leeds. A chance to beat them for the fourth time this season. A Leeds team who have lost four of the last six games. They did bounce back from being hammered 5-0 by Arsenal to beat Middlesbrough in midweek though.

I am still trying to get through to Radio Birmingham, to have a go on their Sports Quiz. I know the answer to the qualifying question is 2-1, but the number is continually engaged. At least I now know the Radio Birmingham phone number off by heart. The qualifying question is very easy, which is probably why the line is always engaged. I hate that bleep. I want to hear a ringing noise. The qualifying question is, 'What was the score when Villa played Leeds in the first game of the season?' Definitely 2-1 to Villa. Shaw and Morley scored, after Eamonn Deacy had given away that penalty. Another 2-1 win today would be good, but I think we might score more than two. By the time I get on the radio somebody will have probably got all five questions right. I certainly know three of the five. Number three, 'Who won the 1976 FA Cup?' is Southampton. Mike Brearley was the England cricket captain before Ian Botham and Ben Nevis won the 1980 Grand National. I remember the horse's name because we went to Fort William for our holidays two years ago and I climbed half way up Ben Nevis. It was too misty to go any higher. Must admit I will have to guess on question two. 'Who won this year's Rugby League Challenge Cup?' I am sure it is either Wigan or Hull Kingston Rovers. Seem to recall catching it on TV with Eddie Waring from It's a Knockout commentating. Question five I have absolutely no idea of at all. 'In which year did Roger Bannister break the four minute mile?' I've rung Grandad and he thinks it was about 1950. Still, the BBC Radio Birmingham phone is engaged.

It's now 3:05 and I have been trying to ring for 40 minutes. No goals at the Villa yet. Dad promises to tell me if there are. I am sure I will hear the goal horn though. I am sick of that engaged bleep. But wait, it's ringing. Success at last. Just need somebody to answer it now. Oh, they have. A lady just said, "Hello". Very unprofessional. There is a pause. I decide to go straight for it and announce. "Villa 2 Leeds 1". The lady seems a little confused and wants to know who I am. So I tell her politely my name, age and that I support Aston Villa. It seems I must have dialled the wrong number this time. She doesn't work at *Radio Birmingham*. I dial the number slowly again and this time it is engaged again.

Dad tells me somebody has got three of the five questions right in the quiz. But they didn't get Mike Brearley or Southampton. They said Tony Greig and Manchester United. Both are definitely wrong. They also said 1954 for Roger Bannister's four minute mile so that must have been right. They also gave Hull Kingston Rovers for the Rugby Challenge Cup. Great, I know the five answers. I just need to get through now and I can win. The prize is two tickets to see 'Team Fiat' play at the Aston Villa Leisure Centre. Dad said he will go with me if I win as he has never seen a basketball match live.

It's ringing again. Yes, right number this time and my qualifying question is right. Oh, I can hear a goal horn. They say I am next on. Dad comes to phone to tell me Leeds have taken the lead. The Argentinian player Sabella has scored. Well, they took the lead last time and we beat them. At Villa Park we will soon pull it back. I have been told to make sure I turn my radio down. Dad and Mum are listening in the front room and Dad is going to try and record his son on the radio.

Oh, just my luck. The Walsall fan on before me, Clive from Essington, has got all five right. He has won the basketball tickets. That means I am going to be the first to try and answer five brand new questions. Worse still the prize is a book about Birmingham City. I am a Villa fan why would I want that. I don't even know anyone who supports Birmingham. Grandad jokes that the Villa have lost the FA Cup more times than Birmingham City have won it. This is because it was stolen from a shop in Birmingham when we won it back in 1895. They never did find the stolen cup. A copy had to be made.

I am feeling quite nervous, but make it clear to the presenter that I am a Villa fan and that I think we will still beat Leeds. First question is fairly easy. 'When did Villa last win the League?' I know that, it's 1910, of course. Second question is not so easy. I am going to have to take a guess. Wish I had counted when I was watching them with Haystacks last week. I am going to say there are seven. Yes, I think there were seven players in a netball team. No idea! He's now asking how many medals Great Britain won in Boxing at the Olympics. A horrible sport. If you can call men hitting each other a sport. He is rushing me now. I am saying three. 'What is the maximum break in snooker?' I know this one. It is 155. Haystacks told me. If your opponent misses and you can't play a red you can start with a free ball. So say pot the yellow as a red. So if you then get a black you can get eight more than the normal maximum of 147. So that is 155. I tell the presenter 155 feeling rather pleased with myself, he didn't catch me out. Last question and if my guess for the boxing was right I might have a chance. Easy! 'Which county does cricketer Vic Marks play for?' Somerset, my team. I might have won a blooming copy of a Birmingham City book. He's saying I did very well especially as I am only thirteen. I will ignore that patronising comment. Come on tell me, so I can go and get my lucky radio turned on. No Blues book for me then as I only got three right. I suppose not bad for brand new questions.

Mum wanted me to hear the tape back of my radio stardom, but I didn't want to hear my own voice so I am now upstairs in my bedroom, with my lucky radio. It's nearly 3:30 now and the Villa are still losing. Next contestant has only got two right. They're going backwards.

The equaliser! Yes, Villa level almost within five minutes from turning my lucky radio on. Gary Shaw has scored his tenth league goal of the season. He could score even more than Andy Gray did in 1976-77 season at this rate.

Disappointing result for the Villa. Only drawing 1-1 with Leeds. I really thought they would win. The Sports Quiz was a con as well. Another Walsall fan won and he said the maximum break in snooker was 147. I feel like ringing and complaining, but it would probably be engaged for the next half an hour. The other one I 'supposedly' got wrong was the boxing. The answer was actually one, but I really don't care. He's welcome to a stupid book about blooming Birmingham City. Maybe Dad will still be willing to go and see Team Fiat play?

Mark isn't happy as Wolves lost 2-0 at home to Brighton. Mark is right, Brighton really are Wolves' bogey team. I am trying to think who the Villa's bogey team might be. We struggle against Manchester United.

The scores haven't gone too bad today. Ipswich did win at home to Leicester, but Forest lost 3-0 at home. Liverpool could only draw at Crystal Palace and the Albion - Arsenal game ended in a draw. There seems to be plenty of draws at the moment. My grandad says that Jimmy Hill wants to change the points system because there are too many draws. Some odd idea about three points for a win. So a win is three times more important than a draw. I don't think that will ever happen. If that was the case the Villa would now have 40 points not 28. I think it's stupid and would just make teams defend more when they are winning by one goal. Grandad says things in football do change though. He was very anti changing from goal average to goal difference a few years ago but now he is starting to get used to it. Goal average always seemed far too complicated. Some league tables went to three decimal places.

So after eighteen games we are four points clear of Ipswich and we have the best goal difference in the division at +18. If it was goal average still, it would be 2.2. Interestingly Ipswich would have a goal average of 2.45 but their goal difference is only +16. Mr Walker could use this for a whole Maths lesson. If somebody has a goal average of 2.45 and a goal difference of +16 then how many goals have they have conceded? It doesn't matter, all that counts is we are still top. Just got to hope Ipswich don't win their two games in hand.

5:20pm Wednesday 19th November 1980

Finally I have my left arm back. Fracture Clinic today, saw them cut the plaster off with some really big scissors. I was slightly scared for my safety at one point. My arm looks very pale compared to the rest of me but seems to have healed well. I still can't do Games for a few weeks but at least I will be able to climb the ladder up to the Lighting Galley. Also, I finally finished my Metalwork goalkeeper this afternoon, so I am now placing it on my bedroom window ledge. Maybe I need to weight the base on the left post more as it seems to be leaning quite a bit. Bellington was thrown out of the Metalwork lesson today and sent to Miss Thatcher's office. He will probably blame me for it tomorrow, but it wasn't me who told Mr Harpwell. Bellington had whacked me hard on the base of my back with his pump. The next thing I knew was Mr Harpwell going berserk and shouting about how dangerous it is to mess around when there is hot metal about. We didn't see Bellington again all afternoon.

It's been a long day and I am feeling tired, but need to stay up to watch Midweek Sports Special. The England - Switzerland World Cup qualifier is on. I have avoided the *Nine O'clock News* in case they told us the score and I haven't been on Ceefax all night. After losing in Romania we need to win. England have two points from our two games, but Romania have three and Hungary haven't even played yet. I think if England lose tonight Ron Greenwood might be sacked. It was bad enough not qualifying for the 1978 Finals in Argentina, but if they fail to qualify again…. Wales are doing better than England. They have won both their first two games 4-0 and are playing Czechoslovakia tonight. It seems very odd though that we have five teams in our group, yet Group Seven only has Poland, East Germany and Malta. I know only one team qualifies from that group but anyone can beat Malta.

Why is Ron Greenwood so anti-Villa? Brian Moore goes through the team. Mick Mills and Paul Mariner both from Ipswich and Mills is captain. Phil Neal and Terry McDermott from Liverpool. Even Second Division Trevor Brooking is in the team. Kenny Samson and Tony Woodcock from Arsenal. Villa are higher than all these teams. Peter Shilton from Forest. I suppose I am happy with Shilton in goal, I never understand when they pick Ray Clemence. He always seems to let the ball in between his legs. How can Ron Greenwood still pick Dave Watson at 34? He's surely too old. Pity the Villa centre-halves are both Scottish. Bryan Robson at least proves that Ron Greenwood has heard of the West Midlands. England need a winger like Tony Morley. Steve Coppell isn't a winger.

Wembley looks quite lively. I can't wait to go there with Villa. England are winning thanks to a cross by Steve Coppell. It was an own goal, but Coppell made it. The noise is different to league games. Long haired Paul Mariner has made it 2-0 now, so England look like they will win.

Trying to get to sleep after watching England narrowly win 2-1. It certainly wasn't a great England display. Swain, Gibson, Mortimer, Shaw, Withe, Cowans and Morley would all improve that team. Surely Cowans, Shaw and Morley will get picked in the next few games. I can't sleep. It's odd without my plaster cast and

I am worried about what Bellington might have in store for me tomorrow.

That's twice Grace Taylor has looked round at me this morning. Once she definitely smiled. Looks like she had her hair cut at the weekend. Looks several inches shorter at the front. Last week you could only just see her eyebrows, now they are totally on display. Maybe I should be brave and compliment her on her new hairstyle. But what if I am wrong and it hadn't been cut? My own fringe is getting far too long. Hate it when it starts to get in my eyes. Also it is so greasy at the moment. It's no fun this being a teenager malarkey. I wonder what style Grace would like me to have. Perhaps I could have it curly, like that bloke out of Dexy's Midnight Runners or a Kevin Keegan perm.

9:18am Friday 21st November 1980

Mr Walker is in a strange mood this morning. Perhaps he is still taking Forest's 3-0 home defeat to Spurs last Saturday really badly. His blue shirt today is more creased than Albert Steptoe's face. He just isn't himself. He's trying to tell us something about rehearsals for the 'Mikado', but nobody is listening. Bellington has most of class's attention, he's seeing how many paperclips he can fit in his left nostril. Apparently he has managed 26 so far. I'm sure he must have larger than average sized nostrils. Interestingly, Grace Taylor is the only girl who seems disgusted by Bellington's antics. She starts screaming for him to stop. Mr Walker continues to repeat (to himself) the times of the rehearsals. This really is a very odd form period. I have this sense of doom. A feeling that something very bad is about to happen. Bellington has managed 30 now. I didn't know he could count that high. His left nostril is now sticking out at a very unnatural angle. Was I the only one thinking that those paperclips would need to be sterilised before they could go near any paper again? Mr Walker is getting louder with 'Mikado' talk and really getting rather cross. I wouldn't be surprised if he didn't rip his creased blue shirt open 'Hulk' style soon. All the class except Grace Taylor and me are now egging Bellington on with a chorus of Roy Castle's Record Breakers theme tune. I wonder if there is a world record for the number of paperclips inserted in one nostril.

BANG! Mr Walker explodes. He runs across the classroom to Bellington and whacks him right on the back of the head with his fist. Paperclips go shooting everywhere from Bellington's nose followed by a wave of blood. The whole class are silent and in a state of disbelief. The usually mild-mannered Mr Walker is trying desperately to regain his composure while a very shocked Bellington is trying to stem the flow of blood, while trying to detach the final paperclip that is now firmly wedged up his nose. One thing for certain, this is not going to be enhancing Mr Walker's teaching career. Bellington is stunned and it takes him nearly two minutes before he threatens the now shaking Mr Walker with both his dad and the police. Perhaps we will all end up being witnesses in a Mr Walker versus Bellington court case. That would be so difficult. I mean obviously I am on Mr Walker's side, but I couldn't lie in court especially after swearing on the Bible. Mr Walker did bash Bellington, with excessive force. I'd have to say that Bellington deserved it. Susan Talbot is trying to clean splatters of blood off her desk that had been propelled a good ten feet from Bellington's nose. James McMullan though is stopping her, claiming that this is now a crime scene. I think he has been watching too much Quincy. The only person who seems to be more caring about Bellington than McMullan is surprisingly Grace Taylor. Obviously the rumours are right, she is his girlfriend. She is now holding his arm and leading him out of the classroom.

Ten minutes have now gone since Bellington and Grace left. Mr Walker hasn't said a word he is just sitting slumped at his desk. The rest of us are all just too scared to talk. Partly fear of whether Mr Walker might explode again and also because we really are struggling to take in what has just happened. Silence is broken when Headmistress, purple-haired Miss Thatcher, stomps in. We all quickly get to our feet, but our scary leader doesn't make eye contact with any of us. Instead she just squeals, "Mr Walker, now!", then marches a crumpled Mr Walker away. It's as if his execution awaits.

Lunchtime, Spud and I are filling in Pincher, Noddy and Tucker on the sensational events of the morning. Of course, news has already reached all the classes in the school, but the stories have been even considerably more dramatic than the real shocking incident. Apparently Pincher's class had been told that 'Bellington had a knife and that Mr Walker had whacked him on the head with a chair.' There was also talk of brain damage, but we all thought it would be difficult to tell with Bellington. One thing that's true though is that Bellington, Mr Walker and even Grace Taylor have not been seen since. Why would Grace be missing all morning?

2:48pm Saturday 22nd November 1980

Villa are away at Liverpool and I'm struggling to tune my lucky radio in to Radio Birmingham. Really has been a very odd few days. Yesterday, no sign of Mr Walker, or Bellington. We had a supply teacher called Mr Thomas-Ball who seemed to think we were all about seven. Don't know why he needs two surnames. Grace Taylor was missing all day, but nobody was saying anything. It didn't make the Express & Star, so it couldn't have been that serious. I checked the front page as well as reading the back sports pages just in case.

Feeling a bit tired this afternoon as I stayed up late to watch a fundraising appeal programme called Children in Need on BBC1 and BBC2. They were raising money for disadvantaged children in Great Britain. Terry Wogan and Esther Rantzen were presenting it. Apparently it's been on the radio in previous years but never on telly before. They think the final total of donations might reach £1,000,000. A whole Trevor Francis. I would send some money myself but it need it for my Atari fund.

This doesn't sound like Radio Birmingham. It is a bit crackly but they are running through the Villa team. Gary Williams is playing number three. If we can beat Liverpool at Anfield I really will think we can win the League. I recognise that broad Black Country accent, it is Tony Butler. So this must be BRMB. Maybe BRMB can bring the Villa luck, so I will listen to it today. They're playing that music that they play at the Villa. My dad did say what it was last time we were there. Something about a Silent movie star. My grandad thinks Tony Butler is a Wolves fan, but I think he has a soft spot for the Villa. I bet he's met all the players. I did listen to his Friday night phone-in the other week until it got that the reception was too bad. A Villa fan called 'Acker' seemed to be mouthing off too much, so Tony Butler told him to 'get on his bike' and then banned him for three weeks. 'Acker' was suggesting that Albion fans would be throwing themselves in 'the cut' after the Villa beat them. We didn't beat them though, it was 0-0.

Wolves are losing to Boro, Albion are beating Leicester and Villa are holding Liverpool after an hour. It is goalless when an excited Tony Butler shouts, "Goal at Liverpool". He's having us on though, the reporter who we can only just hear on his telephone line is as shocked as we are at the suggestion of a goal. Villa have come close though.

Just two minutes later and there is a goal at Liverpool. Blooming Kenny Dalglish has scored. Oh well, Liverpool have only lost one league game all season and they haven't lost at

Anfield in the league since Jan 1978. As Tony Butler points out that was to Birmingham City. Mind you we did beat Liverpool 2-1 there on Bonfire Night in 1977, so you never know. Tony Butler is telling us Villa fans to get our prayer mats out now. I heard him say that before when the Villa were losing.

Seems that Terry McDermott and Ray Kennedy are running the show against us. At least we will still be top even if we do lose, but it will mean Liverpool are just three points behind us and will still have a game in hand. Come on you Villa!

A very excited Tony Butler is sending us back to the BRMB reporter at Anfield. He is not saying there is a goal though. Yes, one all. Allan Evans has equalised. Brilliant news.

Ten minutes left and Villa are on the attack. If we can score and win this we will be seven points ahead of Liverpool. Seven points ahead of a team who have won the league in four of the last five seasons. In fact in my football life I can never remember Liverpool not being first or second so being seven points ahead of them will be very special. I feel very nervous.

Must be nearly full-time now. Come on Villa, you can do it. I would be happy with a draw though. At least David 'Super Sub' Fairclough isn't on the bench for them.

"Goal at Anfield", Tony Butler yells, nearly blowing the speaker off my lucky radio. But all you can hear is the crowd. I think it is bad news. Yes, it's that flaming big bottomed Scottish star Kenny Dalglish has got his second of the game.

Depressing, our first league defeat in twelve games. First one since the other blooming Liverpool team beat us in September. It's made worse because Ipswich have won, again, they have beaten Mr Walker's Forest. He really is having a miserable week. Hope he's alright. Ipswich now have two games in hand on us and are only two points behind. Liverpool are now only three points behind and Arsenal are catching us, just four points behind. Even Haystacks' Baggies are closing the gap. They are now just five points behind, with a game in hand. Thank goodness they haven't brought that silly three points for a win in yet. At least we are well ahead of Wolves. Actually Wolves are getting quite near the bottom in 17th place. Surely Andy Gray and co. can't be relegated, a year after winning the League Cup?

8:10 Saturday night and we're all sat round the telly to find out the answer to 1980's biggest question, "Who shot J.R.?" Dallas is a favourite of mine and I am glad that J.R. Ewing isn't dead. He was shot in March, at the end of the last series. Really could have been any of his enemies. I think it is Dusty Farlow though, Sue Ellen's lover who disappeared in the plane crash. Mum is convinced it is Sue Ellen herself who pulled the trigger. Haystacks has been saying all week that it is Vaughn Leland, a banker J.R. swindled lots of money out of. Tucker has an 'I Shot JR' tee-shirt he got on his holiday in Morecambe. Spud is still disgusted that The Baron Nights used the tune from Gary Numan's 'Cars' to record their 'We know who dunnit' song. We will soon all know who shot J.R. Ewing. They say this is going to be one of the biggest ever television audiences.

J.R. is by the Southfork pool in a wheelchair. Looking in good nick for somebody recently shot. He thinks Sue Ellen is going to kill him. He has managed to stand up. Not a very butch blue dressing gown. Sue Ellen says she is just looking for Kristin, her sister. I think J.R. was having an affair with her. Her surname is Shepherd, but I don't think Sue Ellen's maiden name was Shepherd. Oh Kristin has arrived and Sue Ellen says Kristin tried to frame her. Yes, Sue Ellen went to the office with J.R.'s gun, but says she was too drunk. As usual. It was Kristin though who took the gun off her and shot J.R. It was Kristin Shepherd who shot J.R. Ewing! I didn't expect that. I knew it wasn't Sue Ellen though. So J.R. is now calling the Dallas police. They must have a hotline from Southfork, the number of times they suddenly arrive. But wait, Kristin has just revealed she is pregnant with J.R.'s baby. So J.R. isn't going to phone the police. He doesn't want his child being born in prison. So at least we now know who shot J.R. The only mystery now is what happened to Mr. Walker. I guess we'll find out Monday morning at school.

9:05am Monday 24th November 1980

The return of Bellington and he's taking great delight in telling everybody that Mr Walker has been sacked. This really is the worst news. Two of the girls are crying at this revelation. Typical of Bellington to come out on top. The supply teacher Mr

Thomas-Ball is in charge again and continuing to treat us like primary school children. He even insists on us all saying 'Good morning Mr Thomas-Ball' when he reads our name out on the register. I bet he doesn't even like football. I am going to miss Mr Walker.

As we are leaving the form room, Bellington decides it's time to celebrate his Liverpool team's win over Villa by punching me several teams while tunelessly singing 'You'll never walk alone'. He thinks it's funny to then change the words to 'You'll never work again, Mr Walker'. I don't suppose Bellington will ever get a job. Mind you with unemployment rising so fast at the moment, will any of us? That last Bellington punch really hurt. My arm pain is eased though by a gentle tap on the shoulder by Grace Taylor. She whispers in my ear. Her lips nearly touching my ear. Whilst contemplating if this counted as a kiss, I realised what it was she was whispering. I must admit I hadn't really been paying attention at first, as I was too busy enjoying the feeling of her blowing in my ear. It was about Mr Walker. It seems that Bellington's lying and that Mr Walker has not been sacked. She asks me to meet her in the Library at dinner time so she can fully explain it all to me. This is becoming a habit.

As agreed I meet Grace Taylor in the Library, trying to make sense of what she is very nervously telling me. I have questions to ask about her relationship with Bellington, but Mr Walker's future, at the moment, is more important. I need him for my O-Level Maths next year. Listening carefully to the very pretty Grace Taylor, I try not to stare into her eyes too much.

Just as Grace is explaining what had really happened to Mr Foster, Noddy appears from nowhere, grabs me by my now bruised arm and starts to excitedly ask if I have heard about Mr Walker. Noddy goes on to say how last Wednesday Mr Walker's dad had a massive heart attack and that's why Mr Walker was behaving so oddly on Thursday and why he lost it big time with Bellington. I turned back to Grace for confirmation of this and another chance to gaze into her eyes, but she'd gone. Noddy appeared to be well informed. Apparently he had been talking to Mrs Cresswell-Farrington. He always was her favourite. So where is Mr Walker now? Noddy knows everything. It seems that when Miss Thatcher came to fetch him it wasn't to tell him off it was because she had just received a phone call for Mr Walker to tell him his dad had died. Mr Walker is off for a few days arranging the funeral. Poor Mr Walker. I ask Noddy about the Bellington incident, but Noddy claims that it was never reported. That seems very strange to me, but I am sure Mr Walker has much more important things to worry about than Bellington. I can't imagine one of my grandfathers' dying, let alone my dad. Must be dreadful deciding if you are going to bury them or burn them. Think I would rather be buried just in case I am still alive. You get nearly a week before they bury you.

Spud is really gloating this morning and I am actually quite happy he is. He is gloating because incredibly last night Wolves produced their best performance of the season. They beat mighty Liverpool 4-1 at Molineux. Spud keeps pointing out that as Liverpool beat us on Saturday then Wolves are much better than the Villa. A point my very happy brother also pointed out when he arrived home from the match yesterday. Even Emlyn Hughes, the former Liverpool legend, scored for Wolves. But for once I don't mind the team in Old Gold winning. It means Liverpool have blown their game in hand on us and they are still three points behind.

Always exciting to stay up to watch Sportsnight on a Wednesday. Tonight is one of my favourite of the year though. It is the annual Daily Express 5-a-side tournament from Wembley. Well, Wembley Arena. You couldn't really play 5-a-side on the enormous Wembley Stadium pitch. Villa often do well in the 5-a-side. It says in the Daily Express that they are entering this year, but Ron Saunders isn't keen on sending any of his star players as they have to play Arsenal on Saturday. Also the reserves were playing Albion and the youth team were playing Fulham tonight so I don't know who will be representing the Villa.

The BBC are showing Villa playing Tottenham first. That's interesting, Villa have got some star names playing after all. They have Kenny Swain, Allan Evans, Des Bremner and Peter Withe playing. Quite a big tall team for 5-a-side. Hope Withe and Evans can keep the ball down. They have also got Noel Blake who is one of the biggest black men I have ever seen. I don't really think he is made for 5-a-side. He starts as sub though. Who is that little bloke in goal? It isn't Jimmy Rimmer or even reserve goalie Nigel Spink. Apparently, his name is Kevin Poole. He looks like he should be at school.

Well, somehow we are into the second round after beating Spurs 2-0. Some good saves by Kevin Poole. I am feeling tired, but will stay up until the Villa are out. Probably won't be long as Man United next.

Some Show Jumping now before the semi–finals. Villa having beaten Manchester United 2-0 face Arsenal in the second semi-final. Hopefully a cup of dad's special hot chocolate in my Villa mug will keep me awake.

Chelsea are into the Final so let's see if we can join them. That's number five, the Villa are on fire. 6, 7.... Wow 7-1 that was a real pounding. Same again on Saturday at Villa Park please. No way am I going to bed yet. We have a final to win. Up the Villa.

Watching Kenny Swain lift the cup I feel very proud. What a night. Four games, four wins, fourteen goals and only one against. The 3-0 Final win emphasising Villa's domination. Maybe we will be back at the real Wembley in May to lift the FA Cup. Who knows perhaps it will see Villa complete the double like they did in 1897.

Spud is in a great mood this morning and not just because he knew all the answers in the unexpected RE test on Judaism. The main reason is this weekend he is going on his first date with Carrie Campton. Perhaps the term 'date' is stretching it a bit, as it is just painting scenery together for the 'Mikado'. There will be other people there, but Carrie has agreed for Spud to walk her home afterwards. Even though it is about three miles out of his way. I am pleased for Spud. He deserves some happiness. It isn't even December yet and already Spud is asking my advice on what to buy Carrie for Christmas. Well, Haystacks has got a girl and now Spud so I guess we are all starting to move to a new phase in our teenage lives. Perhaps I will be next, although Pincher is the pretty boy of the group. I don't think Tucker or Noddy are mature enough yet for girls. I guess being Walsall fans they are still a couple of divisions behind the rest of us. I wonder if I will ever see Walsall in the First Division in my lifetime. Then again will I ever ask Grace Taylor out in my lifetime? If Spud can be brave enough to ask scary Carrie Campton out, surely I should be able to ask Grace Taylor out. Yes, she might be going out with bully Bellington but that doesn't mean she won't go out with me. I mean, Janet Hogan went out with Matt Andrews and his brother Stephen even though she was supposed to be going out with Carl Presley. I think I would rather Bellington didn't find out though. Really don't want to have to explain any more bruises to my mum.

If Villa beat Arsenal at home tomorrow I am going to ask Grace Taylor out on Monday.

3:01pm Saturday 29th November 1980

Villa have just kicked off at home to Arsenal and I am dressed as an elf sitting outside Santa's Grotto, in the middle of Bilston. Why does my church insist on having their Christmas Sale on a Saturday afternoon? It isn't even Advent yet. Quite a queue of children. Wish Santa would hurry up. That little spotty one looks like he's about to wee himself. The Grotto looks very impressive with lots of white polystyrene squiggles on the floor and white bin liners pinned all over the ceiling. I helped my dad and brother to build it. Mark made the enormous polar bear that has frightened quite a few of the smaller children. Come on Santa. Let's get this next family in so I can listen to the radio. Difficult to hear though against the tape recording of Christmas 'Spinners' songs that is playing. It is only 3:10 and already three of the dads have asked me what the Wolves score is. Wolves are at home to Stoke, surely they will win that one. Albion are at Spurs, Walsall are at home to Sheffield United, if anybody cares. Sheffield United have certainly tumbled. They used to always be in the First Division in the 70s, when Tony Currie was their star player. Listening discreetly to Radio Birmingham whilst taking the money off the excited kids. All I ever keep hearing is, "goal at Fellows Park". Lost count of the score, but I think Walsall are losing. Still no goals at Villa Park. I can't believe how excited little Amy (from

Sunday School) is about seeing Father Christmas. I am sure she'll be heartbroken if she finds out it's only Cyril, the Organist, in a red dressing gown with cotton wool beard.

That's it. Santa has no naff gifts left so 4pm and time to close up. Feel like a really mean elf turning these children away. At least I can put the radio on louder and listen to most of the second-half now, while we pick up all the polystyrene squiggles and rip all the bin liners down. I have never known such a sweaty Santa, it really smells in here.

Goal horn and it is another one at Walsall. It's 3-3 now. Another goal horn straight away. This time Molineux and Wolves have taken the lead against Stoke City. Come on Villa we need to beat the 'Gunners'. Yet another goal horn. It is going mad. This time it is Villa Park. 1-0 to the champions elect. Super winger Tony Morley has scored yet another cracker. Apparently there is snow on the pitch, but a Morley - Gary Shaw one-two before Morley gave Pat Jennings no chance. I sing 'We are going to win the League' in a deserted Santa's Grotto.

Oh the reporter is saying that captain Dennis Mortimer has just sent the screamer against the crossbar. It is all Villa. Good news also is that Ipswich's game against Middlesbrough has been postponed because of snow. Villa will be lots of points clear at the top tonight at this rate.

I am now sat on the floor by Santa's red cushioned seat feeling quite tearful. It was going so well until Brian Talbot scored an equaliser for Arsenal. Final score was 1-1 so I guess I won't have to ask Grace Taylor out on Monday. I wonder how Spud's 'date' with Carrie Campton went. He will be frozen walking her home in this weather. At least he will find out Wolves won 1-0 when he gets home. I bet Tucker and Noddy enjoyed the 4-4 draw at Walsall. Haystacks will be celebrating Albion winning 3-2 at Tottenham. They really are catching us now. Perhaps I won't be winning the bet at the end of the season. Which manager named Ron will come out on top at the end of the season? Disciplinarian Ron Saunders or flash champagne-drinking Ron Atkinson? I must keep the faith. The Villa will finish the top Midland team. Anyway, there's still the FA Cup to come.

12:32pm Sunday 30th November 1980

The first Sunday in Advent is an odd day. It is too early to start feeling Christmassy even though yesterday I was helping Santa. We have been to see my dad's parents on the way home from Church and Grandpa just didn't seem his normal self. I hadn't seen him for a few weeks, but today he just looked much older. He didn't get up from his chair the whole time we were there and my parents seemed more attentive to him than usual. We still chatted about the football. He didn't stay up to watch the Villa on Star Soccer last night, so it was left to me to explain how unlucky the Villa were. The smashing Mortimer shot deserved to be a goal. Pat Jennings was well beaten.

Sitting on the floor reading the 'Pink' Sporting Star, my mind is still on Grandpa. His eyes looked quite dull and something was definitely not right. Dad hadn't said a lot since we came back. Perhaps I should ask him about Grandpa, but it might upset him and Match of the Day starts in half an hour.

Today as well as being the first Sunday in Advent is also St. Andrew's Day. So happy St. Andrew's Day to our three Scottish Villa players. Well, four if you count Alex Cropley. Not sure if he will be at the Villa much longer. Never did really recover from that broken leg. But happy St. Andrew's Day to Allan Evans, Ken McNaught, Des Bremner and Alex Cropley. I don't think Des Bremner looks very Scottish. Ken McNaught certainly does. You can imagine McNaught as some great mad Scottish warrior in a kilt. Noddy says that his uncle heard that Ken McNaught has been playing with a great big cut on his leg that needs to be stitched before every game. His uncle says they sometimes tape it up inside his sock to keep the stitches in place. Mind you Noddy's uncle also says that Brian Clough is going to replace Ron Greenwood as England manager. I don't think the Football Association would let a loudmouth like Cloughie into Lancaster Gate. He might play Peter Withe though, as he did so well for him at Forest. A forward line for England of Withe and Shaw with Tony Morley on the wing. Then Dennis Mortimer commanding midfield and Gordon 'Sidney' Cowans spraying his wonderful passes all over Wembley. Two fullbacks under the famous Twin Towers could be Kenny Swain and Colin Gibson. Cloughie would pick Forest keeper Peter Shilton before Jimmy Rimmer though. But six Villa players in the starting England eleven would be pretty good. Just hope England don't try and poach Ron Saunders from us.

In the Sunday People it says that Norwich new manager Ken Brown has paid £100,000 for a nineteen-year-old defender called Dave Watson. Not the old Man City one who now plays at Southampton, but one from Liverpool's reserves. Seems a lot of money for me for someone with no experience.

Really good Tales of the Unexpected tonight called 'Parsons Pleasure'. A crooked antiques dealer was masquerading as a clergyman. He was claiming to be collecting old furniture, he came across a farmer who gave him an antique piece worth a fortune. Still like seeing the silhouettes of the naked ladies dancing at the start of the programme. I wonder if they recorded it with them dancing naked. Bet that was fun to be in the lighting gantry for.

End of November Top of Division One		
Aston Villa	Pl: 20 Po: 29	+17
Liverpool	Pl: 20 Po: 27	+17
Ipswich Town	Pl: 17 Po: 26	+17
Wet Brom	Pl: 20 Po: 26	+9
Arsenal	Pl: 20 Po: 25	+10
Man United	Pl: 20 Po: 24	+13

Villa November League Results	
1st Leicester City (h)	2-0 Won (Shaw, Cowans)
8th West Brom (a)	0-0 Draw
12th Norwich City (a)	3-1 Won (Shaw 2, Evans)
15th Leeds United (h)	1-1 Draw (Shaw)
22nd Liverpool (a)	1-2 Lost (Evans)
29th Arsenal (h)	1-1 Draw (Morley)

Chapter Five (December)

Funny that even at thirteen I am excited about opening the first window on my Advent Calendar, even though I have opened the same cardboard window every year since I can remember. I have left it until after school to open window one and sure enough the trusty angel is still there. Still not sure if the blond angel is male or female, but I don't suppose it matters in Heaven. I suppose I need to start thinking about writing a Christmas list. I would love a Villa white away top and maybe a new Villa duvet cover. I suppose I really should ask for money to help my Atari Fund, it has stopped the last few months. No, I want presents to unwrap on Christmas Day, Space Invaders can wait a bit longer. A TV gantry tower with a cameraman on for the Subbuteo would be good as well.

9:17am Tuesday 2nd December 1980

Mr Walker is back and quite chirpy this morning. All the girls seem especially pleased to see him. Bellington is quieter than usual, but Mr Walker is joking with him. I think Mr Walker is keen to make amends for bashing him. The 'Mikado' performances are now just two weeks away so Mr Walker is keen to get us experienced with the lighting. We will have to attend all the rehearsals from now on including the Dress Rehearsal. This is good news as Grace Taylor will be there at every rehearsal playing her clarinet in the orchestra at the front of the stage.

Lunchtime and Spud is showing Pincher, Tucker and me the scenery he painted with Carrie Campton on Saturday. It's really good, although Tucker is surprised to find some of it is still wet. Hope that red paint washes off my blazer. We are all keen to know how Spud's date went. But I am suspecting not that well as Spud has been grumpy all morning. Also the fact that Carrie Campton walked straight past him in the dinner queue did not bode well. In fact, not only had she walked passed, but she quite clearly exaggerated looking completely away from Spud.

Spud is trying to convince the three of us that the date went well. It was like the 'Summer Nights' scene in Grease, as we tried to get information out of Spud. You could image Carrie Campton with her girlfriends having a similar chat. I think Spud is suggesting there was a kiss. Well, an attempt at a kiss. I don't think he got very far. Apparently because it was -1 degrees. Spud gave Carrie his leather jacket, well his borrowed brother's leather jacket, as they walked back and Spud was frozen. When they got to Carrie Campton's house Spud was hoping to be invited in, but Carrie shut the door. He had to ring the bell to get his brother's leather jacket back. I don't know why he is so obsessed by Carrie Campton. She is so stuck up and isn't even very pretty. Spud could attract a much nicer girl. As long as it isn't Grace Taylor.

Tonight's rehearsal of 'Mikado' is turning into a total fiasco. Music teacher Mr Pemberton has just totally gone ballistic with the choir for coming in late on 'Comes a train of little ladies' and part of the scenery that Spud made came tumbling down after Yum Yum caught her heel in it. The lighting is going very wrong as both Pincher and Noddy are missing. Pincher hasn't been at school all day and Noddy went home ill this afternoon after going to see the nurse. So Haystacks, Tucker and me are trying to get all the light fades and spotlights right. Tucker is really struggling, he keeps fading the steel blue lights instead of the straw yellow ones. We will never get this right on the night. Mr Pemberton is now asking Spud if he will try to sing the same tune as the rest of the choir. Carrie Campton is saying that she is not used to working with such amateurs.

The disastrous rehearsal is finally over and Noddy's dad has come to see Mr Walker for some reason. He was picking up Noddy's little sister, Elizabeth, who is one of the choir. Mr Walker doesn't look happy. Lots of shaking of his head. What has Noddy done now?

So both Noddy and Pincher won't be doing the lighting for 'The Mikado' because they have got chicken pox. Triple whammy for me, as I am pretty sure I haven't had chicken pox. I will have to check with my mum when I get home. So two men down and I was with them both all yesterday. I need to remain spot-free and we will still need extra help up in the gantry. Mind you after tonight's rehearsal the stage in darkness might not be such a bad thing. I don't think any song got through to the end without Mr Pemberton shouting.

Now to get home to see the end of Top of the Pops because Abba are number one with 'Super Trouper'. I haven't seen the video yet, but very appropriate a song about a big light when I am working as part of a lighting crew.

10:00 Saturday 6th December 1980

So cold today. Hope the Villa game at Boro isn't postponed. Dad says there's snow forecast. Peter Withe is suspended for reaching twenty disciplinary points. He is going to miss three games. We need to win today. We can't go a fourth game without a win. Perhaps David Geddis (Withe's replacement) will find the net. Can't believe we have to rehearse 'The Mikado' on a Saturday either, although I'll be home for kick-off unless we get snowed in. It will be a struggle without Pincher and Noddy and less fun. Especially as Tucker always misses his cue to fade. Pincher was easily the best of us. We will miss him probably as much as the Villa will miss Peter Withe.

Dad was punctual as always so I am the first of the lighting team here. Haystacks and Tucker are supposed to be coming together as Haystacks has to walk past Tucker's house to get to school. Tucker though is always late. Even though he lives the nearest to the school, he often arrives after the late school bus pupils. Tucker blames his frequent lateness on his close proximity to the school. He claims as he only lives five minutes away that if he is late there's no time to catch up.

Oh, there is Grace Taylor walking into school. Maybe I can catch her eye and say hello. I could tell her about the chicken pox epidemic, ask her how she would like to be lit or just find out if she thinks Villa will win at Boro. Damn, she isn't alone. Unfortunately her rumoured boyfriend Bellington is right behind her. What is Bellington doing here? Surely Mr Pemberton won't let him watch the rehearsal?

Finally Haystacks arrives followed by a very out of breath Tucker. It seems Tucker was watching Sally James on Tiswas in his pyjamas and forgotten totally about the rehearsal, until Haystacks started banging at his door. Up in the gantry Mr Walker is waiting for us looking at his watch, like Clive Thomas about to blow the full-time whistle at the end of an important match. Haystacks always goes on about how in the World Cup Final game between Brazil and Sweden Thomas blew full-time seconds before Zico scored what would have been the winning goal. Brazilians still aren't fans of the Welsh referee.

Mr Walker wants to ask the three of us something very important. I have the feeling we aren't going to like this. He did say 'ask', but it seems more like 'tell' to me. I'm surprised even Grace Taylor down in orchestra didn't hear me shout, "No". Mr Walker has decided that as we are two men down, we need a substitute. Somebody who could join the team with only a week to go before the show. Tucker is thinking who they could ask, but it's too late. Bellington has already been asked by Mr Walker. I think Mr Walker is trying to smooth over things with the boy he bashed a week ago. It seems Bellington agreed yesterday, that's why he is now climbing up the gantry steps. What a nightmare! He will probably end up pushing me off the gantry and I will land on top of poor Spud in the choir. Bellington is thick and will never master these difficult controls. It will be a complete farce.

It's now snowing a blizzard at Middlesbrough and they are midway through the second-half, still goalless. I need Villa to win to make this day at least a little bit bearable. Bellington wasn't quite so much of a pain as I had feared this morning, but still made me very nervous and took all the enjoyment out of being in the lighting crew. I know it was his first time, but he made so many mistakes. Worst of all he kept trying to blame me for the fact that Nanki-Poo was in total darkness for most of his solo.

As BBC Radio 2 have second-half commentary from Ayresome Park (Boro's ground) it means that BBC Radio Birmingham broadcast the commentary only going away for goals in the other West Midland games. Albion are at home to Leeds and Wolves at Arsenal. Goals everywhere but the commentary game. Bryon Butler is commentating but now struggling to see the play through the blizzard. He tells us that Jimmy Rimmer's wife, Christine, had a baby son in the early hours this morning. Congratulations to Jimmy then. Bet he would like to keep a clean sheet for his new son. Hope the team coach can get back alright tonight in the snow, for Jimmy's sake.

Albion are losing now, so this could be the chance for the Villa to put a gap between us and Haystacks' team. Just ten minutes left. Radio commentaries make me so tense, as I really don't know how close to the goal the ball actually is. Middlesbrough seem to be doing all the attacking. We need to win though, we've been doing poor lately, despite being top of the league.

Oh no, Boro have scored. Australian Craig Johnston has given them the lead with only eight minutes to go. This really is a rubbish day. Looks like the paperboy has forgotten to deliver my Roy of the Rovers too. What else can go wrong today?

Hold on, a chance for Villa. Mortimer good run, plays in Gary Shaw. YESSS!!! One each, we are not giving up our place at the top of my League Ladder. Before Boro have even kicked off I am colouring in a square by Gary Shaw's name on the 'My Team Performance 1980-81' chart. Shaw has now scored thirteen goals this season. Certainly not an unlucky number. It's only 6th December. He could score 30 this season. More than 30 would be a challenge as there are only 30 squares by each scorer on the chart. Still two minutes to go, shall I be brave and fill in the league position graph? It has been a flat line down since October 22nd. I shall get my Aston Villa FC ruler ready.

Another late goal and Jimmy Rimmer beaten twice on the day his son was born. Shearer gets the winner and we have lost again. Fourth time this season and second straight 2-1 away defeat. Worst of all Liverpool have won at home to Spurs so

Liverpool are now top. I suppose second to Liverpool is pretty good, but we haven't won now for four games. I am not going to update the tabs on my league ladder today. Villa can stay top for another day.

5:10pm Sunday 7th December 1980

Just watching the Villa - Middlesbrough game on Match of the Day. Grandad did his usual joke. "Perhaps they will win this time". Villa look very good in our all white kit with claret and blue trim. I prefer it with the light blue shorts though, must get away top for Christmas and maybe the socks. Looks very cold. Both goalies are wearing tights under their shorts, well they look like tights. Jimmy Rimmer seems to look better in tights than Jim Walker does. I bet it wasn't much fun playing in that blizzard. The snow didn't stick though, so no need for the orange ball. Great ball from Mortimer and Gary Shaw slots the ball between the Boro keeper's legs. Great goal. Commentator calls Shaw, "A goal machine". I can't watch the Middlesbrough winner, I shall just pretend it ended 1-1 and that we are still top of the league.

Liverpool are on top on goal difference. They have +18 to our +16. Ipswich are two points behind us after they drew at Manchester City, but they have only played 18 games. Three less than our 21. We are half way through the 42 game season. 29 points is not bad. Crystal Palace only have 10 points at the bottom. They have lost five of their last six games. They might start improving, Jimmy Hill has just told us that they have today appointed former Man City manager Malcolm Allison as their new boss.

5:45pm Tuesday 9th December 1980

I have spent far too many hours in the company of Bellington today. As if form period and Metalwork were not enough, we now have the last but one rehearsal for 'The Mikado'. He tries to criticise my fading skills. It wasn't me who misread steel for straw in scene four. Tucker is dreadful and Haystacks spends the whole time trying not to sneeze. I shall be glad when this show is finished. Bellington even has the cheek to suggest Grace Taylor is fat. Mr Walker seems to be treating Bellington like some prodigal son at the moment. While Bellington seems to have forgotten the beating that Mr Walker recently gave him.

Some moments in your life probably stay with you forever. Some moments are a shared worldwide experience. This is both of those. Difficult to take in, but the radio is now backing up everything Dad has just told me as we drive home from the rehearsal. The Beatles legend John Lennon is dead. The man who, with Paul McCartney, wrote songs like 'Yesterday', 'Let it be', 'Roll over Beethoven' and 'Yellow Submarine' was shot in America last night. My dad seems upset, but then he should be, one of our greatest British pop stars has been assassinated. A man who had just featured so heavily in my Music Project. My brother, a real Beatles fan, is going to be devastated. How could anybody shoot a man who was so keen on peace? John Lennon never hurt anybody. The worst thing he did was stage a sit-in in bed with his wife Yoko. He is, well was, a music icon. It would be like somebody killing Bjorn from Abba. Lennon was 40, and they say shot outside his home in New York City. He was pronounced dead on arrival at hospital. Nobody seems to know why. The man who shot him did give himself up and has been arrested. Seems like he might have been a fan. John Lennon had a five-year-old son called Sean.

All the news tonight is of Lennon's killing. I feel quite sad about this. At least I got to write my Music Pop Project about him before he died. I wonder if he was a Liverpool or Everton fan. I might not like it but perhaps fitting that Liverpool are top of the league on the day he was shot.

11:11am Wednesday 10th December 1980

Talk at school today is not about 'Mikado' opening night (tomorrow) but about John Lennon's shooting. Most of the children do seem quite upset, it even gets a mention in Miss Thatcher's assembly. Insensitive Bellington did try to re-enact the shooting with a pen top and an elastic band. Not surprisingly he wanted me to play John Lennon. The gunman still hasn't been named, he told onlookers, "I have just shot John Lennon". In last night's paper it said Mr Lennon staggered up six steps into the vestibule after he was shot, before collapsing. How stupid that the Americans let people carry guns. I am glad I live in Britain.

Grace Taylor is crying at break time by her locker. Thinking it must be over John Lennon I am trying to tell her I understand and about my Pop Music project. Sadly I guessed wrong, it is actually because her pet hamster, Bam Bam, has died after having a big lump on his back. Still I am having my longest ever conversation with Grace, I am cheering her up a bit. Wish I had a hanky I could whip out like a real gentlemen. Grace Taylor's eyes are so perfectly circular and such a great shade of brown. I wonder if she has noticed my nice blue eyes. Our conversation goes on to how nervous we both are about Thursday's opening performance. Grace says she has bought an extra four clarinet reeds in case she runs out. I just pretend I know how clarinets work, but really have no idea what purpose these reeds play. Oddly, Grace strokes my right arm, tells me not worry and that Kenny won't let me down. As she walks away it clicks that she means Bellington and the lighting crew.

Curtain up in just ten minutes now. I am busy reading all the cues on the script. Tucker seems to be the most laid back of us all. He seems more interested in finishing his Geography homework that is due in tomorrow. Haystacks looks worried, probably because Georgina Ramsey is sitting in the audience right next to Karl Slater, the boy she threatened to snog. Mr Walker isn't his normal self either. Not surprising as yesterday was his dad's funeral. In fact the only person behaving normally is Kenny Bellington. Well, not really normal for Bellington as he isn't poking and thumping me. This is a new side to Bellington. He seems quite determined to get it right. He asks me a few questions to check he fully understands some of the changes. He even wishes us all good luck as Mr Walker announces five minutes. All the seats in the audience are now full. Tickets have sold out for both nights. With each school family allowed a maximum of four. Although this hasn't stopped Carrie Campton from getting over 20 for her family and friends. Tickets were 50p each, but it is rumoured that Carrie's Mum paid more than £2 for some of hers. Seems it helps being one of the school governors.

We can see Spud in the off-stage choir and he gives us a thumbs-up. At least as he is off-stage he hasn't got to wear one of those ridiculous red dressing gowns. They look more like mini Santa Clauses than Japanese characters. Their faces though have all been plastered with white makeup, which makes them look like Santa Claus ghosts.

Grace Taylor looks especially pristine in her neatly ironed uniform, her clarinet looks the shiniest of all the clarinets in the orchestra. I try to catch her eye, but at that point Tucker correctly brings all the house lights down.

Brilliant show. The lighting crew excelled with only three real mistakes. Two of them unfortunately mine. Bellington did really well and was actually very supportive of my blunders. One of them was during the second encore of 'Three Little Maids from School are we'. I was admiring the brilliant clarinet playing of Grace Taylor at the time. All those clarinet lessons she goes to certainly paid off. Spud seemed to sing quite tunefully, although I have never seen anybody sweat quite as much. As expected Carrie Campton stole the show and didn't she know it. Her solo gets the biggest applause. It is quite a buzz being involved in such a great show and unlike 'late comer' 'Bellington; Tucker, Haystacks and me got our names in the programme. Carrie Campton will be cross, she is down in the programme as Garrie Campton. I am surprised she didn't go on strike.

We are giving Haystacks a lift home and he is asking my mum if she thinks the three spots that have come out on his stomach this evening are chickenpox. Looks like there will just be three of us tomorrow night.

10:32pm Thursday 11th December 1980

I am worn out and shattered after two sell-out shows. I think tonight's was even better than the first night. The audience demanded three encores and even we got applauded in the lighting gantry. It really was hard work especially without Haystacks. I have to say that Kenny Bellington did very well. Maybe he isn't quite as bad I thought. The only conflict came when he made me say that Liverpool are more likely to win the League than Aston Villa, while holding a stapler to my left ear. Trying to wind down before bed now, but I really am still on a high. Keep singing 'Three Little Maids from school'.

6:02pm Friday 12th December 1980

Express and Star has an interview with Archie Gemmill, the Birmingham City player ahead of tomorrow's big Birmingham derby tomorrow at Villa Park. To think I cheered Gemmill when he played for Scotland in the World Cup in Argentina. Now he is really slagging off the Villa. Saying they aren't good enough to win the title. He is probably right, we haven't won for four games and Peter Withe is still suspended.

4:06pm Saturday 13th December 1980

That's it long enough, we need a goal and the second-half is already ten minutes old. Time for my lucky radio, even if the aerial is broken. It still works, just have to turn it upside down occasionally. Frank Worthington has a chance, but apart from that it has been all Villa. Tony Morley hit the bar in the first-half when he cut in from the Trinity Road Stand side. David Geddis had a chance as well, but the reporter thinks they are really missing Peter Withe. You can't play with two blonde-haired pretty-boy strikers.

Ipswich are playing Liverpool so they both can't win. This is our chance to go back to the top. Problem is I don't know if I want Ipswich or Liverpool to win. I suppose Ipswich winning would put us top, but then they already have three games in hand on us. Albion losing at Coventry so that is good and Arsenal are somehow losing to Sunderland. It seems Malcolm Allison is weaving his magic already, his Crystal Palace are thumping Norwich.

Finally I have got my lucky radio tuned in. I had to turn it upside down and open the window. Blues keeper Jeff Whelan has just made a brilliant save from Gary Shaw. Birmingham did think they had just scored. A goal by Berchin was disallowed, quite rightly, for offside.

The goal horn. it's off to Villa Park. I can hardly breathe. Lots of sounds of celebration. It's a goal by David Geddis. 1-0 to the Villa. Well done the lucky radio. It was right in front of the Holte End apparently. Now we just need to hold on.

Another goal at Villa Park. Surely we haven't let the Blue Noses back in. Yippee!! Gary Gary Shaw. He has scored another goal. This time Geddis hit the post and Shaw half volleyed it in. 2-0 to the Villa. Liverpool are still drawing with Ipswich. We could be top again. Up the Villa!

Radio Birmingham reporter says it is all Villa. David Geddis should have had four, but as the reporter is handing back to the studio Geddis does score again. Villa rampant. Blues destroyed. 3-0.

22 games played and we are top of the league. What a day. Ipswich 1 Liverpool 1. My Roy of the Rovers comic has arrived and on the front cover Roy has been shot, wearing his Melchester club blazer. The headline is 'ROY RACE SHOT!' with blood dripping down the 'SHOT' part. Looks like a man's hand holding the gun. At least it can't be wife Penny then. What a month! First J.R., then John Lennon and now the most famous fictional footballer of all has been shot. I can't wait to read the cartoon

inside, but more important things first. Sorry Roy. For first time ever the draw for the 3rd Round of the FA Cup is going to be live on the telly. The biggest football cup in the world. This year I just know it's going to be the Villa's year and somehow I will get a ticket to the FA Cup Final. It stands to reason Aston Villa will be there, it's the 100th FA Cup and Villa hold the record for winning it seven times. It might be a staggering 24 long years since we last won it, but come May I have a real feeling there will be claret and blue ribbons on the famous trophy and not West Ham this time.

Walsall are out of the FA Cup after losing 3-0 at Carlisle today. Non-League Enfield are through and St. Albans City got a draw with Torquay. I would prefer to play a Third or Fourth Division team. I don't want the embarrassment of not scoring lots against a non-league side.

We are normally ball number two, it hasn't come out yet. Liverpool are at home to Scunthorpe or Altrincham. Mr Walker's Forest are at home. Please don't draw the Villa next. They will play Bolton Wanderers. Albion are at home next and have drawn Grimsby Town. Why couldn't we have had that draw? Hope we don't have to play Wolves. Everton at home to Arsenal that'll be a good game. Glad we have avoided Arsenal. Next one out is Ipswich Town. That is certainly one to avoid. I wonder who they will get. NO!!!! It is ball number two and as I predicted that is Aston Villa. A very difficult tie, but we owe them one for beating us at Portman Road earlier in the season.

Non-League Enfield will be disappointed at having to go to Port Vale. Wolves are away to Stoke City. Last season's winners West Ham are lucky as they have Wrexham at home.

I am sure it's Vic Guthrie who has shot Roy even though it is him calling the ambulance. Everyone is now arriving at Melchester General Hospital. Roy Race can't die! He's like J.R. Ewing and Captain Scarlet: indestructible. He has brain damage and is in a coma. Knowing Roy Race he will probably still score a hat-trick in the cup game next week. Blackie Gray has been made Caretaker Player Manager. I don't usually fill in the marks out of ten at the bottom of each story, but this has been a good week so I'll give it nine out of ten. The Roy of the Rovers cartoon is the only one in the comic that is ever in colour. I guess it is favouritism, they must print those pages separately. There are two pages of messages from celebrities to Roy saying 'Get well soon'. Who is there that I recognise? Morecombe and Wise have both written messages. As well as the Radio One DJ Mike Read. The footballers include Trevor Francis, who has very neat writing and blooming Ipswich forward Paul Mariner. Managers Alf Ramsey and Lawrie McMenemy have also left messages. Hope Roy does get better.

As Villa stuffed Birmingham so well I am for once going to fill in the 'My Team's Performance – This Week!' page in my comic. I need to find out who the referee was though. Will have to look carefully when it's on Match of the Day tomorrow. Goalscorers: Geddis, Shaw and Geddis again. My marks out of 10 for our performance is 9. Not 10 because they didn't score in the first-half. 'My comments on the match' I am going to put 'Great improvement and back TOP OF THE LEAGUE'. I put the last bit in capitals so it stands out. The 'Famous Football Funnies' page this week really aren't very funny. One cartoon has two subs on the bench. The normal No. 12 and the other player wearing 99 on his back. The best joke is probably from Darren Alanville; it has a couple getting married with the vicar. The Bride says, "Does all his worldly goods include his football season ticket?" I shall have to start thinking where I am going to keep my season ticket safe when I have it next year.

Surprise surprise, Gordon Stewart has kept another clean sheet in 'The Safest Hands in Soccer'. Still don't think it's very believable having a good Scottish goalkeeper. One of my favourite stories is still 'Tommy's Troubles', maybe it is because Tommy Barnes is the same age as me. He and his mate Ginger Collins have formed their own team called Barnes United. I expect Ginger wanted to call it Collins United, but that would make you think it full of boys named Colin.

Definitely though, my all-time favourite strip in Roy of the Rovers is 'The Hard Man'. John Dexter is like Allan Evans. Nothing gets past him at the back and he scores goals. The chubby little bald track-suited Hungarian manager is so funny. Today Danesfield are playing a Norwegian team in the European Cup. A few of the players have got seasick. Be great if Villa did win the League this year and ended up in the European Cup next season. I can dream. In the Christmas issue next week are Rod Hull and Emu plus Daley Thompson. That'll be interesting.

2:35pm Monday 15th December 1980

Last week before we break up for Christmas and everyone is extra lively. Even our French lesson is full of laughter. We are discussing what we will be eating on the trip in February. I will not be eating snails even if they do try to disguise them by calling them escargot.

Haystacks is back at school, Mum was wrong it wasn't chickenpox but insect bites from up in the lighting gantry. He still managed to get Friday off school, but had to go Christmas shopping with his nan. Anyway, lunchtime and Haystacks is frantically giving out invites to his Birthday/Christmas Party, which is this Friday night. It's at his house. They have recently had an extension and a downstairs toilet, so plenty of room. He has already invited his girlfriend Georgina Ramsey and it looks like she has had a big say on the invitation list. Glad that I made the list but we will have to smuggle Spud in as he hasn't made it. A number of girls from Georgina Ramsey's class do appear to have been invited despite the fact that Haystacks doesn't seem to know who they are. Haystacks had wanted it to be a Blake 7 themed party, but Georgina Ramsey called this geeky. So now it is a 'Christmas Pantomime Fancy Dress Party'. So we all have to dress up as pantomime characters. Talk about short notice. Georgina Ramsey apparently already has a 'Sleeping Beauty' costume that she will be wearing. Haystacks is going to be her 'Prince Charming'. Just hope he hasn't got to wear the tights. Georgina Ramsey is letting Haystacks invite four girls from our year although he isn't allowed to pick Donna Sutton because her boobs are too big and will distract us lads. Haystacks has already invited Frances Coulton and Beverley Cartwright. Well, they invited themselves really when they heard about the party. Beverley Cartwright is going to be the Wicked Witch as she has a costume that she wore at the Halloween Disco. That leaves two places left for 3rd Year girls and both Spud and I know ideal ladies for Haystacks to ask. He could ask the ego that is Carrie Campton (or Garrie as we now calling her… behind her back) and, of course, he can ask the beautiful Grace Taylor. Haystacks wasn't against the idea but gave the invites to us to ask the girls ourselves. That wasn't the plan!

Monday night and watching Peter Duncan lighting the second candle on the Blue Peter Advent Ring. Just three Blue Peters now until Christmas. Spud tried to make one last year, but he ended up setting the tinsel alight and it came crashing down landing on a his very scared Jack Russell dog who has been nervous ever since. I need to work out how to ask Grace tomorrow to come to Haystacks' party. I am nervous already just thinking what to say. How do I start the conversation off? Maybe I ask Carrie for Spud and he asks Grace for me? No, that is an even scarier thought.

I practice saying "hello" to Grace in front of my Aston Villa mirror. The motto, on the round mirror, 'Be Prepared', has never been so true. I can hear boss Ron Saunders telling me, 'Go on Jonathan give it 110% and with the Villa fans behind you anything is possible'. But is asking Bellington's girlfriend out really the best idea?

9:27am Tuesday 16th December 1980

Great news this morning. It is my lucky day. Bellington is off with chickenpox. I won't see him again until 1981. My chances of getting a 'yes' from Grace Taylor are surely enhanced by Bellington's spots. Well done Noddy and Pincher for passing the chickenpox on.

Lunchtime and we're outside listening the chart countdown on Radio 1 with Gary Davies. Seeing if Abba's 'Super Trouper' is still top. Spud is really pleased because Carrie Campton has said 'yes' to the party. She is going to wear a big cloak she has and come as 'Little Red Riding Hood'. You would never call Carrie Campton little though. So Spud's really excited. Tucker was not so pleased though as his parents said he couldn't come to the party. He is still grounded for accidentally breaking several of next door's greenhouse windows when his Peter Powell kite dive bombed it.

John Lennon is now number one with a song called '(Just Like) Starting Over'. I suppose it was expected after the sad events of last week. Apparently, his wife had him very quickly cremated without a real funeral. I am sure God understands. Not a very Christmassy song, although still a lot more bearable than the St. Winifred's School Choir, 'There's No-one Quite like Grandma' which is now number two. 'Imagine' and 'Happy Christmas (War is Over)' by John Lennon are both also in the top twenty. He certainly liked his brackets. I quite like the one at number three though by somebody called Jona Lewie. It is 'Stop the Cavalry'. Great beat and very Christmassy. We need to record it for Haystacks' party. Maybe I could dance to it with Grace Taylor. Should I do my slow or fast dance to it?

Nearly home time and I still haven't asked Grace Taylor to the party. This is a chance, she is alone by her locker and I am going to mine in the next aisle. I am just too shy though. Missed another chance. I have missed more chances today than David Geddis did before he scored his first goal on Saturday. David didn't give up so I won't.

Just as I am planning my next attack Grace Taylor comes over to me by my locker and smiles. Had she heard about the party and was waiting to be asked? She reached into her Puma bag and pulled out a magazine. She then explained it was the Christmas copy of 'Look-in' and she had got it for me as there is a bit about a Villa player in. Flipping heck, this is unexpected. She hands me the 'Look-in' which was open at a page about the great Gordon Cowans. Grace Taylor must like me. She is giving me, or loaning me, a magazine that's cost 15p. I actually think she has purchased it just for me. Mr Walker would be impressed, it has a picture of 'The Police' on the front. Grace was walking away before I had even said 'thank you'. With my locker still wide open I run after Grace.

I am sat on my bed, in my Villa pyjamas, reading my 'Look-in' magazine that still smelt of Grace Taylor, feeling pretty pleased with life. Not only were the Villa top of the league, but I had asked Grace to Haystacks' Pantomime Party and she had said 'yes' straight away. In just 72 hours' time I will be going on my first ever proper date.

It is the first time I have really seen a 'Look-in' magazine and I actually quite like it. It has more comic strips than I expected. All of programmes are from ATV. It calls itself a Junior TV Times. My grandad has TV Times, but that is just really full of what's on ATV. I will have to show Spud this tomorrow as it has got a picture of his idol Gary Numan. It says he drives a white corvette, drinks Coke and likes messing around with synthesisers. In the inside cover is 'Serenade to Spit'. There's other Tiswas stuff on that page including a short and to the point letter (from a C. Newham of Ringwood). It reads 'Please could you flan my brothers, Harvey and Mark'.

On the telly I don't find Benny Hill funny, but I am reading the Benny Hill Page just in case Grace asks me about it at the party. 'Stewpot's Newsdesk' has got some ideas of what to buy different family members for Christmas. It seems Lego is always good for younger brothers and sisters. Ed Stewpot is also giving advice about booing at sports events. He thinks all booers should be put together. Like with the 'No Smoking' section in the cinema there should be a 'Booing Section'.

That's more my thing, a Worzel Gummidge comic strip. Worzel is having a party but the two children, John and Sue, are told the place is haunted. They can't let Worzel down though so they confide in Aunt Sally.

After a comic strip on The Smurfs which I think is aimed at very small children comes a real informative page on 'The Police'. All about Sting, Andy and Stewart. Apparently Sting likes to escape to his second house in Ireland. Not only is it somewhere to escape, but it seems there are income tax benefits. I didn't know that. Apparently, Sting appeared in an X-rated movie called 'Quadrophenia' when he was younger. I wonder if Mr Walker knows that.

Bosley is hiding in the bushes in Charlie's Angels. He has got a great job working with those pretty ladies. Even as a black and white cartoon they look very glamorous. They're giving those baddies a real kicking. 'Krakk!!', 'Whapp!' and 'Whoomph!' the Angels take down the Mafia. My favourite now is Kris Munroe, played by Cheryl Ladd. Although, I did used to be a Farrah Fawcett-Majors fan. Maybe now she has split from Bionic Man, Lee Majors, I might have a chance with her if things don't work out with Grace Taylor.

Two pages on Gordon Cowans. The reason Grace got me this magazine. It calls him 'Golden Gordon' and talks about Villa being top of the league. Not much in it I don't already know, but still a good to read. I'd forgotten his Dad worked for the Villa and I didn't know he used to support Mansfield Town. Some great cartoons showing Sid's amazing passing range. Also there's a sad one, showing how Alex Cropley breaking his leg gave Gordon Cowans his first chance. The No. 10 shirt is now Sid's for many years, I think. He really can become a world great. Maybe in 1986 Gordon Cowans will captain England to World Cup glory. How many other players get two whole pages in 'Look-in'?

Just 'Sapphire and Steel' and 'Mork and Mindy' to read now before I go to sleep. "Na-Nu Na-Nu"

9:25pm Wednesday 17th December 1980

What a game that must have been at White Hart Lane and what a great result for the Villa. Eight goals. Tottenham 5 Ipswich Town 3. Ipswich have lost the first of their games in hand. Well done Tottenham, you have made this a very good Wednesday for all us Villa fans. It says the Tottenham goals were scored by Crooks, Hoddle, Perryman, Ardiles and Archibald. Five different goalscorers, that is impressive. Mariner scored twice for Ipswich and Eric Gates got the other one. It was 3-3 at one point. Apparently very wintery conditions.

Can't believe I agreed to this. Mum's sewing some tights into one of her old bras. Well, if it wasn't an 'old' bra before it certainly is now. Spud and I are going to Haystacks' party as the 'Ugly Sisters'. Spud seemed quite keen on the idea when Tucker suggested it. But I didn't think we were going to take it this seriously. We have both got big wigs to wear. For some reason my grandad had them in his coal shed, I didn't ask why. It should be a really good party but I will be so hot in this big dress and I will struggle to get through the door in this hooped girdle. I can't believe that at thirteen I am going to have to wear make-up for the first time tomorrow night. Apparently, it isn't Spud's first time, but then he is a Gary Numan fan. I don't think he's quite a 'New Romantic', but he has worn a little makeup at concerts. Trying on my busty bra now and it's quite tight on the shoulders. So glad I was born a boy. This certainly isn't comfortable. Mum thinks my left boob needs more padding. I think the right one is just too big. Even Lynda Carter as Wonder Woman didn't have one that big.

9:15am Friday 19th December 1980

Registration, the final one of 1980, but still no Pincher, Noddy or Bellington. Strangely also no Grace Taylor. My date for the big party tonight is obviously running late this morning. Spud is really looking forward to the party and us dressing up, but worried that his bright orange dress is too short. We thought it would be clever if Spud wore Wolves colours and I wore the famous Villa claret and blue. I am going to wear my really long Villa football socks under my dress.

At lunch and I am getting worried by the lack of Grace Taylor. This is not looking good and I have no way of getting in touch with her. At least she has Haystacks' address, but why haven't I seen her all morning? Tucker notices that Haystacks has several cuts on his face and is examining them as I ponder over the whereabouts of Grace Taylor. It seems to celebrate turning fourteen today that Haystacks borrowed his dad's razor and has had his first shave. It appears it didn't go too well. At least being a late developer I won't have to do that for quite some time yet. Perhaps when I can I should grow a Dennis Mortimer style beard.

Spud kicks the side of the lockers hard and really is fuming. There is now quite a large dent in the green metal. Luckily no teachers are around and Tucker manages to talk a small First Year into not going to tell. I have not seen Spud this angry for days. Finally he has calmed down enough to tell us why he attacked the defenceless locker. Carrie Campton is again the reason for the outburst. Carrie has just told him (well, sent Bonny Sidwell to tell him) that she won't be coming to the party, as she has to go to a 'grownup' Christmas Party instead. Poor Spud, but I still think there of lots of nicer girls for him than Carrie Campton.

It is confirmed. Both Spud and I will be dateless tonight. Mr Walker tells the whole class that Grace Taylor is the latest chickenpox victim and that any of us who have never had it should be really careful to stay away from those who have until the very last spot has gone. All my hopes for tonight dashed. I hadn't felt this down since Kenny Dalglish scored that late winner against us in November. Also, despite posting 43 Christmas cards in the school post-box I have only received 28 back and today's was the last delivery.

Dressed as the two Ugly Sisters Spud and I are uncomfortably sitting on Haystacks' stairs. It hasn't been a bad party. Haystacks' mum had done some ace food, but there seemed to be more for Georgina Ramsey and her Second Year friends than for us. Spud is getting too hot so he has taken his bra off. With his orange and black striped dress he looks like a stretched bee. It feels very strange dressed as a woman and not having fabric between my thighs. Makeup is a pain as well. I have got lipstick around my tiptop and my eyes now look like a panda. Probably best Grace Taylor isn't here to see me like this. I might be getting carried away, but I didn't really want our first kiss to be with me wearing lipstick and a busty bra.

Georgina Ramsey and her friends are dancing in the extension. Me, Haystacks and Spud are now in Haystacks' bedroom. First time I have seen his Baggies bedroom. He has an Albion bean bag and even West Bromwich Albion wallpaper. There is a big double page poster of Cyrille Regis on the front of his wardrobe. The three of us are playing Football Top Trumps. We have managed to bring the final two plates of sausage on sticks up with us. Having great fun sticking the used sticks into Spud's discarded bra. I wonder how many cocktail sticks you could stick into one of Wonder Woman's bras.

Haystacks plays his Kenny Dalglish card. He is confident that 132 League Goals will mean he wins the hand. This is my chance though as I have Malcolm MacDonald with 189 League Goals. Just waiting on Spud first. He has only got Peter Ward of

Brighton though. Ward has only scored just 41 goals. So the round is mine. Well played Big Mac. Haystacks is moaning though because it doesn't include all the goals Dalglish has scored this season. Did he really have to bring the two against the Villa up? He still wouldn't reach 189 though. It is time to give Haystacks the bumps. Fourteen and one for luck. I just hope his bedroom floor can take it. Happy Birthday to Scott Hastings. The first of us to reach fourteen.

2:49pm Saturday 20th December 1980

Brighton away today and still no Peter Withe, but we should win. Gary Williams is in at left back and Eamonn Deacy back on the bench. At least Peter Ward isn't playing for Brighton. Former Villa player John Gregory is though. He scored for them at Villa Park when we went top. They also have Mark Lawrenson playing for them who some of the bigger clubs are watching. Ipswich are at the Blues and Liverpool at home to Wolves so all the main games are on Radio Birmingham. For once it would be good if all the West Midlands teams won. I have entered Guess the Goals with sixteen goals, but that was before I heard the Baggies game with Everton had been called off due to a frozen pitch. It's very cold today. Glad I am inside. I have put a blanket over Snowy's hutch.

How can we be losing at Brighton? It was a goal by Michael Robinson just on half-time. I even have my lucky radio on. Can't believe it. I wonder if it is too late to ask my parents for a new radio for Christmas. We haven't scored in the first-half of a game since 15th November. Ron Saunders needs to start shouting at them before the game instead of waiting until half-time. In fact we have only scored one first-half goal in the last nine league games, amazing considering that we are top of the league. Although we might not be if we don't score in the second-half. Just added it up and we have scored 39 league goals so far this season, but only 10 in the first-half. We score very nearly three times more second-half goals than first-half ones. Is that because I only tend to put my lucky radio on in the second-half or are the players not giving 110% in the first-half?

Maybe it is all part of Saunders's tactics. We let the other team think they have a chance and then blitz them in the second-half. We need one of those blitzes now. Come on Villa, you can win this game. I just want the Villa to be the Christmas number one. Liverpool are winning at home to Wolves, thanks to a Ray Kennedy goal so at the moment they are heading back to the top.

Ipswich are murdering Birmingham at St. Andrews. Sounds like the Bluenoses aren't even trying. Mariner, Wark and Brazil have all scored. We really need to find an equaliser, but it doesn't seem as if it happening today. David Geddis has had to go off, defender Eamonn Deacy has come on. Very early to have to use the sub. I expect Allan Evans is going up front. Gary Williams could go in middle with Deacy going to his normal left-back position. Amazing that we still have only used just fourteen players all season. Perhaps Ron should have put Terry Donovan on the bench instead of Deacy so he could have brought a forward on. If we don't win today I think Ron Saunders should go shopping over Christmas. I don't want him to sell any of the fourteen but maybe buy another striker as I sadly don't think Brian Little is coming back. I wouldn't mind Garth Crookes from Spurs, or Norwich's Justin Fashanu. Fashanu has scored twelve goals already this season and Norwich are in danger of being relegated. Only our Gary Shaw has scored more.

Beaten by Brighton & Hove Albion. A team who started the day in the relegation zone with just 14 points. It's a disgrace. Glad there is no school on Monday. As I write 0-1 on the chart I feel sick. If only Peter Withe had not been suspended. Liverpool, Ipswich, Forest and Arsenal have all won. I bet even the Albion would have won if they had played. Liverpool, Bellington's team, will now be top of the First Division on Christmas Day. Ipswich are only a point behind us and still have two games in hand. Really is a depressing day. Not so depressing though for Wolves captain Emlyn Hughes apparently. Despite his team losing to his old club 1-0 today the radio is reporting that when he was leaving the field Eamonn Andrews was there waiting with his big red book. So most of the Liverpool and Wolves players are now on their way to the studio to record This Is Your Life.

Really not sure if I like Cannon and Ball, this Christmas Special just isn't funny on ATV. Mum wants to watch Search for a Star next, so I think I will go and list which stickers I still need in my 1980 Football Sticker Album. Haystacks says that the new

Panini 1981 album is out next week. I am determined to get all the stickers this time. But I can't waste my money as I need to start adding to my Atari fund.

6:10pm Sunday 21st December 1980

Dressed as an Ugly Sister on Friday night and now 48 hours later dressed as a Shepherd in the Nativity at the Church Candlelit Carol Service. I am certainly very adaptable. Not quite sure how I agreed to be in charge of these little shepherds. Most of which seem to need the toilet just as Mary is going to give birth to the baby Jesus. Which is why I forget to pass the Cabbage Patch doll to the Angel Gabriel at the correct time. At least the congregation find my expert throw of the baby across the stage funny. Gabriel does a catch that Ian Botham in the slips would have been proud of.

11:32am Monday 22nd December 1980

Brilliant, the Alpine Pop Man has been with the Christmas pop. We get twelve bottles instead of the normal six today. There's even some Dandelion and Burdock.

12:40pm Wednesday 24th December 1980

Even at thirteen I am excited that it's Christmas Eve. It still seems a very long time until Christmas Day. Maybe I am too old to be watching Rainbow, but Christmas brings out the child in us all. Anyway, Finger Bobs has finished. Choice next between

Clapperboard on ATV and Why Don't You on BBC1. I really can't stand Why Don't You. Why have a TV programme that tells you to switch off TV and do something less boring instead? Why don't they just try harder and make a more exciting programme. At least there is a 'Lassie' film on later.

Grandad has arrived for Christmas with some very large presents. Have no idea what he has got us and he is giving no secrets away. He is staying with us for two nights. He has brought with him the Christmas editions of both the Radio Times and the TV Times. I still think it is odd that the BBC call their magazine Radio Times even though it is mainly about their television programmes.

Christmas at Robin's Nest was very funny. I loved the way Albert (with his one arm) was trying to help Robin Tripp put the tinsel up. Hope Albert hasn't really left though to open his own business after he inherited all that money.

Even on Christmas Eve we still have Coronation Street. Len Fairclough is trying to talk Emily into going to the police to report her bigamist husband, but she isn't sure. She always has a hard time does Emily Bishop. Annie Walker is telling Elsie Tanner what is wrong with Christmas today. She believes money is to blame and that people were happier at Christmas when they were poor. Eddie Yates is now making my grandad chuckle by asking Fred Gee what happened to the gifts the Wise Men gave to Baby Jesus.

We need to use the video now as Grandad wants to watch Val Doonican. I don't like Val Doonican at the best of times, but this year it's a nostalgic one about years gone by. It is going to be a long Christmas Eve night. We are recording the London Night Out Christmas Special on ATV. Which sounds much more exciting. It has got Hot Gossip in as well as, Bernie Winters with Schnorbitz, the St. Bernard dog.

6:58am Thursday 25th December 1980

Christmas morning and my parents have still put some presents in my Villa pillow case for me to open. Good to see a selection box in there. Most of my Christmas presents are under the white Christmas tree in the front room, we will open these after the Queen's Speech, but the rest I can open now. Looks like a record. Yes, the new Abba album 'Super Trouper'. The 1980 'Shoot Annual' and a pack of three VHS 180 minute video cassettes. What is this smaller one, it's quite heavy? Wow, a real Sony Walkman. A Stowaway TPS-L2. I didn't expect that. It's got really cool earphones with sponges on the ends. I have got some Villa sweatbands as well. Just like Peter Withe wears, when he is not suspended.

As Mark lights the brandy on the Christmas pudding I make two wishes. Now Mark's sixteen it seems that the tradition of lighting the pudding has been passed to him. My wishes are quite varied. The one is the traditional Villa to win the FA Cup. I think the league would be asking a little too much, but getting past

Ipswich and winning the Cup Final would do me. The second wish is maybe more important.

We had been to see Grandma and Grandpa before lunch and Grandpa really was not well. He didn't say much at all, but just looked in pain. He is getting more poorly each time we visit. He gave me and Mark some money for Christmas. A pound note each, but Grandpa then fell asleep. Grandma said she was only going to give him a small Christmas dinner. They weren't even having turkey. So my second Christmas wish is for Grandpa to start getting better. I know he is 72 now, but still I want him to be well again.

Come on Queen Elizabeth the Second, get your speech finished please. It is all very interesting hearing about the Queen Mother's 80th birthday celebrations, but I want to see what my Grandad's present is under the tree. It looks a very odd shape.

Dad has his Christmas hat on as he is distributing the presents to us. Fairly making sure that Mark and I have similar size piles. We both have football socks for our appropriate teams. I have 'The Game' by Queen cassette to play in my new Sony Walkman. Another selection box. This time from my Auntie and Uncle. Some racing car Top Trumps and a Villa ruler and pencil set are the next two presents I open.

Now to the two presents from Grandad. Mark has already opened one of his, it's a kit model boat. My first one is very heavy and some kind of book. Wow, yes a complete 'Encyclopaedia of British Football'. It is written by Phil Soar and Martin Taylor and is enormous. It has every statistic you would ever need in it. Now I can know as many facts as Haystacks. On the front it has got Ian Wallace, of Coventry. Colliding with Peter Shilton as Kenny Burns looks on. It really is a great book. There is still this other present from Grandad to open though. It is lighter and I have no idea what it can possibly be. Grandad is watching me closely whilst trying on his new Christmas slippers. He's struggling to get his left foot in one.

I didn't expect it to be a model. Mark is the creative one not me. It is a wooden kit clock to make that fastens to the wall. How am I supposed to build that? There are pages and pages of instructions.

The last present as always is a combined one for me and Mark from our parents. This is always a surprise and this year Mark's letting me unwrap it. Well he had lit the Christmas pudding. It looks like a board game and rattles when I shake it. It is not a game I recognise. It is called 'The Fastest Gun' and looks like a cowboy board game. It looks really good on the box with roulette-style holes that the plastic coloured cowboys fall down if they lose a gunfight.

Reading my 'Encyclopaedia of British Football' in bed with Freddie Mercury singing through my Sony Walkman headphones I am reflecting on what a very good Christmas Day it has been. One of the best since I stopped believing in Santa Claus. The cowboy board game's been great fun. I even won the first two times against Mark. Admittedly he then won the next four, but still I think I was the victor. I had even made a start on building my clock. Fiddly and I did get lots of glue on my fingers, but I think I can do it.

1:26pm Friday 26th December 1980

Cold turkey, chips and pickles eaten, just time to work on building my clock before the football starts. I could probably have had it finished before 3pm if I wasn't watching 'Billy Smart's Christmas Circus' at the same time. Mark and Dad have gone to see Wolves at home to Brian Clough's Forest. Villa are at home to Stoke City. Stoke beat Leicester at home last Saturday but they haven't been doing that well. Apart from perhaps Adrian Heath and Lee Chapman up front Stoke haven't got any decent players.

At last a goal in the first-half for Villa. Peter Withe is back and he has scored after 38 minutes. The reporter says that Gary Shaw should have scored, but the Stoke keeper Fox made a superb save. Luckily for Villa the big man then smashed in the rebound. So Villa are a goal up at half-time. Liverpool are only drawing against Man United so we could yet get level with them. Alan Brazil has scored for Ipswich again. They are 1-0 up against their local rivals Norwich City. Spurs against Southampton looks to be a good game. At half-time it is 2-2 even though Southampton are without Keegan.

Oh dear, Dad and Mark won't be happy. Wolves are losing 4-1 and Colin Brazier and Geoff Palmer have both scored own goals. Grandad says, "So Wolves have scored three goals and

Forest only two". I need to explain to Mum that Wolves aren't actually winning. Albion are still goalless at Sunderland. Villa need to hold on to this one-goal lead. I really thought we would score more than one against Stoke. That's it, full-time. Villa have won 1-0. Need to find the final score from Old Trafford now. Tottenham - Southampton ended up 4-4. Another eight-goal thriller for the White Hart Lane crowd. Steve Archibald scored so that means he has now scored more goals than Gary Shaw. No goals Man U - Liverpool though. That's not too bad, but I think Liverpool are still top. We both have 33 points and a goal difference of +19, but as Grandad points out Liverpool have scored more goals. I think I will call it joint top though. Ipswich beat Norwich 2-0 so it is now getting very close at the top. Tomorrow everyone plays again. Hope they didn't have too much turkey yesterday.

10:22am Saturday 27th December 1980

The Daily Express seems to have labelled today Christmas Saturday. I am just carefully fastening the very delicate fingers to the face of my finished clock. The mechanism is all working and now I can see if it keeps good time. Dad is mincing the leftover turkey up to make his annual turkey rissoles. Villa are at Forest today which is not going to be easy. Forest are, of course, the reigning European Champions and have Ian Wallace and Trevor Francis up front today. Funny that on the front of my 'Encyclopaedia of British Football' Ian Wallace is playing against

Forest before his big move. I still think Forest's best player is winger John Robertson, but Mr Walker always raves about John McGovern.

Great, the clock hands are going round. Don't believe it, Peter Withe is injured and David Geddis is playing again. He has only been back for one game. That is going to make it difficult for us to win. Liverpool should win at home to Leeds. Ipswich have a difficult game at Arsenal though. Arsenal are 4th now just above Forest. 7th place Albion are at home to 6th place Manchester United. So apart from Liverpool all the other teams in the top seven are playing another team from the top seven.

Great start for the Villa. Seems like a bizarre own goal after 15 minutes, scored by Larry Lloyd. I think it is a good time to eat the lion bar out of my selection box.

Good news from Highbury. Ipswich are a goal down. Former Wolves player Alan Sunderland is on target. Not sure who I want to win at The Hawthorns, but Peter Barnes has put Albion two-up against United. Nearly half-time and Wolves are still 0-0 at Man City, but Paul Bradshaw has made some outstanding saves according to the reporter Hugh Porter. Oh, there goes the goal horn. Blooming Trevor Francis has equalised against us. I think this is going to be difficult.

Super Gary Shaw has put us back in front. Come on Aston Villa this will be a great win. Liverpool are still being held at Anfield by Leeds. We are going back to the top. Ipswich have drawn level at Arsenal but as long as we win it will have been a brilliant Christmas. Just five minutes left now.

Wolves have gone to pieces at Maine Road. 4-0 suddenly to Man City. Tommy Hutchison has scored two. That is eight goals Wolves have conceded in just over 24 hours. Albion look to have won. Cyrille Regis has scored their third. It sounds like they have torn United to pieces. Remi Moses and Bryan Robson dominating the Albion midfield. Another goal horn, but where? Martin O'Neill has drawn Forest level. Seems like sloppy defending by the Villa boys. Disappointing but I would probably have taken a draw at the start.

Nothing has really changed today. Villa, Liverpool and Ipswich have all drawn. So we are still behind Liverpool on goals scored. The next league game is at home to Liverpool, that's going to be very interesting. So top of the table only has one change and that it Albion going above Manchester united.

So at the end of 1980 the top six teams are separated by just five points and 6th place Albion have a game in hand on all teams above except Ipswich. Ipswich have still played two games less than the rest of us. This is turning out to be one of the most exciting leagues ever.

5:05pm Monday 29th December 1980

At last the start of the new series of Grange Hill. There is a new head called Mrs McClusky who seems determined to shape the school up. A slightly less frightening version of our

Headmistress Miss Thatcher. Poor Justin is having problems with his overprotective mother. She seems to think Grange Hill is a bit rough for him. Tucker is trying to win £10 for the best cover for the new school magazine. Some new faces too, including Claire Scott who looks quite pretty. Trisha Yates and Cathy are forming some kind of protest group against the rising Tuck Shop prices.

According to John Craven, on Newsround, Breakfast Television is on its way. Television will start at 6am on ITV from January 1983. We will be able to watch it before we go to school. Doesn't sound very exciting as it will be a lot of news it seems. It will be called TV-AM. There is also talk of BBC announcing their own Breakfast Television as well soon. People seem quite excited by the idea. Also it seems in a big shakeup ATV is going to be broken up into two different Midland regions. Hope that doesn't affect Star Soccer.

11:56pm Wednesday 31st December 1980

New Year's Eve and I have been allowed to stay up this year. Just a few minutes left. My clock is working well and saying about three minutes to midnight. Been a funny evening. Gail gave birth to a baby boy on Coronation Street and the last ever episode of Citizen Smith was on. The end of Wolfie and 'Tooting Popular Front'. Wolfie and Ken went to visit Shirley in Italy. Unfortunately Shirley has a new boyfriend. The closing scene saw 'Wolfie' driving away on his scooter with a message painted on Shirley's boyfriend's posh black car 'Merry Xmas Shirley, Power to the People'. It has been a month of my favourite programmes finishing. Shoestring finished last week.

Here comes Big Ben. Happy New Year!!! Here comes 1981, just three years away from the infamous 1984. I think 1981 might be a very good year for Aston Villa FC.

End of December Top of Division One		
Liverpool	Pl: 25 Po: 34	+19
Aston Villa	Pl: 25 Po: 34	+19
Ipswich Town	Pl: 23 Po: 33	+19
Arsenal	Pl: 25 Po: 30	+9
Forest	Pl: 25 Po: 29	+13
West Brom	Pl: 24 Po: 29	+7

Villa December League Results	
6th Middlesbrough (a)	1-2 Lost (Shaw)
13th Birmingham City (h)	3-0 Won (Geddis 2, Shaw)
20th Brighton (a)	0-1 Lost
26th Stoke City (h)	1-0 Won (Withe)
27th Forest (a)	2-2 Draw (Lloyd (og), Shaw)

Chapter Six (January)

3rd Round of the FA Cup the greatest day in the footballing calendar. The date that the mighty Aston Villa start their journey to Wembley and hopefully their 8th FA Cup Final success. Up the Villa.

Peter Withe is back in a full-strength Villa team, but Ipswich are at full strength as well. The two Dutchmen Muhren and Thijssen are both playing. With Gates, Mariner and Brazil up front as well as midfield goal machine John Wark they have a scary amount of goal power. Scoring against them will be difficult as Paul Cooper has a habit of saving penalties and Craig Burley is Scotland's right back. Two centre-halves Terry Butcher and Russell Osman are real rock hard lumps. I suppose best hope is that Mick Mills is getting old. He looks like he is in his 50s. Hopefully Tony Morley will skin him alive down the left.

This is going to be difficult now we are a goal down at half-time. We need to equalise and get them back to Villa Park on Wednesday night. Dad says he will take me if it is a replay. Wolves look like going out as well as they are losing 2-1 at Stoke. Albion are cruising at home to Grimsby. Non-league Altrincham have managed to score at Anfield but are still being well beat. Not many shocks around although Second Division Bolton have made it 3-3 at Nottingham Forest. I thought Second Division Chelsea might give Southampton a better fight than they are. Manchester City are smashing Crystal Palace and QPR are drawing at home to Spurs. Last season's winners West Ham are being held by Fulham from Third Division. West Ham are now top of the Second Division and certain to get promotion. I should get to see Trevor Brooking playing at Villa Park next season.

I hate Paul Mariner. I am trying so hard not to cry in my bedroom. It is impossible to hold back the tears any longer. The New Year, 1981, which promised so much, has left me heartbroken on only its third day. My pillowcase is getting wet with my head buried in it and my eyes and nose now running like Niagara Falls. My dream of FA Cup glory shattered again. Beaten 1-0 by Bobby Robson's Ipswich. Wolves got a late equaliser so they live to fight another day. Will I ever see Aston Villa in an FA Cup Final? This was surely our best chance for years.

Watching 3-2-1 is normally quite pleasurable, but not this Saturday night. It has a Wild West theme tonight and Lionel Blair from Give Us A Clue is in it. Doc Holiday has changed his gun for a big stick. Mum thinks this could be a holiday. She is thinking because he is called 'Doc Holiday' the stick could represent a stick of rock from the seaside. Dad reminds her they haven't read the clue yet. Lionel Blair has now pretended to die after being hit on the head. He is well enough to bring in the clue though. It is a gun and the rhyme is 'I will put an end to all your cares. The prize is what the Sheriff wears'. That's got us thinking. The Sheriff wears a badge so maybe that is part of the prize. Mark is thinking it's a star and the star of the show is Dusty Bin so this one is Dusty Bin. He could be right. They have already lost the car.

The tall bloke in the kind of suit my Dad wears has been rubbish so far. They are reading the 'Visiting Card' clue again. 'Don't rush in you could go bust. But your prospects are bright if you don't bite the dust'. Dad thinks that one is Dusty Bin. I think I am with Mark though. They should lose the gun that Lionel Blair brought in. The woman has decided to go for the gun. She thinks the Sheriff wears a tin badge and tin sounds like bin. Think I preferred Mark's version. They are both right though, it is Dusty Bin. I wouldn't mind winning Dusty Bin, he looks ace. They have just wheeled him in wearing a cowboy outfit. How cool does he look? Imagine having that outside our house instead of that black plastic round bin with the top that keeps going missing. So at least they'll get a decent prize now. The clue was that Dusty Bin was the only tin star on the programme. They get some stars on this show. There was Diana Dors and now Alvin Stardust. He is a cowboy in a shootout outside the bank. Joke about the getaway horses getting away wasn't funny. Nor was the 'Chicken Tonight' gag. Maybe I am feeling too sad to laugh today. Alvin's clue is an American silver dollar. Mum thinks it is a holiday again. The rhyme is, 'Half my name is not the prize but it comes back C.O.D.'. Even I can guess that one. C.O.D. backwards is 'Doc'. The character's name was Doc Holliday and as half the name is not the prize take off the Doc bit. It leaves 'Holliday'. Surely they will choose that one now as the car has gone.

The silly couple rejected the clue Alvin Stardust left. It was a holiday in America for two weeks. I was completely right, but Mum says she knew it was the holiday. What are they taking home then? They have gone with the 'Visiting Card' one that Diana Dors brought in. They have won jewellery, not very exciting. But apparently the four gold nuggets are worth over £1,300. Blimey, that's lots of money. Nearly as much as the car would have cost. Hope they don't get mugged on the way home.

4:50pm Sunday 4th January 1981

Barry Davies doesn't have to sound so pleased when he is commentating on that Paul Mariner goal. He believes Ipswich could win the double and the UEFA Cup this season. Why are the Villa always on Match of Day when they lose? They really didn't play well yesterday. To be honest, Ipswich could have won by more.

David Coleman is now getting excited as Middlesbrough are beating Swansea 5-0 at Swansea's Vetch Field ground. Swansea are second in the Second Division but I don't think they are good enough for the top flight yet. The first game on was Everton knocking Arsenal out. Grandad fell asleep during that one.

The gang are all back at school post-chickenpox. Pincher and Noddy are comparing who had the most spots. Pincher with his fair complexion still has lots of signs of where the spots were. Noddy had one on his eyelid which still has a nasty blister. They don't seem to have had much fun over Christmas as they were both covered in calamine lotion. Tucker keeps trying to touch Pincher where he can see remains of spots as he wants to have two weeks off school. The five of us and Mr Walker are in the small Maths room at 12:30 ready to listen to the fourth round draw. I really couldn't care less now my Aston Villa are going to have a free Saturday at the end of January. Spud, Pincher and Haystacks though are keen to hear who their local teams will be playing.

Wolves are the fourth ball out and Spud cheers as they are away at Watford. Singer Elton John is chairman there and they got promotion from the Third Division last year. Haystacks frequently raves about Watford's manager Graham Taylor.

Mr Walker sucks on his teeth as Forest are drawn at home to Manchester United. Cloughie against Sexton. Haystacks is not happy at WBA being drawn away to Boro. Tie of the round next is Everton at home to Mersey rivals Liverpool. As this is announced Tucker decides it would be witty to whistle the theme to The Liver birds which confuses Pincher who wonders why Tucker is whistling the theme to Cuckoo Waltz.

Ipswich are lucky again. They have to go to Shrewsbury. Although Haystacks believes the small Gay Meadow pitch will not suit Ipswich. Haystacks is as always full of facts. Why does an Albion fan know so much about Shrewsbury Town? He informs us that they have a player-manager called Graham Turner and also that there is a river behind one of the stands and on match days a man in a boat is on hand to retrieve lost balls that fly over the stand. Tottenham have an easy game at home to Hull. Noddy as a Walsall fan tells us how bad Hull are. It seems Hull City are bottom of the Third Division. Man City against Norwich could be a close game. I really am not interested in this meaningless cup though. Hopefully clubs like Liverpool, Ipswich and Albion can get distracted by it and we can steal the League title whilst they're not looking. Of course Liverpool and Ipswich have European games to distract them as well.

Bellington is back and is taunting me that Liverpool are going to thrash the Villa on Saturday. Oddly it was more teasing than real taunting. It was almost light-hearted. The kind of banter I have with Spud about the Villa and Wolves. Maybe Bellington was mellowing or was I just getting better at dealing with it? It had been rumoured last term, but Mr Walker confirmed it in registration today, that James McMullan (Bellington's mate) has left the school. His family have gone to live in South Africa. Apparently his dad was offered a big promotion. Hope my dad never gets a big promotion. I certainly don't want to live in South Africa or anywhere that is more than 30 miles from Villa Park.

Grace Taylor is not yet back from her chickenpox but she did only start the last day before the holiday. Hope the chickenpox doesn't leave any scars on her smooth silky skin. For some reason I decide to ask Bellington how Grace Taylor is. He looks at me with a look of horror. Before saying, "she should be back on Wednesday, but what's it to you?" I think I have overstepped the mark here. Obviously working on a lighting gantry with someone does not permit you to enquire about their girlfriend's health.

The front of the Express & Star tonight is all about the police catching the 'Yorkshire Ripper'. He is Peter Sutcliffe, a 35-year-old lorry driver from Bradford. It always mentions people's ages in the paper. Our Head, Miss Thatcher, was in it last week and it said she was 53. I am sure she is older than that. The lorry driver was arrested on the 2nd in Sheffield, but has finally today been charged. He is a mass murderer, who is believed to have murdered thirteen women and attacked seven others across northern England since 1975. I wonder how many people you have to kill to become a 'mass murderer'. The police have done very well to catch him.

Nine o'clock and at last the start of the new series on BBC2 that my brother and Haystacks have been saying is going to be great. Apparently Mark has listened to it on the radio and read the books. Haystacks has recorded every radio episode. He played some to me and Spud at his party. It seems quite funny in places but I didn't really understand it. The programme has an enormous title. It would take ages to guess on Give Us A Clue. It's The Hitchhiker's Guide to the Galaxy.

The programme starts with a computer screen with that normal green on black computer writing. The words on screen are the time 06:30. Somebody is up early. It now says 'Destruction of Earth Due 11:46:00'. That's not good. Apparently 'The Hitchhiker's Guide to the Galaxy' is the best and most important book in the Universe. It has the words 'Don't Panic' in large friendly letters on the cover. Poor Arthur Dent, in his dressing gown, is not happy because a bulldozer is about to knock down his house. Haystacks was right this is really clever and funny. It keeps finding information from the book. Apparently, the best drink in existence is the 'Pan Galactic Gargle Blaster'. The effect of drinking one is like having your brain smashed out by a slice of lemon wrapped round a gold brick. Arthur Dent has just rather surprisingly discovered that his best friend Ford is not from Guildford at all, but from a small planet somewhere in the vicinity of Beetlejuice. Ford has ordered six pints of bitter and told the delighted barman to keep the change from a fiver because the world is about to end.

That was a brilliant half an hour. I can't wait for the second episode next Monday. The first episode ended with Arthur and Ford, having escaped the destruction of Earth on a Vogan Spaceship, about to be thrown off it with the threat of the Vogan Captain reading poetry to them first. At least they know where their towels are and have babel fish in their ears.

10:20pm Tuesday 6th January 1981

Mark and Dad are back having seen Wolves get through to the Fourth Round, thanks to a 2-1 replay win against Stoke. Elsewhere West Ham still couldn't beat Wrexham even after extra-time, so they will replay again on a neutral ground. Forest won at Bolton so Mr Walker's team will play Manchester United providing United don't lose at home to Brighton tomorrow night. Bury and Fulham must replay again as well. Coventry knocked out 'dirty' Leeds.

9:27am Thursday 8th January 1981

Grace Taylor is back and looking just as lovely as she did in 1980. I didn't know that she had her birthday over the holiday until Mr Walker asked her if she had still had a good birthday despite the spots. So my second love is now fourteen. When I say second love I mean after Aston Villa Football Club. That is taking the club as a whole and not treating the Reserves and youth team as separate loves. So if we do get together I will be her 'Toy Boy'.

I did try to ask Grace how she was and wish her a belated 'Happy Birthday', but she was distant. She thanked me for asking before walking straight away. There was no eye contact and no apology for not coming to Haystack's party. She was behaving oddly.

Both Haystacks and Spud are having girl troubles. Georgina Ramsey has told Haystacks that she thinks he needs to grow up. Which is good coming from a Second Year. Georgina Ramsey was cross that Haystacks spent so long in his bedroom with two Ugly Sisters at his birthday party instead of socialising with Georgina Ramsey's friends. Pincher thinks Haystacks should dump Georgina Ramsey. As for Spud, he keeps phoning Carrie Campton's house, but only ever gets to speak to her nan who always refers to him as young Master Hogan. Spud is convinced that Nan never tells Carrie he has called. Tucker gives me one of his famous looks that silently says so many words. Silent movie star Harold Lloyd has got nothing on Tucker. It was obvious that Tucker thought Carrie Campton was deliberately avoiding Spud. We really need to get Spud interested in a more suitable girl. Such a pity Spud isn't coming with us to St. Malo next Wednesday. Pity also that Grace Taylor isn't and an even bigger pity that Carrie Campton is.

11:48am Saturday 10th January 1981

Grandad has got me some francs for my France trip next week. There are fifty francs which is apparently about four pounds. I am excited about going but very nervous as well. Have a feeling I might get travel sick on the ferry and probably in the coach. We will be travelling through the night. Should be good with Pincher, Haystacks, Tucker and Noddy. Now what I really want before I leave the shores of Great Britain is for Villa to be top of the league. I can then tell French people I meet that I support the best team in England. For that to be true we have to beat the champions Liverpool this afternoon.

Liverpool have beaten us the last three times they have played us. Last time we played them, at Villa Park, Brian Little scored but we still lost 3-1. The best Liverpool game I can remember though was 15th December 1976 when we beat the reigning champions and top of the table team 5-1. All the goals came in an amazing first-half when we ripped them to pieces. The forward trio of Andy Gray, John Deehan and of course Brian Little had the Liverpool defence for breakfast, dinner and tea. Jake Findley played in goal for us and an unknown defender called Charles Young played, but they both had nothing to do. Same today would be very nice.

On the Ball isn't giving us a hope against Liverpool. They all seem to think Liverpool are going to run away with the league now. Come on Villa, let's show them that we are not beaten yet.

The radio reporter says Villa have a new electronic scoreboard today at the Witton Lane End. It seems that it will be used to show half-time scores instead of the traditional letters. I can't wait for next time I am at Villa Park so I can see that. Reporter also points out that Liverpool have only lost once in their last 31 games in all competitions.

Colin Gibson is back at No.3 so Gary Williams is on the bench. This is a game Villa need to win. Apparently Scotland manager Jock Stein is in the crowd watching Allan Evans, Ken McNaught and Des Bremner. Probably some Liverpool players too. Liverpool are wearing their traditional white away shirts with black shorts. Irwin and Money at the back for Liverpool so we might get some chances. Graeme Souness is fit though. Don Shaw is the referee, he never seems to like the Villa.

Ipswich are at home to Mr. Walker's Forest today so perhaps they will slip up.

The Villa - Liverpool game sounds very frantic, but Villa dominating. Dennis Mortimer they say is running the midfield. Phil Neal is at centre-half for Liverpool for some reason. I bet he won't like jumping against Withey. Reporter thinks Villa might have had a penalty if Gary Shaw had fallen when he was kicked. We are Aston Villa though we don't dive. Now 'Sid' Cowans has just missed. Come on Villa.

Goal at the Villa. Yes, Peter Withe has done it. Tony Morley skinning the full-back pulled it back for Gary Shaw. Ray Clemence saved from Shaw, but Peter Withe tucked the rebound away. We are top of the league, singing we are top of the league. A long way still to go in this game though. Only twenty minutes gone.

Wolves are beating Middlesbrough, Kenny Hibbitt has scored and Martyn Bennett has given Albion the lead away at Leicester.

Jimmy Rimmer has just saved from Ray Kennedy, but you can hear the Villa faithful singing to the Liverpool fans, "You're not champions any more". Sounds like Mortimer is organising Villa well, but Liverpool starting to get on top. We need to still be winning at half-time. Reporter says McNaught nearly scored with a header after Morley short corner to the magic wand-like left foot of Gordon Cowans. I bet if Cowans was Scottish he would have 50 caps by now.

Half-time and winning 1-0, time for a quick wee. Albion two-up and Wolves one-up. Birmingham are still goalless. Ipswich against Forest is goalless as well. Villa Park is full with only 40 below 48,000, yet only about 16,000 at the Wolves. I suppose people can only afford to go to the more glamourous games these days. The Villa have only been averaging around 30,000 this season despite challenging at the top.

Commentary on the Villa second-half and the crowd are making so much noise. Wish I was there. Liverpool are having more of the ball, but Villa are still having some good counter-attacks. Kenny McNaught has just been booked. He has been shown the yellow card and it might be one of the last. FA decided yesterday to remove the cards later on in the season because they are too aggressive. Wolves have scored a second goal. Oh that was close. Mistake by Liverpool with a short back-pass, but Peter Withe couldn't get it past Clemence. Villa starting to get chances though. This game is so vital for the whole of our season. A great break by Allan Evans. One-two with Gary Shaw and it just goes wide. Now Kenny Dalglish has a chance. Straight to Rimmer that is a relief.

Kenny Swain is breaking forward. He back heels it to Gary Shaw. Shaw through to Dennis Mortimer who is onside. It is Mortimer against Ray Clemence. Mortimer has rolled it past

Clemence. The cheers of the Villa fans makes my lucky radio crackle. Aston Villa 2 Liverpool 0. Sounded a brilliant goal. Another super Villa team goal.

What a great day. Villa now two points clear of Liverpool and a goal difference two better. Unfortunately Ipswich beat Forest 2-0. Muhren and Mariner scoring. So Ipswich also have a +21 goal difference like us, but they are only a point behind us and have two games in hand. Arsenal and Albion both won again, but we are top of the league after 26 games. I can go to France with my claret and blue head held high. Vive la Villa!

5:05pm Sunday 11th January 1981

At Grandma and Grandpa's watching the Villa beating Liverpool on Match of the Day. Grandpa seems a lot better today. Apparently he had some liver for his dinner. The thought of it makes me want to heave, but at least he is eating. Looks like the Villa really did play well. Cracking goal by the skipper. David Coleman commentated on his goal so well. Haystacks wants to be a commentator when he grows up. I need the toilet but it is freezing and my grandparents have only got an outside toilet.

Really odd to think that growing up my dad had to have a bath in the kitchen in a tin bath and go outside to the loo. Grandpa has got a special seat now by his bed with a hole in that has a potty built in. Think I will just hold my wee in. Hope they have proper toilets in St. Malo. Tucker says you have you go in a hole in the ground. It is odd seeing the Villa shirts in black and white again.

The next game is Chelsea against Sheffield Wednesday from Second Division not sure what the score was in this game. Chelsea are one of the poorer London teams although my grandad said that Jimmy Greaves used to play for them. I suppose the most famous former Chelsea player now is Kenny Swain. He should be playing for England. That's funny. Chelsea have a player called Bumstead.

10:05am Monday 12th January 1981

Grace Taylor is being friendly again to me today. She even apologised for avoiding me last week. She claims it was because she was embarrassed about her spots. Spud jokingly said just that she fancies me. Still don't know what she sees in Kenny Bellington. I wanted to mock Kenny about our victory over Liverpool, but I wasn't that brave. Mr Walker did comment on the Villa being top at registration when he called my name out.

11:23pm Tuesday 13th January 1981

We managed to bags the backseat on the coach. Pincher and Tucker are both deep asleep and the coach is in darkness. Haystacks, Noddy and I are playing racing boat Top Trumps. The only light we have apart from the headlights of the occasional passing vehicle is from Noddy's digital watch he got for Christmas. Noddy is very proud of his Casio Alarm Chromo watch because it tells you the date, has an alarm and is water resistant. Although, his Mum has warned him not to get it wet. He has also brought the instruction booklet with him so he can reset the time when we get to France. My watch has the 24-hour clock on it which Miss Tully has told us the French always use.

She has been encouraging us all the speak French on the journey but it is far too late at night for French speaking. We didn't leave Walsall until 10pm and will be travelling across the Channel on a ferry during the night. Hope the ferry has better lights than Noddy's digital watch.

Miss Tully and Mr Walker seem to be sitting quite close to each other, three rows in front of us. I note that she isn't speaking in French to Mr Walker. Haystacks found out yesterday that Miss Tully's name is Sindy, like the doll. As Mr Walker is called Ken she should really have been Barbie. We couldn't start calling her Sindy now though as she's affectionately known as Madame Cholet. I do think Mr Walker is quite taken with her though. Perhaps romance will blossom in France.

What a crossing! My head won't stop bobbing up and down and my stomach is very empty as most of its content is now polluting the English Channel. Tucker was first to be sick. Sadly he didn't reach the side of the boat. Haystacks was next, although he then proceeded to demolish a Mars bar. Pincher looks even paler than usual and refuses to open his mouth, while Noddy is trying to read the tiny writing in his Casio digital watch instruction leaflet. It was quite a pleasing sight though to see Carrie Campton being dramatically sick just behind the lifeboats. Certainly it has been a rough crossing. I am still very surprised we weren't all given life jackets.

We are now in France. A place called Calais and are about to have another five hours in the coach to St. Malo. Mr Walker says it is quite a pleasant journey along the coast, but really with the taste of sick still in my mouth the last thing I want is a long coach trip. Especially when we are driving on the wrong side of the road.

It looks quite a grey place and the people in the cars do look very French and miserable. I suppose it is only 6am though. Mind you Miss Tully says the French don't have AM. If I remember right we have to say 'du matin'. Then it goes to 'de l'après-midi' from midday until 6pm. I am not sure if I am saying that right. Think I will avoid mentioning that time of the day. Then after 6pm it is 'du soir'. Very odd. French kids must be very smart to understand this and they have to give everything a sex. Mind you Tucker has said that the French are sex mad. He reckons there is a good chance we might see a French film with nudity in as French telly is full of it. His uncle often goes to the South of France and there are lots of topless women there. Weather looks miserable at the moment. Be very surprised if we see any topless women.

That's all you want in a coach that smells of sick. Carrie Campton leading a chorus of 'Frère Jacques'. I don't know how Pincher can sleep through this racket. Mr Walker is trying to sound intellectual and telling Miss Tully, with his hand touching her leg, that Frère Jacques was a monk named Jacob. I wonder what 'ding, dang, dong' translates to. Haystacks does a brilliant 'ding, dang, dong' in the style of Leslie Phillips from Carry on Nurse. I don't think Carrie Campton appreciated this comic twist to her chorus.

Well there's a beach, but it isn't like Blackpool. St. Malo is smaller than I expected. Lots of seagulls but they do sound different to back home. Perhaps they have trouble understanding the good old British seagulls. We have been here less than an hour and I am already feeling homesick. So far from my family and news of my beloved Villa.

St. Malo is, as Mr Walker is reading to us, a walled port city in Brittany. Now the sun is up it is looking more appealing. Lots of big old buildings all with windows in the roofs. Each house seems to have at least four floors. The sea looks very green and there are some huge boats in the harbour. Or are they ships?

Mr Walker shows us on the map where we are. Tucker is quite excited to find there is a place called 'Brest' quite nearby. The sea is crashing against the wall of the harbour and it is quite cold. Why couldn't we have come in the summer?

Pincher and Noddy are sharing a bedroom and the other three of us are in the room next door. Feels odd sharing a bedroom again. The real problem though is our room sleeps three, but there is one single and one double bed. So two of us are having to share a bed. We did rock, scissors, paper for a few rounds but kept drawing. So in the end Tucker suggested that as

Haystacks was the oldest that he should be allowed a bed to himself.

It feels really strange being in bed with Tucker. We have put a line of cushions between us though. Haystacks is snoring, but I can't sleep the room is full of other strange noises. Mostly due to the incessant creaks of the wooden shutters. Also the constant noise of passing police sirens. The sirens might be more tuneful than our English ones, but I feel like any second Inspector Clouseau will come bursting into the room. I still can't believe that Peter Sellers died last July. I love the 'Pink Panther' films. So sad to think there will be no more made. My favourite scene is still the one with the begging 'minky'.

The French police sirens are now louder and as I look out of the window I can see three French police cars. I suppose that should be 'trois françaises police voitures'. Probably a 'Le' or 'La' sex thingy in there. Tucker is with me but Haystacks is still snoring away. His snores still sound very English. Tucker points out that the French policeman, who is smoking a very short cigarette, has a gun on his belt. Not quite sure what has happened, but there appears to be somebody lying down.

Tucker is convinced they have been murdered. I think he has been watching too many James Bond films. The policemen are talking very loud in French and there are now people from most of the hotel windows looking out at the scene. Tucker says he just heard the word 'mort' which he is pretty sure means 'dead'. Certainly the person lying down is not moving.

A French ambulance arrives next. I can't believe Haystacks is sleeping through this. I really need a wee now but I am not going to go into the corridor and miss what is happening. Anyway the flush on the toilet seemed very different to ours at home.

7:32am (French time) Jeudi 15th Janvier 1981

At breakfast around the large kitchen-like table all the talk is of the possible murder in the night. At thirteen I might well have just seen my first dead body. Who would have thought I would have to leave England to see it. They say England in our recession is a pretty violent place, but it seems nothing compared to across the Channel.

The breakfast is disappointing. I was hoping for some bacon and maybe a sausage, but we just have bread and a big bowl of coffee. I hate coffee anyway but even my Dad wouldn't want it in a bowl. Guess no chance of a good cup of tea. My Villa mug seems so many miles away.

This French school is difficult. Even Miss Tully is struggling to understand what the teacher is saying. The French children all seem excited to see us. Noddy just keeps saying 'Bonjour' to everyone he meets. We have been told so many names, but because they aren't normal names I am struggling to remember many of them. Pincher chuckles though when one of them said his name was Pierre. We have had endless French lessons about Pierre and his bicycle at Dieppe.

He seemed to always leave it at 'La Gare'. Noddy and Tucker though have both remembered the name of one French Schoolgirl called Célina. Yes, I can see with her short blonde hair she is very attractive, but the two Walsall fans are acting like they haven't seen a pretty girl before. Just a pity my Grace Taylor isn't here. Hope she is having a big argument with boyfriend Bellington now.

Saturday afternoon and as the Villa are kicking off against Coventry City at Highfield Road we are sat in a dark, smoky café in St. Malo. Mr Walker has just tried to order me and Haystacks two Coca Colas but comes back with two bowls of hot chocolate. What is it with these French and putting drinks in bowls?

We are waiting for Tucker and Noddy who seem to have got lost. They were both following after Célina last time we saw them. They might be best friends but since Célina came on the scene they have been having more fights than Tom and Jerry. I think Célina's English Is better than she makes out even if she thinks Fellows Park is a meeting place for men.

Pincher has had enough, he wants to start heading back to the hotel. We have been walking around the streets of St. Malo for ages and still haven't found an English newspaper to find yesterday's scores out. Never before have I not known if the Villa have won or lost 24 hours after they have played.

I feel ashamed to call myself a fan. It is nearly tea time so we will have to go back. I wonder what strange meal awaits us tonight. Hope it isn't snails or frogs legs or worse still a horse. Really odd how they serve everything up separately. Last night I waited a good ten minutes for some vegetables to arrive to go with our fish only to find it is a different course. Really missing some proper food.

Pincher thinks we are lost, but I am sure we have been down this street before. It is getting dark though and I could be wrong. All these French streets with their high houses look the same and smell very French. All the roads on the map seem to start with 'Rue' as well. Wish we had gone with Noddy, Tucker and Haystacks now to see Célina play a game where they catch balls in nets on sticks. But finding out the Villa score is more important.

At last a newsagent's, with English newspapers outside. It's The Times but if it is good enough for Uncle Bulgaria it is good enough for me and Pincher. It is behind the glass and we can't see the sports pages so we have to pay for it before we can read it. For some reason it costs three francs. That is over 50p. All the French papers are less than half that price. It has to be done though. I pay for it and Pincher tries to ask the newsagent how we get back to our hotel. The newsagent looks blank and laughs at

Pincher's attempt at French. Still a long way off his sister's O-Level grade B standard.

No idea how a little Womble coped with this gigantic Times paper and why isn't the sport on the back page? Pincher is really starting to panic now about us being lost. I am suggesting we head for the road that looks like it leads to the beach, but I think Pincher is too busy trying to hold back the tears to listen.

I don't believe it! I have paid 3 francs for Friday morning's paper. It is two days old and written well before yesterday's games. This is getting serious. What was the Villa score? We do always seem to beat Coventry. I don't think we have lost to them in my lifetime. Mind you, I have never been this lost in my lifetime. Just a very scared Pincher and me, lost in France. The narrow streets now look so sinister and it is cold and dark now. Even going back to the hotel to eat snails is more appealing than spending the night out here on these dangerous streets.

We seem to have walked for miles, or kilometres as the French use. Still nothing looks very familiar. Pincher suggests stopping one of the policemen and asking them, but I remind him that they carry guns.

Fantastic, a familiar face. As we reach the corner we see Mr Walker holding in his one hand a very wet Tucker and in the other a very annoyed Noddy. It looks as if Mr Walker had just dragged the two off each other. They were probably fighting over Célina. I will never let a girl come between me and my best friend. Mr Walker is now annoyed with Pincher and me for getting lost to go with how annoyed he already was with Noddy and Tucker. The good news though is that we are only yards from the hotel. A hotel with an ambulance outside.

A covered up stretcher is being carried to the ambulance. Followed by an old man with the whitest hair I have ever seen. Tucker said that must be his dead wife under the blanket and the shock has just sent his hair white. How many more people will have to die before I find out the Villa score?

10:39pm (French time) Lundi 19th Janvier 1981

In bed with Tucker on our last night in St. Malo and we are excitingly chatting as Haystacks hits maximum snoring volume. Main conversation is about how Tucker got to help Célina on with her tight sweater after the Lacrosse match.

Tucker has no idea who won the game, but shortly after helping Célina on with her sweater Noddy had punched him. The two of them had then had a major scrap on the dusty ground where a group of old men and berets were playing boules.

The game is like crown green bowling but you don't have to bend down. Noddy and Tucker were then chased down an alley by a very irate boules player who's potentially winning ball Tucker had landed on. The best part of Tucker's story was the bit when he and Noddy ran into a very surprised and embarrassed Mr Walker. Embarrassed because he was snogging Miss Tully. Tucker described it as a full on kiss with Mr Walker's hand almost touching our French teacher's bottom.

My joke, 'I wonder if she wears French knickers' has Tucker is hysterics, but to be honest I don't really know what French knickers are like. The closest I ever get to seeing ladies knickers is when Mum puts her large pants out to dry on the rotary clothesline. Mind you they are tiny compared to Mrs Slocomb's in the Are You Being Served film set in Costa Plonka. That's the film with the inflatable red bra which causes all the attention.

11:30am (French time) Mardi 20th Janvier 1981

Just stopped at a small café on the way to the ferry and Mr Walker has found me an English newspaper from yesterday. It is the Sunday Express and Mr Walker is now reading the classified football results out like the chap does at the end of Grandstand. He is trying to give scores away by the tone of his voice. He has said Birmingham City nil Southampton THREE. Bet Villa will be next unless Brighton were at home. "Coventry City one….", come on Mr Walker! "Aston Villa TWO". Yes!!!

Pincher is satisfied with Wolves drawing away at Crystal Palace and Haystacks delighted that West Brom had won the battles of the Albions by beating Brighton 2-0. Mr Walker was somewhat disappointed to find Forest game against Manchester United had been called off. A draw for Ipswich at Everton is good but Liverpool winning at Norwich is not so good. Not many goals around, perhaps this new three points for a win idea for next season will produce more goals if it gets ratified.

Walsall won at home to Chester so both Tucker and Noddy are feeling happy and have long forgotten Célina. We have all made a pact never to let a girl break up the 'Local Gang' again. I just hope nobody starts fancying Grace Taylor.

On the ferry, a better crossing this time. I am able to read fully the football pages in the Sunday Express. Morley and Withe scored for Villa and Mark Hately for Coventry. It was 0-0 again at half-time, like so many Villa games. With Villa going 2-0 up after 65 minutes. Pity we couldn't keep a clean sheet though. The league table can't be right though.

The Villa are second on goal difference to Ipswich. Both are on 38 points. We are not top it seems that Ipswich have gained an extra two points. I search the paper trying to prove it is a mistake. It isn't. On Tuesday night it seems our rivals Birmingham did us no favours and let Ipswich beat them 5-1. If it had been 2-1 we would still have been top because we would have scored a goal more than Ipswich. Thank you Bluenoses.

10:30am Thursday 22nd January 1981

Back at school and maybe slightly exaggerating the tales from our French adventure. Tucker now claims that he found Miss Tully in bed with Mr Walker. Grace Taylor seems very disappointed that she didn't come with us though. It is really nice to see her again. I think she has a new pair of black shoes. Spud is glad he didn't come though because he has a new girlfriend.

While we were trying to tolerate the very bossy Carrie Campton in St. Malo, Spud has started 'going out' with Janet Hogan. Apparently it all started when Janet told Spud she didn't dislike Gary Numan during Mr Dodd's Physics lesson. Janet does seem to be going for the record of how many boyfriends a girl can have before their 14th birthday, but at least it has put a smile on Spud's face. It seems he has walked her to school the last two mornings. Carrie Campton appears a little perturbed by the news of Spud's new love interest.

3:55pm Sunday 25th January 1981

It's been a boring weekend with no Villa game. I did try and follow FA Cup 4th Round ties, but it just didn't feel right. Wolves drew at Watford, but Baggies were knocked out by Middlesbrough. Liverpool aren't going to win the double this year, they lost 2-1 at Goodison. Ipswich Town are still just in, but they could only draw 0-0 at Shrewsbury.

How can they beat us but not beat Shrewsbury. We would have beaten Shrewsbury. Biggest win though was Manchester City beating Norwich 6-0. It is only two months since John Bond left Norwich for Man City. I bet the Norwich fans hated that.

12:26pm Monday 26th January 1981

Haystacks is all excited this lunchtime because he went to see the basketball team Team Fiat last night at the Villa Leisure Centre. He has now decided that we should form a basketball team. I suppose it could be fun. I quite enjoy playing basketball in Games and I seem to have quite good coordination when it comes to throwing the ball in the basket.

Spud is very keen, but says it will depend on when he is seeing Janet Hogan. He's meeting Janet's parents tonight as they are taking him to Wolves' cup replay. Pincher isn't sure he wants to be on the team as he thinks he is too short for basketball. Haystacks says we need to have a team of six, as that gives us five on the court and one substitute. I bet he is thinking of me as the substitute.

Tucker and Noddy are both excited about the basketball team. Noddy thinks he might be able get his dad to put some cash in. Noddy's dad (Ken) runs the Mobile Shop that stops in the cul-de-sac by us. He sells everything. Only last week we ran out of toilet paper just as 'Ken's Mobile Shop' was sounding its horn. Ken has got big ears like his son.

Spud will be happy, Wolves are now through to the 5th round of the cup. They've beaten Watford 2-1. Ipswich are also in next round as they smashed Shrewsbury 3-0. Wolves will play Wrexham at home in the next round, perhaps this could be their year. Surely Wolves can't spoil my year again.

1:05pm Friday 30th January 1981

Grace Taylor has actually come to sit by me in the Library this time. There I am doing my History homework and she has chosen to sit by me. Now there are four more chairs she could have sat on, but she didn't. What should I talk about? We have done the hellos, so what next? Maybe I should talk about the Villa as it is the topic I know best or should I discuss the fall of the Roman Empire as that is what my homework is about?

Not now! Noddy arrives and excitedly sits by Grace and me. He is bursting to tell me something. I am trying to play it cool, too late, Grace smiles and leaves. Noddy is telling me how keen his dad is to sponsor our basketball team, as I am still watching Grace Taylor and her bottom leave the school Library. Noddy's dad wants us to be called 'Ken's Mobile Trotters'. It hasn't quite got the same ring as 'Team Fiat'.

He sees us wearing 'Ken's Mobile Shop' on our vests that will be brown like his van. I am not sure if Haystacks has really thought this through. I mean, who are we going to play and where are we going to train? According to Noddy though we are going to have a big meeting next Monday night to discuss all these things. More interesting news is that Haystacks apparently has found our sixth player and he is red-hot. I don't suppose he will be the substitute then.

12:14pm Saturday 31st January 1981

Why do we have to have the news between Swap Shop and Grandstand? It isn't as if much happens in January, certainly not on a Saturday morning. The biggest news seems to be about the Spanish Prime Minister resigning. I am surprised he did that when

Spain are hosting the World Cup next year. Surely as Prime Minister he would have been guaranteed a ticket.

Hard game for Villa today, at home to John Bond's Manchester City. Hopefully City scored all their goals in the cup last week. Ipswich and Liverpool are both at home this afternoon. Mark and Dad are at Wolves for the big local derby. It is Wolves against Albion. I think I am supporting Wolves as the Albion are still quite close to us and I want to win the bet for highest placed West Midland team. Mum still refuses to write West Midlands for our address and insists on putting Staffordshire even though the border was moved six years ago. I know Derby and Nottingham are in the East Midlands but where is North or South Midlands?

Tony Butler is in good form today on BRMB. He thinks the Villa will stuff Man City, but that the Black Country derby will be a draw.

No goals at Wolves in the first-half, but Villa going well. We are 1-0 up against Man City. Gary Shaw scoring again after a Peter Withe flick-on was knocked back by Allan Evans. Evans does get forward a lot for a defender. Lucky Liverpool are 1-0 up at home to Leicester because of an own goal from Alexander Forbes Young. Also bad news from Portman Road, Wark and Brazil have put Ipswich well in control against Stoke. BRMB starting to crackle so I need to tune radio to medium wave 206 for Radio Birmingham. Could do with the Villa scoring a few more goals.

Well, a win is a win so 1-0 at home to Manchester City is good. How important are these Gary Shaw goals? That is the fourth game we have won 1-0 thanks to a Gary Shaw goal. "Gary Shaw, Gary Shaw, Gary Gary Shaw. He gets the ball he's bound to score. Gary Gary Shaw". Oh, brilliant! I hadn't realised that Leicester had come back and beaten Liverpool. That is a shock. It means we are four points ahead of them. They have 36 points whilst Villa and Ipswich have 40 points. But as Ipswich scored four today their goal difference is now six goals better.

They still have a game in hand as well. Bobby Robson's team will take some catching. Albion are now seven points behind us so looks like I will be keeping all the betting money for my Atari fund. Wolves beat them 2-0. Mel Eves and Andy Gray getting the goals. Peter Withe is doing well but just what would an Andy Gray/Gary Shaw partnership have been like?

Villa have now played 28 games, exactly two-thirds of the 42 game season. We have 40 points so if we keep going at this rate we will have 60 points at the end of the season. That was how many points Liverpool won the league with last year.

Time to get some sleep then. February starts in an hour. Villa have won every single league game so far in 1981. So let's hope it can continue throughout the whole of February. We have to play Everton, Crystal Palace and then go to the Wolves. Maybe we will be top by the end of February and maybe I will have stolen Grace Taylor from the clutches of the evil Bellington. We might even have formed the 'Ken's Mobile Trotters' basketball team.

End of January Top of Division One		
Ipswich Town	Pl: 27 Po: 40	+29
Aston Villa	Pl: 28 Po: 40	+23
Liverpool	Pl: 28 Po: 36	+17
Southampton	Pl: 28 Po: 33	+16
West Brom	Pl: 27 Po: 33	+9
Arsenal	Pl: 28 Po: 33	+8

Villa January League Results	
10th Liverpool (h)	2-0 Won (Withe, Mortimer)
17th Coventry (a)	2-1 Won (Morley, Withe)
31st Man City (h)	1-0 Won (Shaw)

Chapter Seven (February)

So 'Ken's Mobile Trotters' basketball team has now been formed. Haystacks is running the meeting very well and his mum has given us lots of crisps and fizzy pop. Noddy's dad has agreed to pay for our kits and the weekly hire of the school sports hall. Georgina Ramsey is going to get some of the second year girls to be the official cheerleaders. All sounds quite professional, although the current lively debate over the colour of the kit is reaching a stalemate. Haystacks wants blue and white stripes like the Albion but Noddy and Tucker are fighting for the red of the Saddlers. Spud and I are anti the red because we would look like Liverpool. Georgina Ramsey is suggesting a pale blue colour.

Looks like Noddy's Dad has had the casting vote and 'Ken's Mobile Trotters' will wear all red (they don't do a brown). Basketball players wear sleeveless tops so we will see all Spud's hairy armpits. No sign of any hairs on my armpits. Haystacks also will need a good underarm deodorant as he can get very sweaty.

That sounded like Haystack's doorbell. Who can that be? Too early for my dad. I told him half past eight.

What's he doing here? Bellington walks in and unlike the rest of us he is not in his school uniform. He is wearing a bright

273

orange Adidas tee-shirt. What does Grace Taylor see in him? My worst fears confirmed, Bellington is our sixth player. It seems Haystacks was impressed with how he played in the last Games session. I don't know if I want to belong to a team that has Kenny Bellington in.

7:38pm Thursday 5th February 1981

According to the Express & Star tonight Crystal Palace owner Ron Noades has sacked manager Malcolm Allison. Mr Allison isn't having a good season. Noades has already appointed Wimbledon's Dario Gradi as Palace's 4th manager of the season. Wimbledon have made their coach, Dave Bassett, their new manager. All these teams changing their managers. We have had Ron Saunders since 1974, Villa's centenary year.

11:17am Saturday 7th February 1981

Whose idea was it to train on a Saturday at 11am? Saturday is for football not basketball. I am going to miss Football Focus. They'll probably be previewing the Villa game at Everton. Apparently, Peter Withe is an Everton supporter.

Who put Bellington in charge of fitness training? If he really thinks he is going to make me do ten press-ups I am going home. We haven't even seen a basketball yet. Noddy's Dad is going to Sportsco this afternoon to buy us one. Only one of Georgina Ramsey's friends has turned up and she doesn't seem to have much rhythm. Mind you, spelling out 'Ken's Mobile Trotters' isn't easy.

I am shattered after this morning's training. Gary Williams is playing left-back today in preference to Colin Gibson. Eamonn Deacy played there last game. We have still only used fourteen players this season and three of them have been left-backs. Rimmer, Swain, McNaught, Mortimer, Bremner, Shaw, Cowans and Morley have not missed a game. It said in last night's paper that Pat Heard might play instead of Tony Morley, but Morley is in the team according to the radio. Like Peter Withe, Tony was an Evertonian as a lad. Apparently all his family and friends still support Everton.

Kick-off time then. My lucky radio is on the floor with the aerial extended fully and pointing towards the window. Although the Villa will probably be goalless in the first-half again like most of our games lately. Everton are a good team with ginger-haired Gary Megson in midfield and Billy Wright in defence. That isn't the Billy Wright who played for Wolves, won 106 England caps and is now Head of Sport at ATV, but a younger one. At least John Gidman isn't playing for them. Peter Eastoe is up front though who has scored quite a few goals this season.

Goal horn already and at the Villa game. Hope it good news. Yes, a great stunning goal from Tony Morley. Ron Saunders was certainly right to play him. According to the reporter he dribbled the ball from the half-way line, then cut in from the left and let fly. Goalkeeper Hodge had no chance. 1-0 to the Villa. What a start!

Ipswich are at home to Crystal Palace who have their new manager. Amazingly Palace have taken the lead. Teams always win with a new manager. We could be going back top of the league today. Reporter says it is all Villa at Goodison Park.

Albion are now beating Liverpool. Bryan Robson has scored. Apparently he put the ball right through Ray Clemence's legs. You would think an England goalkeeper would learn to keep his legs together. That's why I think Peter Shilton should be first choice for England.

Another goal, this time Steve Hunt has given Coventry the lead at home to the Wolves. Villa need a second. Another goal at Goodison Park. It was a penalty, given for handball. Sounds very harsh on Ken McNaught but Trevor Ross has equalised for Everton. My lucky radio is letting me down. At least Ipswich are still losing.

Another goal for Coventry. This time Mark Hateley, Wolves are in trouble. The goal horn again. They will wear it out this week. Back to Goodison Park. Oh no, that's not good, the crowd are very noisy. But Villa are back in front. A breakaway goal by Captain Dennis Mortimer. Sounds very similar to the one he scored against Liverpool. Everton 1 Aston Villa 2. The good news also is that this cracking game will be on Match of the Day tomorrow.

Half-time scores in and they look fantastic. Villa winning, both Ipswich and Liverpool are losing. We could be two points clear at the top tonight. I need to relax though and not get too carried away. The ref might be an Everton fan and give them another unfair penalty in the second-half.

This time a Villa penalty. Gordon Cowans won't miss. He never does. Yes! We have a two-goal lead. Blimey, Andy Gray has equalised for Wolves. They have come back from 2-0 down, no wonder Mark is cheering. Nice one Cyrille. Cyrille Regis has made it West Brom 2 Liverpool 0. Paul Mariner has just scored an own goal against Palace. This could be a pivotal day in the race for the title.

How did that happen? Ipswich have somehow come back and beaten Crystal Palace. A great 3-1 win for the Villa, but we are still second on goal difference. It just isn't fair. Four straight wins and still not top. I wonder if we can win every single league game in 1981. Not even Brian Clough's or Bill Shankley's teams managed that. Maybe they are not in the same league as the great Ron Saunders.

Doctor Who was really good tonight. The Doctor lost the Tardis. Still don't know what Kassia's pact with Melkur was. Now watching The Dukes of Hazzard. Bo and Luke have run into Sheriff Rosco and don't realise someone has planted marijuana in the General Lee.

Report completed on French trip. I decided not to include mention of all the dead bodies or the unsavoury antics of the teachers. Mr Walker refused to comment on Friday as to whether Mademoiselle Tully was his new girlfriend. Now time to watch the Villa on Match of the Day. I quite like it on at Sunday afternoon tea-time now. Well, I suppose 4:25 is a bit early for tea as we only had our chicken dinner at half past one. It is good to get to watch it with my grandad. This time at my grandad's house as my parents are at my dad's parents' house. They have called the doctor out to Grandpa again. He hasn't been very good the last couple of weeks.

The Villa game is on first and glad to see Motty is commentating. The second game is Tottenham against Leeds. Spurs always seem to be on. The lower league game is Shrewsbury against West Ham. Although West Ham will be promoted to the First Division soon. It is really hot in my grandad's house. I can't believe he is wearing that pullover as well as his shirt and a tie.

What a goal that was by Tony Morley. Cracking move with Gary Williams and Gary Shaw. That must have a chance of Goal of the Month. It went in like an arrow. I quite like the Villa blue away shorts with the home top. He is a great player, Tony Morley. I bet all the girls like him with his curly hair. Maybe I should ask for a Tony Morley cut next time I go to my grandad's barbers.

That was never a penalty. How could the little fat ref give handball for that? It just bounced up and stroked big Ken's hand.

Even John Motson is saying it is all Villa. You would think we were the home team. They are stroking the ball around like Real Madrid.

Dennis Mortimer must score. Yes, just like the goal against Liverpool. John Motson and my grandad are making that point as well. Ron Saunders under his blanket though doesn't seem to be getting too excited. Mind you he isn't a young chap.

Peter Withe hits the bar with a shot from outside the area. No, I think the keeper touched it on to the woodwork. Everton and Asa Hartford are just chasing shadows. Why does Des Bremner never seem to tire? He is everywhere. My grandad thinks Gary Williams has played well but I tell him all eleven have been brilliant.

That's the penalty then. Gary Shaw chased it and the Everton defender and goalkeeper got in a right mess. In the end the defender, I think it is John Bailey, gave Shaw a pull. Everton try to put Cowans off the penalty by making a substitution first. But another great Sidney Cowans penalty. He should be England's penalty taker.

Great effort from Gary Shaw. A curling shot from miles out. It was only an inch wide. What a marvellous player Gary Shaw is and still only 20. All you can hear is the Villa fans and my grandad's new central heating boiler. The Villa fans are singing, "Now you are gonna believe us, we are gonna win the League". Grandad says the pretty obvious thing, that if they win all their matches they will. I am starting to think we have a real chance.

My parents are still not back from Grandpa's. I am a bit worried. They can't ring though as my grandparents haven't got a phone and it is quite a walk to the phonebox; which is probably vandalised again anyway. So watching the holiday programme with Cliff Michelmore. The little tavernas in the quaint fishing village somewhere in Greece look very appealing. Grandad says he would never fly though. I expect I will fly one day. Seems that a number of people have started to go skiing on their holidays. Very odd.

Finally back home and watching a new comedy called Solo on my bedroom telly before going to sleep. My dad seems really upset about my grandpa. They have to take him to the hospital on Thursday. Felicity Kendall, Barbara from The Good Life, is in this. I think Grace Taylor might look like that when she is older.

Apparently Carla Lane the writer of Solo wrote the Liver Birds as well. The woman Felicity Kendall is playing, called Gemma, has a lovely house rabbit.

I wonder if Mum would let Snowy live in the house. Maybe not. It was bad enough when he came in for an hour at Christmas and chewed through the television aerial and left hidden little poos that looked like currants.

10:52am Monday 9th February 1981

Last week before the half-term holiday and Bellington is asking me to help him with his Maths homework. It is easy as he is a set below me, but do I really want to be helping somebody who threw my Abba pencil case out of the window?

I haven't said 'yes' but then I haven't said 'no' either. I do want to be a teacher and quite enjoy teaching, so part of me is keen, but it's Bellington.

That's three times today that Grace Taylor has come over to speak to me. Wish I knew what to talk to her about and I also wish Spud didn't keep appearing from nowhere. Spud is apparently getting bored with Janet Hogan, all she talks about is tennis and Stephen Duffy. She claimed Stephen Duffy was once in Duran Duran, but I never believed this.

Spud wants to try to win Carrie Campton back. The term 'try to win' is perhaps misleading because I don't think he ever had her in the first place. The idea of winning Carrie Campton as a prize would be a nightmare to the rest of us.

Finally Grace gets me on my own. She seems to want to thank me for helping Kenny Bellington with his Maths. Now what do I do? I think best to just pretend I am helping her boyfriend and then really start helping him. I expect he wouldn't be so keen for me to help him if he knew that I fancied his lovely girlfriend.

The no girlfriend pact with fellow gang members doesn't include Bellington as his only link to us really is being in the basketball team and he doesn't support a local team.

It has been a really good night's telly tonight. Glad I finished my English story quite fast. BBC2 had two great funny programmes on. First the one about the Fawlty Towers hotel.

Basil really was going mad today and ended up in hospital. The bit with the Germans and not mentioning the war even made my mum laugh. She was trying not to. Spud does a brilliant impression of Basil Fawlty. He even does the silly walk.

Not sure which I enjoyed more Fawlty Towers or The Hitchhiker's Guide to the Galaxy. Tonight after the big rocket concert Zaphod, Trillian, Ford and Arthur, still wearing his dressing gown, stole a spaceship that was heading towards the sun. I think Marvin, the paranoid android, is my favourite robot on telly. Better than Metal Mickey any day.

I shouldn't really have my telly on this late at night but I have my headphone plugged in so nobody will know. Just wanted to watch Film 81. Haystacks was telling us all how good the new film with the country singer with the large chest sounded. It is called 9 to 5. So I wanted to hear what Barry Norman has to say about it. The other comedy film looks ace as well. It's called Private Benjamin and has got an actress in called Goldie Hawn. Odd name but she looks familiar. The film is about a rich girl who joins the army. I think it is worth seeing, so will try to get my brother to take me if it is on at the ABC.

6:40pm Wednesday 13th February 1981

Grandpa has to stay in hospital again. He is having more tests. So I am at Grandad's and we are listening to Test Match Special on Radio 3 Medium Wave. It's the 1st day of the 1st test in Port of Spain. Surprisingly Port of Spain is not in Spain at all, but in Trinidad. I bet that causes some confusion amongst the sailors. 'Beefy' Botham and his England team are taking on the best cricket team on the planet, the West Indies.

I think with Ian Botham as captain, England have a chance. Christopher Martin Jenkins is introducing the programme. He sounds awfully posh. I expect a lot of cricket players went to really posh schools. You need big sports fields to play cricket. We haven't even got room at our new school.

I always enjoy watching the Test Match, but it is hard to follow on the radio. Especially as Gordon Greenidge and Desmond Haynes are showing no signs of being out. They have put on nearly 100 already. They will probably declare on 600 without loss. My grandad jokes, "Thank heaven Loss isn't playing". I manage a polite laugh, but I shouldn't encourage him. Another four by Greenidge this time off spinner John Embury. I.T. Botham, Graham Dilley and Mark Old have already been hammered.

My grandad makes the best tea. He has that milk with the cream on top instead of the sterilised stuff that we have at home. He has got one of those clever basket trays you put out for the milkman, with a dial on to say how many pints you want today. My grandad likes to play tricks on the milkman by putting the dial halfway between the 2 and the 3. Oddly the milkman then always leaves three bottles. My grandad never did really grow up. He still has 'Watch out, watch out there's a Humphrey about' stickers on his pantry door. That is so 1976!

150 partnership up for blooming Haynes and Greenidge. Poor captain Botham. Must be heart-breaking to know that when they finally get one of these out then Viv Richards will come in. Hopefully Richards (world's best batsman) will give his best friend 'Beefy' a chance.

We're watching Superstars in the hope that England might get a wicket while we aren't listening. The last programme in the series. The Superstar champions and runners-up have all gone to a place called Eilat. I have never heard of it, but my geography isn't very good. David Vine says it overlooks the Gulf of Aquaba. Gerd Muller, the Germany striker, is taking part. Apparently he has scored more than 600 goals. Even Gary Shaw probably won't manage that in his career.

That's more like it. England have taken three wickets. John Embury has got them all including Greenidge and Haynes. Ian Botham caught Desmond Haynes. Viv Richards is batting so this should be fun 215 for 3. Oh, maybe we won't see Viv Richards. He has just been caught behind by Downton from Chris Old's bowling. Go Botham's England.

8:34am Saturday 14th February 1981

Valentine's Day and mum is joking that the postman is bringing sack-loads of cards for me and Mark. I know I won't get any, but still make sure I am first to the post as it lands in the porch. I perhaps should have sent Grace Taylor one, but last thing I need is a beating off Bellington.

Depressing day really as there isn't even a Villa match. Mark and Dad are off to see Wolves home to Wrexham in the 5th round of the FA Cup. I haven't said but I really hope they lose.

12:31pm Monday 16th February 1981

Monday lunchtime and yet again we are listening to the FA Cup draw. It is the quarter-finals. Spud and Pincher as well as Mr Walker are dreaming of Wembley and the Twin Towers. Wolves beat Wrexham 3-1 and Forest overcame Bristol City. Flaming Ipswich won again and Haystacks thinks they are going to win the double. Forest ball is out first. Mr Walker is excited. That's good they are going to play Ipswich. If anybody can knock Bobby Robson's team out it is Cloughie. Noddy whispers to me to say that it is now official that Mr Walker and Miss Tully are an item. Apparently they were spotted at the weekend together in Woolworths in Walsall by Helen Tranter.

Wolves are away at Middlesbrough. That's a tricky one. Everton are at home to Manchester City.

2:40pm Tuesday 17th February 1981

That was rubbish! Despite a brave 70 from Geoff Boycott England have been well and truly humiliated. They have lost by an innings and 79 runs. It is going to be a very difficult tour and then we have the Ashes here next. I bet Aussie bowler Dennis Lillee is licking his lips already.

3:34pm Thursday 19th February 1981

It seemed like an ordinary Thursday when I got up, but now Grace Taylor is asking me this. It must be a good sign. I don't know who else she has asked to help her at her 'Blue Peter Bring and Buy' sale in the New Invention Church Hall. I will have to see what I can find in my bedroom to bring along. I wonder what Grace Taylor will donate. I might impress Grace by wearing my Blue Peter badge. This could be my chance to get closer to Grace. Only problem is that it is on Saturday afternoon. The time when Villa are playing Crystal Palace at Villa Park.

3:07pm Saturday 21st February 1981

"Shuddup You Face", Bellington shouts for the 100th time today. I am sick of that Joe Dolce song already. Who let Kenny Bellington be in charge of the tape player? Quite a good turnout for the 'Blue Peter Bring and Buy'. More people seem to be doing the 'bringing' than the 'buying' though.

This year's appeal is to buy bungalows for disabled children. I remember two years ago we had to collect used stamps and coins (old money) for health workers on bikes in Tanzania. I still have no idea where that is even though Grace tried to tell me. I am still annoyed that Bellington came. He doesn't seem very keen and is just spending his time reading the 1976 Dandy Annual and sticking 'Blue Peter' labels on any old people that walk by. It is an odd relationship Grace Taylor and Kenny Bellington. I have never seen them hold hands and Bellington is so nasty to Grace.

This is frustrating but I must stay calm. Bellington keeps twiddling my knob and losing my Radio Birmingham reception. The games have kicked off. Villa are unchanged with Colin Gibson on the bench. I don't know if I would choose Gary Williams over Colin Gibson in a home game. Colin Gibson is much better going forward, but then Gary Williams is a much better defender. I trust Ron Saunders though. I think we will score a few today against Crystal Palace.

Is that old gentlemen really trying to haggle for the knitted pink lady toilet roll cover? 10p to help those poor disabled children is surely reasonable. Grace has let him have it for 5p and thrown in a toothbrush. I bet he hasn't even got his own teeth. Bet they come out at night and get soaked in a bowl of bleach like my grandad's do. Was that the goal horn? Where has Bellington hidden my radio?

I can't believe Bellington tried to sell my radio. It might be for a good cause but I need my lucky radio. Thank goodness Grace Taylor stopped him. It was only a minute later that Peter Withe gave Villa the lead. So half-time and we are 1-0 up. Wolves aren't helping though. Despite Andy Gray scoring they are still losing 2-1 at Ipswich. After Ipswich beat Middlesbrough at home last Tuesday it looks like we will never catch them. John Wark just keeps scoring for them. Bellington lied, Liverpool aren't 3-0 up at Brighton. They are actually losing 2-1.

Grace Taylor is very good at this selling and so generous. She not only donated her roller skates but also her skipping rope and her Partridge Family LP.

We must win now. Peter Withe has scrambled in a second. Apparently Crystal Palace are playing in their classy kit with the red diagonal on.

Packing away the remains of 'Bring and Buy' now. I wonder if my dad is outside yet. Maybe the football isn't all over. We have let Crystal Palace score from a Vince Hilaire cross. Come on Villa hold on.

Nearly home now and the final whistle has gone. Villa have managed a 2-1 win, but Ipswich have gone one better and beaten Wolves 3-1. Kevin Beattie, a defender, scored their third. That's 58 goals Ipswich have scored to our 52 and they have let in a goal less than us. At least Liverpool could only draw with Brighton. That means with just twelve games left we are six points ahead of the mighty Liverpool. Sadly, though, two points behind Ipswich.

7:38pm Monday 23rd February 1981

Our first 'Ken's Mobile Trotters' basketball match. We are playing a team called 'Little London'. Their name is wrong on several levels. Firstly, why a place near Willenhall is called London and secondly, their players are anything but little. They even make Haystacks and Spud look small.

Spud has somehow managed to get Carrie Campton to come along and watch us. Georgina Ramsey asked Carrie if she would like to be a cheerleader and Carrie told her very clearly what she could do with her pom-poms and that she was a serious operatic singer not a 'bimbo'. I am not really sure what a 'bimbo' is but suspect is isn't complimentary.

As I expected, I am the player left on the sidelines at the start. Haystacks and Spud play up front with Noddy and Tucker at the back. Bellington is then in the middle. In football you would call it centre midfield but I am not sure what it is called in basketball. Wish Noddy's dad could have got us tracksuit tops as well as these vests. I am freezing. Disappointing also that Grace Taylor didn't come to support us.

'Little London' appear to have brought their own fan club and they seem to be enjoying seeing our new team get annihilated. I think Haystacks' mum has lost count of the score already. Maybe being on the sidelines isn't so bad after all.

At least Bellington has scored our first ever basket. It has only taken us fifteen minutes. Haystacks wants us to join a league, but I feel this performance suggests we aren't quite ready. Still think it is a bit disrespectful for our cheerleaders to start cheering our opponent's baskets though.

Georgina Ramsey is explaining that the girls were getting bored and needed some practice. Oh I am being called on now in place of Tucker. Noddy has been our worst player but as his dad has paid for the kits Haystacks can't take him off.

I think my ten minutes went fairly well. I even stopped two certain baskets. Unfortunately one of them was for 'Ken's Mobile

Trotters'. It has been a good evening though especially if you forget the 122-14 scoreline. Carrie Campton is telling Spud how rubbish we all were. The good news is she doesn't want to come and watch again.

Very sad news on the inside back page of the paper tonight. Surely it should have had a more prominent position. The Villa legend, Brian Little, is calling it a day. He is retiring from the game due to injury. One of the Midlands' most skilful strikers is stopping playing at just 27. The man who won us the League Cup.

It is a good job we have Gary Shaw, but there will only ever be one Brian Little. I hope Villa train him up to be a coach. Perhaps one day he might even manage Aston Villa and lead us to glory. No, perhaps he is too much of a rebel. Think I will retire his headless Subbuteo player as a mark of respect.

8:10am Tuesday 24th February 1981

The Daily Express this morning is full of the royal engagement. Prince Charles is finally going to get married. They say she is a commoner, but she is the daughter of an Earl. Lady Diana Spencer looks pretty and she is just nineteen. Just five and a bit years older than me. Prince Charles is 32. Thirteen years older. He would have been in my year at school when his future bride was born.

I suppose her family don't mind the age gap as he is the future King. So one day we will have a Queen Diana. Mum says if they have the wedding in the middle of July we will get a day off school. The football season will be over by then. I wonder which football team Prince Charles supports. I suppose it should be Queens Park Rangers. Perhaps when King he'll rename them Kings Park Rangers when he becomes King. Pity the Royal Family don't follow the Villa.

4:41pm Thursday 26th February 1981

Gary Shaw played for the England Under-21s last night, against Northern Ireland at Anfield. Shaw scored the only goal of the game after just two minutes. Ron Greenwood must pick him for the full team now.

I can't believe he was the only Villa player in the side. I don't think Dave Sexton likes the Midlands players. The only other one he picked was West Brom's Remi Moses. Anyway, I don't think it is right that he is allowed to manage Manchester United and England Under-21s. He is bound to have favourites. No wonder Mike Duxbury gets in ahead of Colin Gibson. Mr Walker was slagging Dave Sexton off last week for ruining Garry Birtles. The United boss bought him from Forest for £1.25 million and he still hasn't scored a single goal this season. According to my League Ladder, Manchester United are now down to 9th place. They only have a point more than Birmingham.

What's going on in the West Indies? The Test Match hasn't started because the Guyanese government are revoking Robin Jackman's visa. They say it is because he has played in South

Africa. It seems very harsh, but I don't agree with what is happening in South Africa. If an agreement doesn't happen John Craven says we might see no play in this Test Match. At least this is one we won't lose then.

3:20pm Saturday 28th February 1981

It feels odd standing here in the North Bank with all these Wolves supporters. I am trying to stay quiet though as the man is announcing the Villa team. I am giving a small applause that no one can see. Rimmer, Swain, Williams, Evans, McNaught, Mortimer, Bremner, Shaw, Withe, Cowans and Morley are the men who will hopefully get us our sixth straight win and complete the double over Wolves. No Midlands teams has beaten us yet this season and it isn't going to start today.

The North Bank is the smaller of the two terrace ends at Molineux. Opposite is the larger and noisier South Bank. The North Bank though is just Wolves fans, but the South Bank has one side for the away fans. Villa have filled that section. There is a good gap between the two lots of supporters and plenty of lines of very tall policemen. Pincher is in the seats at the side of the pitch behind the dugout. I still think it is more exciting to stand even if it is hard to see when some kid comes and stands on a crate right in front of you.

Wolves are playing well and are at full strength. Andy Gray, John Richards and Mel Eves up front. Their midfield of Peter Daniel, Kenny Hibbitt and Willie Carr is full of experience. I suppose quite similar to Mortimer, Bremner and Cowans but if I was choosing a team from both these teams I think it would contain all Villa players apart from Andy Gray and maybe Derek Parkin for Peter Withe and Gary Williams. Although John Richards has scored more goals than Andy Gray this season.

Oh dear, Wolves fans don't like that, Tony Morley just did quite a nasty tackle on Peter Daniel. Ref's given a foul but I don't think the ref has booked Morley. Daniel is going to have to go off it looks quite serious. I think Wolves fans are going to give Tony Morley lots of abuse now. Norman Bell is coming on for Wolves, their fourth striker. This will be interesting. Jimmy might be busy.

Half-time and no goals, but Wolves have done a lot of attacking. It's a real Midlands derby day today. Albion are playing Birmingham just a few miles away. I expect there's no police holidays today. According to the boards the Albion are losing 2-1 at half-time. Ipswich are winning 1-0 at Coventry. They really are unstoppable at the moment.

Time is running out. I suppose a draw isn't too bad, but if Ipswich win we'll be three points behind them. Villa have had more of the ball lately but Wolves could still score. Must be about seven minutes left now. Be typical for Andy Gray to score. Oh no, mistake by Allan Evans. He's given the ball to Andy Gray. He is going to win it for Wolves. He's hit it over!!

Gary Shaw has been very quiet. Ooh Tony Morley has won a corner for Villa right in front of our stand. Must try not to look too excited. Dad is furious that John McCall gave the corner away too easy when he could have put it out for a throw-in.

Gordon Cowans is taking the corner. All Wolves defenders back. Only Shaw, Evans and Withe in the penalty box for Villa. Ron Saunders isn't gambling too much. Evans goes up for the header, but he's beaten to it by George Berry. Chance though. Paul Bradshaw is nowhere in the Wolves goal. It's there! Peter Withe with a free header into an empty net.

He couldn't miss. My feet are jumping but I am staying calm. The Villa fans in the South Bank opposite are going crazy. I wish I was there, instead of in with these moaning Wolves fans who are venting all their anger on both George Berry and Paul Bradshaw. We are going to win surely. Andy Gray is walking back to the halfway line. I bet he wishes he was still wearing the claret and blue.

Back in the car and I am certainly the happiest person there. We have beaten Wolves twice this season. Peter Withe's third goal in two games has given us another two points. March starts tomorrow and we have won every single league game this year. Six wins out of six. But Ipswich have won six and drawn one in 1981. The radio reporter is purring at their latest 4-0 thumping of Coventry City.

Watching Star Soccer and the Villa beating Wolves. The Tony Morley tackle on Peter Daniel didn't look good and apparently Daniel has a suspected broken leg. He won't be playing in the FA Cup quarter-final next week. Tony Morley is not a dirty player, he just didn't time it right.

The league table shows it really is Ipswich or us in the race for the title. Albion are 4th but seven points behind us. Wolves are 18th and really struggling. They are only four points clear of the relegation zone after Norwich won today. Crystal Palace look doomed. Seven points off safety it would take a miracle for them to survive.

End of February Top of Division One		
Ipswich Town	Pl: 31 Po: 48	+37
Aston Villa	Pl: 31 Po: 46	+27
Liverpool	Pl: 32 Po: 40	+17
West Brom	Pl: 31 Po: 39	+13
Forest	Pl: 31 Po: 37	+15
Arsenal	Pl: 32 Po: 37	+8

Villa February League Results	
7th Everton (a)	3-1 Won (Morley, Mortimer, Cowans)
21st Crystal Palace (h)	2-1 Won (Withe 2)
28th Wolves (a)	1-0 Won (Withe)

Chapter Eight (March)

Watching Match of the Day with Grandpa. He is feeling quite a bit better today and even had a walk in the garden. I think he is starting to get better. He even stayed up to watch Wolves - Villa highlights last night.

Yes, there it is! Tony Morley's goal against Everton is one of the ones nominated for February Goal of the Month. Easily the best goal. Grandpa says I should enter and have the chance of winning £100 of Premium Bonds. You need to send a postcard with your name and address on the left hand side and your top three goals in order on the right. The January winning goal was the Paul Mariner one against us in the FA Cup. Tony Morley's goal is ten times better than that one.

It's official, Spud is going out with Carrie Campton. Spud is asking us advice on what he should buy Carrie for her birthday on Friday. Typical of Carrie Campton to agree to be Spud's girlfriend just four days before her birthday. My advice of a Villa scarf did not get any response.

Pincher suggests a box of Milk Tray because a lady loves Milk Tray. I wouldn't call Carrie Campton a lady. Spud seems keen on buying her the Gary Numan single 'She's Got Claws'. Now that is a scary thought. Noddy, who is currently trying to follow a cheat guide for his Rubik's Cube, informs us without looking up, that girls like smelly things. Spud asks, "What about some talc then?" For once Bellington offers some help. He says he will look at what smelly things Grace has got left over from the 'Bring and Buy'. Spud is chuffed by this. He better make a donation to the appeal though if he does get something from the leftovers.

Bellington seems to have started hanging around with us more lately. It still feels odd, but I suppose he has got nobody else. I have started giving him the Maths lessons as well but it is going very slowly. It will be a long time until we get on to quadratic equations. Why do some people just not get algebra? If I am going to be a teacher though I am going to have to learn how to cope with the less abled children.

5:57pm Friday 6th March 1981

I hate doctor's waiting rooms. They are always so full of old people. Why did I mention this stabbing pain in my stomach to my mum? I am sure it isn't anything serious. It does hurt though. Odd how many of the people the receptionist seems to know. It is as if they are regulars. I haven't been here since I was at Junior School.

I don't think they have decorated since or changed the magazine. That Woman's Own is from 1978. Wait, that's a new one. Brilliant, a Shoot magazine from 14th February this year. It has got super Gary Shaw with his tongue out on the front cover. Looks like it is in the away game at Ipswich as he is wearing the blue shorts and the player half off the edge has an Ipswich badge on. I haven't seen this magazine. I cancelled by Shoot at home so I could save 25p a week for my Atari fund. Says on the front cover "I'M LAZY' confesses Villa goal-ace GARY SHAW'. I don't think he is lazy on the pitch. Perhaps he means at home. I wonder if he still lives with his parents. Perhaps he doesn't tidy his room up. He is kicking one of the balls with the red bands round. Oh dear, there in a Birmingham team picture inside.

First two pages are all about Forest going to play in the Tokyo Cup in Japan. They have to play Nacional of Uruguay in the Intercontinental Cup because Forest won the European Cup. It decides who the best club side in the world is. It'll need to be a big cup to fit the title Intercontinental Cup on. If Villa win the League this year and the European Cup next year they will play in the Intercontinental Cup. I think this stomach pain is making me think extreme thoughts. Apparently an English club has never won it.

Ray Clemence is talking about Liverpool's second leg of the League semi-final coming up against Manchester City. That was ages ago. Liverpool have to play West Ham in the final a week on Saturday. Another wrong team in claret and blue at Wembley.

Ken Brown, the Norwich manager, says that neighbours Ipswich and Aston Villa are both not good enough to win the League. He thinks Liverpool will still win it again. I bet he has changed his mind now they are eight points off the top.

The Gary Shaw page at last. That chubby ginger lady has only just gone in (to the doctor) so I should have enough time to read it. She looked like she has lots of things wrong with her. Wish Mum wouldn't keep asking me about my pain every two minutes. Gary Shaw wants to reach twenty goals for the season.

Well he already has sixteen, so that's going to happen. Also he wants to work harder and make more diagonal runs into the penalty box. He is learning lots from Peter Withe and thinks the glory days are heading back to Villa Park. It has been a long long time since glory days. We haven't won the league since my grandpa was a small boy.

That's worrying I can name all but two of the Birmingham City team on the picture. Villa fans would probably disown me. Jim Smith has even less hair than my dad. Do I really want to read about Paul Mariner? Seems when he joined Ipswich from Plymouth Argyle, no idea what an Argyle is, he could have joined Haystacks' Albion.

His home debut was then against West Brom and he helped Ipswich win 7-0. Blimey, hope Villa never let seven goals in. They would have had to write SEVEN after the number 7 on the BBC teleprinter that day as people wouldn't have believed it.

That woman is still in with Dr Pennington. How long does she need? These stomach pains are getting worse. That's a cracking picture of Jimmy Rimmer sharing a joke with Kenny Swain in the 'Life at the top' section. I didn't realise Rimmer was lacking his two front teeth. I expect a lot of goalkeepers have teeth knocked out.

Wow, you can buy a digital watch with your football team's name on for only £9.75. An Aston Villa one would be ace for my birthday. This pain is getting unbearable. I expect this is what childbirth feels like. Flipping heck, Diego Maradona, the Argentine superkid is worth more than Steve Austin. His club Argentinos Juniors have turned down an offer of $6 million from Barcelona for him.

I think there are about two dollars to every pound. So that is over two Andy Grays. They aren't allowed to sell him though until after the 1982 World Cup. If seems... ouch... that the Argentine FA gave Argentinos Juniors a loan to keep Maradona in Argentina. I have to grit my teeth to try and ride these stabbing pains.

Even the Bionic Man would struggle with these pains. Argentinos Juniors can't afford the loan repayments though and are looking to sell him for $10 million, but no team in Argentina can afford that. I don't think Ron Saunders would want him in the Villa team. I am sure he isn't as good as Sid.

In 'Ask the Expert' somebody has asked if any player has scored three penalties in one First Division match. The answer is three people. First one was a Villa player called Billy Walker (isn't he Annie Walker's son in Coronation Street?) against Bradford in November 1921. Then Charlie Mitten of Man United did it against the Villa in 1950.

Oh, the chubby ginger woman is out now. I must be next. The Americans never do get football. It says that when the North American Soccer League kicks off on March 28th teams will get up to fifteen points for a win depending on how many goals they score. If we had that, even Crystal Palace would have a chance of still winning the league.

Dr Pennington has been our family doctor all my life, although he never seems to be well. I suppose smoking that pipe continuously doesn't help. He is pushing my belly very hard whilst asking Mum about how all the various members of the family are. She is telling him how ill my dad's dad is. That pushing is really hurting me. Perhaps I should scream out. That's better it doesn't hurt on the other side.

Friday night and I am in absolute agony in a hospital bed. For the first time in my life I will be spending a night in hospital. Thank you Dr Pennington. They think it might be appendicitis and quite a cute one at that.

A doctor will come round soon and see if I need my appendix taken out. I really have no idea what an appendix does. If only we hadn't spent so many months doing biology of plants. I know plants haven't got an appendix. It really does hurt though and I feel sick. Just as well as I have a 'Nil by Mouth' sign above my bed. My sickness could be the fear of being sent to hospital though. It isn't even a children's ward. Lots of old men with pyjamas on with cords holding them up. Dad has gone back home to get my Villa pyjamas. Mum is sitting by the bed looking very concerned. Half of me just wants rid of the pain but the other half is just fearing an operation. What if I don't wake up afterwards? I might never get to have an Aston Villa season ticket. From Heaven will I be able to see Villa Park and see if we do win the League?

The doctor thinks my appendix is rumbling and is also concerned that I haven't had a poo since before the Villa beat Wolves. A week ago. I have tried. They are going to leave it until the morning before deciding if they need to cut me open. But they've given me two laxative tablets to try and make me go. The pain is getting worse and I just can't get comfortable.

7:13am Saturday 7th March 1981

I hardly slept yet the nurse woke me up at 6am. Surely being ill you should at least be allowed to sleep in. It's the weekend as well. Villa are away at Sunderland. The pain and all the old men snoring kept me awake. I can't believe that the nurse made me wee into that grey cardboard thing.

Despite sitting on the loo for ten minutes I really can't go. The pain is still as bad as ever. Maybe it isn't appendicitis and just constipation. So maybe they won't need to cut me open.

Doctor suggests that it isn't an appendix problem but a bowel blockage. If I don't go soon they will have to open me up and see what is causing it. He has instructed the sister, who looks so like Joan Simms, to give me two suppositories.

How am I going to swallow those? Oh, they don't go in my mouth. Shouldn't they close the curtains first? That feels very odd.

Ten past twelve now as I sit here again on the loo trying to push without success. The pain is very bad, but the Villa game starts in under three hours. I really need to get out of this hospital.

These pains are still bad, but at least I am back under my own Villa duvet with my lucky radio on. Maybe I was wrong to lie and say I had been to the toilet, but they didn't check. Surely I will go soon and the doctors didn't think it was appendicitis. Just feel bad having lied to my parents.

If pains get worse I will tell them the truth. Villa are unchanged again and playing well even though Ron Saunders is missing because he has been taken ill. We have a lot in common me and Ron this weekend.

Roy MacLaren and Tony Barton are in charge of the team today. They are doing well. Allan Evans gave us the lead after just two minutes from a great Tony Morley cross. A second goal now from skipper Mortimer. Sounds like a super pass by Gordon Cowans after good work from hardworking Gary Shaw. Twenty minutes gone and 2-0 at Roker Park.

This could be a cricket score. Admittedly a cricket score from a team who have been bowled out very cheaply. Perhaps we could score SEVEN for the first time in my Villa-supporting life. Hopefully Withe or Shaw will score soon. Maybe Kenny Swain, Gary Williams and Ken McNaught will all get their first goals of the season and Jimmy Rimmer can take a penalty.

Ten minutes to go and Villa are trying to hold on to a 2-1 lead as I am holding on to my very painful stomach. So much for cricket scores. I thought we could catch Ipswich's goal difference up whilst they were playing in the FA Cup today. Just need to win. They are obviously missing Saunders shouting at them. All the FA Cup quarter-finals, including Wolves at Middlesbrough look to be going to replays. Oh no, Spurs are now beating little Exeter.

A 2-1 win was not bad but now Ipswich have a game in hand on us. We are level on points but they have goal difference nine goals better than ours. We have now won seven straight games. Every league game in 1981 won and only one more win for a club record. My stomach pains are still really bad. I need to shout my mum.

9:40am Monday 9th March 1981

For the first time at Secondary school I am off ill. Still haven't had any bowel movement. I won't be getting a 100% Attendance Certificate from Miss Thatcher this year. Mum says if no better tomorrow I am going back to hospital. I bet Pincher, Spud and Mr Walker are huddled round Mr Walker's radio at school listening to the semi-final draw.

Forest still have to replay at Ipswich, but if they get through they will have to play either Man City or Everton. That means Wolves or Middlesbrough have to play Tottenham with their two Argentinians. I have got this feeling it is Wolves' year. I can see Andy Gray scoring an FA Cup Final goal to go with his League Cup final one. Who knows, in August it could be Aston Villa against Wolverhampton Wanderers in the Charity Shield at Wembley. So wish this pain would go away.

2:18pm Tuesday 10th March 1981

Last thing you want to watch when you're off ill from school is programmes for schools and colleges. Do I really want to watch Japan: The Crowded Islands? The stomach pain is certainly not as bad now I have been to the toilet a few times. Don't feel as sick either. Let's see if there are any chocolate biscuits in the biscuit tin.

I need to start building my strength up. Think I shall work on my Villa scrapbook before Jackanory and Animal Magic are on. I need to put in the article about Tony Morley's Goal of the Month winner against Everton.

Mark is really buzzing after seeing Wolves get to the FA Cup semi-final. A packed Molineux saw them see off Boro 3-1 tonight. Glad he's happy, but would probably rather they had gone out.

So Ipswich are going to play Manchester City at our ground in the semi-final on 11th April. Spookily the day they should have been playing us there. Our league game, which could be the title decider, has now been put back to Wednesday 14th April. Wolves are going to play their semi-final at Hillsborough, Sheffield Wednesday's ground.

5:00pm Thursday 12th March 1981

A few transfers around today. Everyone seems to be signing goalkeepers. Norwich City have signed 22-year old Chris Woods. He was the one who played in place of Peter Shilton for Forest in the League Cup final against Liverpool in 1979. He was unbeatable. Also Liverpool have signed a goalkeeper. No idea who he is. Says he is a 23-year-old from Vancouver Whitecaps and plays for Zimbabwe. His name is Bruce Grobbelaar and he has cost £250,000. It says he is going to replace Ray Clemence. I can't see Clemence ever leaving Liverpool.

In the paper it says a new BBC comedy, called Sorry, is starting starring the little one from the 'Two Ronnies'. I might watch that.

9:51pm Saturday 14th March 1981

It's been a long week. I feel fine now and I am actually looking forward to seeing the gang at school on Monday. I wonder how they got on with the basketball game last Thursday. Be good to see Grace Taylor as well. I wonder if she noticed I was off ill. There will be lots to talk about. I mean my night in hospital and today's incredible game with Manchester United. I can't wait to watch it on Star Soccer in ten minutes.

I think Manchester United always suit their away kit of white shirts and black shorts. I have never liked Gary Bailey though. The 5th game unchanged for the Villa. Beautiful goal by Peter Withe with his head. The move involved Williams, Mortimer, Cowans and Swain. So easy for the Villa. The pitch looks very muddy and lacking grass. Morley is running rings around Nicholl and has earned a corner. I wonder if this is where we score again. Hope they don't take a short corner.

My grandad always goes mad at those. No, Tony Morley whips it in. Peter Withe, as commentator Hugh Johns says, turns 180 degrees round before smacking the ball in hard and low. 2-0. The Villa were well on the way to equalling the club record for straight wins then. Manchester United had lost the last six away games. No wonder Dave Sexton is under so much pressure. Silly free-kick for Kenny Swain to give away early in the second-half. Good cross by Steve Coppell though. McIlroy hits the bar but lucky Joe Jordan gets a free header.

Poor defending Villa. Ron Saunders will not be happy. The game should have been all over by this point. That was a fine try by Cowans. Could so easily have flown passed Bailey. That was a decent second goal by Joe Jordan. Coppell and Wilkins combined well. But Villa shouldn't have let a two-goal lead slip.

Gary Shaw puts us back in front from a Mortimer cross right in front of the Holte End. Apparently the crowd today was the highest of the season. Over 42,000. They certainly chose a thrilling game to go to. No, that wasn't a penalty. Ref says Gary Williams has brought down Steve Coppell. It was just a tangle. Gary Williams was on the floor. Good to see no complaining from the Villa boys. Pity Jimmy couldn't save McIlroy's penalty. Yes, Hugh Johns, it is 'unbelievable'. Manchester United have not scored in their last five games and now score three at Villa Park. We should have won, but as Dad says, "You can't win every game". Although Ipswich seems to be able to. They beat Tottenham 3-0 today. So they are now a point above us and twelve goals better off. Oh and have played a game less than us.

On Wednesday 1st April Villa Park will see some silverware as our ground has been chosen for the League Cup Final replay (Liverpool against West Ham). They drew 1-1 at Wembley today. Both goals came in extra-time. Alan Kennedy scored in the 118th minute and then with the last kick Ray Stewart equalised for Second Division West Ham. Villa Park will certainly be busy in April. FA Cup semi-final, League Cup Final and possibly a title decider. It really is the best club ground for major games. Makes me very proud to be a Villa fan.

12:17pm Monday 16th March 1981

I was only off a week, but in that time Spud and Carrie Campton have split up and so have Haystacks and Georgina Ramsey. So all the gang are single again. Carrie Campton apparently didn't like the bubble bath that Spud got her for her birthday. Haystacks decided that he was sick of being told what to do by a Second Year girl. Other news includes a whooping defeat for 'Ken's Mobile Trotters' and that the Krunchi Puffs in the Tuck Shop have gone up to 8p. They had been 5p forever.

5:10pm Thursday 19th March 1981

Today is a memorable day. Goldie the Labrador on Blue Peter has had puppies and Grace Taylor told me that she was worried about me last week when she heard I had been rushed to hospital.

To raise funds for 'Ken's Mobile Trotters' we are organising a sponsored basketball throw. The idea is to see how many baskets we can each score from the free-throw line in five minutes. So I am going round all of my family looking for sponsors. My grandad has offered me a staggering 10p per basket. I said I could score twenty but he didn't seem to mind. My dad's parents were very generous as well. I know they haven't got the money my grandad has but still gave me a 50p donation. Grandpa was coughing a lot tonight and seemed unable to get warm. He really needs to eat more. I am concerned about him but he seemed more concerned about my recent illness. I still feel guilty for not admitting that I had lied about going to the toilet.

12:45pm Saturday 21st March 1981

Peter Withe is missing again for the Villa today. We are going to miss him at White Hart Lane after his recent goal blast.

The game was being billed as Withe and Shaw taking on Crooks and Archibald. Now it will be Geddis and Shaw. David Geddis has scored three goals in five games this season though. There are some good games today. Mr Walker is going to watch Forest play at Albion. Ipswich go to Old Trafford.

Man United haven't won in eight games. Jimmy Greaves thinks another defeat today and Dave Sexton will get the chop.

Half-time and my lucky radio is being anything but lucky. Villa a goal down to a Garth Crooks goal. At least Ipswich are only drawing 1-1 in Manchester. Albion are beating Forest thanks to an own goal. Wolves are 1-1 at Leeds. 'Chopper' Harris scored for Leeds and John Richards equalised for Wolves. My guess for the goals prediction of seventeen is looking a little low today.

First league defeat of the year. Beaten 2-0 at Tottenham. Typical, both Crooks and Archibald score. Our sixth defeat of the season. Thank goodness for Jimmy Nicholl getting that winner for Man U against Ipswich. I think today's defeat will be costly for us though. I am sick of us being 2nd in the league.

Southampton, Albion and Liverpool all won so they have all closed the gap. Southampton are now only five points behind us in 3rd. Luckily Keegan's men have played two games more. They only have six left to play. We play them at Villa Park next week as well. Albion are six points behind us with a much worse goal difference. That bet should be safe, but we have to play them in three games time. Our games are very hard.

In the next five games we play four of the top six teams and our last game of the season is away to 7th place Arsenal. We might be struggling to reach the UEFA Cup. At least if Liverpool win the League Cup replay there will be another place in the league for UEFA Cup. I am starting to sound really negative. I need to be more positive. Today was only our first defeat in ten games.

Time to forget about football and watch the last Doctor Who with Tom Baker in. I did think he was rubbish at first with his stupid long scarf, but now I think he is probably my favourite Doctor Who. I can't believe after seven years they are replacing him with a vet. Peter Davison, Tristan from All Creatures Great and Small, is going to take charge of the Tardis. That is just going to be so wrong. He was never any good at putting his hand up a cow's bottom so how will he cope fighting the Daleks?

12:56pm Tuesday 24th March 1981

Bellington is doing better with his Maths and we seem to be more on the same wavelength now. I was actually quite proud that he got 17 ½ out of 20 on his trigonometry homework. He really seems to have got how the logbooks work now. Just got to show him where he lost his 2 ½ marks. Still find it strange that there is no real affection shown between Bellington and Grace Taylor. Maybe they think nobody knows they are a couple.

Studying the Great Fire of London in Mrs Cresswell-Farrington's History class but my mind is all over the place. I need to try and concentrate more. Forget if Peter Withe will be fit to play against Southampton at the weekend. Concentrate on the Great Fire of London and Pudding Lane. Quite hungry actually I could eat a nice pudding just now. One of my dad's famous bread and butter puddings with lots of thick creamy custard on. After my mum has had the skin of course. Or one of my mum's apple pies with apples from Grandad's garden. No, need to concentrate on the events of 1666. Isn't it odd how all the major events happen in years ending 66? The Battle of Hastings. I wonder if one of Haystacks' (Scott Hastings) ancestors started it. Then the fire and then the most famous 66 of all, 1966. The England World Cup win. I wonder how many in this class can name all eleven heroes that day. They are the kind of facts that should be taught in the History syllabus. Let's see if I can do it. So Gordon Banks in goal, before he lost his eye.

George Cohen was a full-back. Captain Bobby Moore, the two Charlton brothers, Nobby Styles and little Alan Ball. Then obviously Geoff Hurst, Roger Hunt from Liverpool and Martin Peters. Peters only stopped playing at Sheffield United two months ago and now he is their manager. That's only ten players. I am missing one. I think it is a defender. I have got all three West Ham players Moore, Hurst and Peters. Who haven't I got? Perhaps Tucker will know. I shall pass him a note saying, "Who were the England full-backs in 1966?"

Ray Wilson, of course. Still very surprised that Mrs Cresswell-Farrington knew that. But then she is a History teacher.

She wasn't very pleased to catch me passing a note around in her lesson though. But it could have been worse. I was fearing my first detention. Instead we have to write 400 words briefly describing the Great Fire of London. Perhaps I can mention it happened 300 years before the World Cup win and include the team and goalscorers. It is probably treason to say it but I really don't think the fourth goal crossed the line. I wonder if any great event will happen in 2066 when I am hopefully 99.

9:34am Friday 27th March 1981

Mr Walker has asked us if there are any topics we would like to discuss in our form period today and that has started a very heated debate about nuclear bombs. Grace Taylor is very passionately protesting about countries having nuclear bombs. She is so up to date with current affairs. Grace claims that both the Soviet Union and France have been testing nuclear bombs. Not sure how, or indeed, where, you test a nuclear bomb.

Bellington is saying the school should have a nuclear shelter for when the four minute warning goes off. I don't understand why the Cold War is called the Cold War as I expect it'd be very hot if a nuclear bomb went off. Grace is very much in favour of us all joining CND. She draws the logo on the blackboard. It stands for 'Campaign for Nuclear Disarmament'. I suppose CFND wouldn't sound as good. I must ask Grace Taylor more about this as she is obviously very passionate about it despite many of the class thinking we should have nuclear bombs. I expect Grace would get on well with Tucker's Aunty Carol.

11:40am Saturday 28th March 1981

Adam Ant is answering questions on the phones on Multi-coloured Swap Shop. He looks quite a sight with white stripes across his face and a red waist-coat with black leather trousers. I really don't think with my chubby thighs that leather trousers would look good on me. Anyway, Mum would probably shrink them in the tumble dryer. That's a good question from John Kendall. He has asked how they got the name of the group. I have always wondered that. That's a boring answer though, but Adam apologised for it being boring. He said one of the guitarists came one day and suggested they called the group 'The Ants'. Adam Ant looks loads cooler than Noel Edmonds does. Mr Ant seems a really nice chap though. Not wild like his songs are. He says his hobbies are going to the cinema, reading and going for walks. What's he going to offer for a swap then? A Frontier Tour t-shirt and neck scarf. Not very exciting but his pirate belt buckle he wore on the tour is pretty fab. That could clip on my school trousers belt. I am sure that would impress Grace Taylor. How do I know the answer to that question? He has asked, "How many different species of ants are there in Great Britain?" I will have to look 'Ant' up in our red encyclopaedias.

That's a blow still no Peter Withe to play against Southampton this afternoon. We need to win this game at Villa

315

Park. Looks a good Southampton team though. Kevin Keegan, Mick Channon and even World Cup winner Alan Ball are in their team. As well as former Villa captain Chris Nicholl. I bet he gets a good reception. I remember in 1976 Villa played at Leicester and Chris Nicholl scored all four goals that day in a 2-2 draw. I bet no other Villa player has ever scored two goals for us and two own goals in the same match. He scored one for each team in each half. Southampton are on a good run and were even mentioned on Football Focus. They have won their last four league games.

Ipswich are at home to Sunderland today, but they must be getting tired with all the games they have played lately. This will be their 7th game this month. They are through to the UEFA Cup semi-final as well as the FA Cup semi-final. We could do with Liverpool losing against Arsenal today, if they do then they will definitely not be completing a hat-trick of League titles.

Disastrous start for the claret and blue. Four minutes and Allan Evans has done a Chris Nicholl and scored an own goal. What was he thinking? This could really be the day that our championship challenge collapses never mind Liverpool's. I am not going to resort to my lucky radio just yet. I will listen on the tuner for half an hour more. Surely my radio can't make a difference. I wish Peter Withe was playing.

I'm going to have to go upstairs now and put my radio on. Only five minutes until half-time and we are still 1-0 down. At the moment nobody is going to be happy on Saturday. Albion are losing, Wolves can't even beat Leicester and Mr Walker's Forest are a goal down. Walsall were beating Chesterfield but I think they are drawing now. At least Ipswich are only 1-1 with Sunderland according to Ceefax. Muhren has scored for them. I am sure if they weren't allowed any Dutch players they wouldn't be half as good as they are.

The goal horn sounds within seconds of turning on radio and it is a goal at Villa Park. ... The equaliser, another great Tony Morley goal. Played through on the halfway line by David Geddis. Then Morley raced forward and rifled the ball past the Southampton goalkeeper. That's more like it Villa.

Back to Villa Park again, blimey. Two goals in three minutes. The Holte End are loving this. David Geddis has scored right in front of them. Another classic Villa break. This time the pass came from full-back Gary Williams. What a radio! What a team! Half-time and we are winning and Ipswich are only drawing.

I hate Ipswich Town. Villa have won 2-1 and Ipswich have to outdo us and win 4-1. Weren't Sunderland even trying? Paul Mariner scored two and the other Dutch player Thijssen scored the other one. At least Arsenal beat Liverpool 1-0 thanks to Alan Sunderland. Baggies and Wolves both lost. Walsall won a seven-goal thriller so Noddy and Tucker will be cheerful on Monday.

Checking the league tables to update my league ladders. We have been second to Ipswich now for over two months. Still one point behind and now they have a +15 goal difference better than ours. We need to score more goals. They have scored 70 goals in the league this season compared to our 60 and they have still played a game less. They play their game in hand against Leeds United this coming Tuesday.

Forest are third now because they came back and beat Norwich. They are still eight points behind us though and only have six games left to play. In fact if we get just seven points from our last seven games then the worst we can finish is 2nd. We should really end up in the UEFA Cup. Wolves losing at home to Leicester means that Wolves are now only four points clear of Leicester who are inside the relegation zone. I can wind Spud and Pincher up about that on Monday.

10:11am Sunday 29th March 1981

Sunday morning and for the first time lots of people are running around London in the country's first official Marathon. Following on from the success of the New York Marathon over 7,000 people are running 26.2 miles. It is going to end at a place called Constitution Hill, but not for over two and a half hours. Apparently over 20,000 people applied to run. At least the weather has stayed quite fine for them.

The men's Marathon is just finishing. An American and a Norwegian are going to tie as they are crossing the line holding hands. You would never get Coe and Ovett doing that in the Olympics. The winning time is just under 2 hours 12 minutes. That seems pretty quick. I suppose there wasn't much traffic around being Sunday morning and no shops being open.

That can't be right. It says in the Sunday People that Rupert Murdoch, who owns The Sun, has just bought The Times newspaper group. Surely he can't own both, they are poles apart. You would never catch Great Uncle Bulgaria ogling a topless lady on page three.

Also in my grandad's paper it says there is going to be a new political party formed. It seems that four Labour MPs think that Labour has become too 'left wing'. So Roy Jenkins, David Owen, Shirley Williams and Bill Rodgers are breaking away to form a party called the Social Democratic Party. SDP for short. I think they will be like a Socialist version of the Liberal Party. Glad I don't have to vote. Politics seems very confusing and boring. Why can't all the parties just work together?

Watching the Villa on Match of the Day and that was another cracking goal by Tony Morley. Perhaps he could win Goal of the Month for the second month running. They could rename the feature to 'The Tony Morley Goal of the Month'. I think his Everton goal was probably a better goal though. That goal started further back and could end up being Goal of the Season.

Grandad is asking me what I want for my 14th birthday next Saturday. I excitedly remind him that Dad and Mum are buying me my first ever season ticket for the 1981/82 season. He asked me how much more money do I need for my Atari fund. I suspect I am still about £30 short, but I need to look at second hand ones in the newspaper. There is no way I can afford a new one unless I save until I am 21.

9:12pm Monday 30th March 1981

Yet another high profile shooting. This time it is the American President. The old western actor Ronald Reagan has been shot. They say it was an attempted assassination. Like Kennedy all those years ago. Certainly been a year for shootings. JR, John Lennon, Roy of the Rovers and now the President of the United States. Reagan was leaving a speaking engagement at the Washington Hilton Hotel when he and three others were shot. The gunman must have fired a lot of shots. Reagan is alive, but has been rushed to hospital and is being operated on. The gunman was arrested at the scene. There were reports that one of the President's main men, James Brady, had been killed, but now it seems he is still alive, just.

5:31pm Tuesday 31st March 1981

Great news! Mum has just told me a son of a teacher at her school is selling his Atari Console and four games, including Space Invaders, for £120. Now I have got £95 saved up so nearly there. Mum says she has spoken to Grandad and he will give me £20 towards it for my birthday. That means I am only £5 short. Even better news is my parents will give me the final £5 because I was so good over my stay in hospital. Feel slightly guilty about this, but I am getting an Atari so who cares. The only slight worry is that the fund includes the money from the top Midlands team bet. There is surely no hope of Albion catching us now, even if they beat us next Wednesday. No, I will gamble and give Mum all the £95 to buy the second-hand Atari with.

Yet more good news when I turn on Ceefax. Final result Leeds 3 Ipswich 0. Ipswich have blown their game in hand. They might still be a point ahead but we have played the same amount of games. I still believe. Not so good reading through is West Bromwich Albion 2 Everton 0. Oh dear, that means Albion are now only six points behind us. That game next week is getting so important. Bryan Robson and Ally Brown scored for the Albion.

Now what April Fools shall I play at school tomorrow morning?

End of March Top of Division One		
Ipswich Town	Pl: 35 Po: 53	+39
Aston Villa	Pl: 35 Po: 51	+27
West Brom	Pl: 36 Po: 45	+15
Forest	Pl: 36 Po: 44	+19
Southampton	Pl: 37 Po: 44	+18
Liverpool	Pl: 34 Po: 42	+17

Villa March League Results	
7th Sunderland (a)	2-1 Won (Evans, Mortimer)
14th Manchester United (h)	3-3 Draw (Withe)
21st Tottenham (a)	0-2 Lost
28th Southampton (h)	2-1 Won (Morley, Geddis)

Chapter Nine (April)

Pincher has started having the Match football magazine. It doesn't seem as grown-up as Shoot but still a decent lunchtime read. Just reading about Ipswich's John Wark and his amazing penalty record. He has scored 26 out of 28 penalties for Ipswich. Obviously refs are very generous with penalties for Ipswich.

I still think Sid Cowans is a better penalty taker than John Wark. Dennis Mortimer is writing in this magazine and is surprisingly suggesting Gary Shaw is not yet ready for the full England team. He does think that England should try Sid, Glenn Hoddle and even Albion's Bryan Robson in their midfield.

Sadly, Dennis thinks his chances of a full cap have now gone, but is really happy to be captaining the England B team. I still think he might get an England call-up yet. The skipper does seem pretty sure we will win the League though. Wish I was as confident.

Noddy is trying to identify the three bearded chins on the quiz page. Ricky Villa is definitely right and Peter Daniel of Wolves, but I don't think the third one is Steve Archibald. Haystacks is saying Garry Birtles and as always Haystacks is right when we check the answers. Just hope he is right in his prediction that his West Brom will beat Ipswich on Saturday. That would be a great birthday present for me.

Kevin Keegan is predicting his old club Liverpool are going to find Bayern Munich very difficult team to beat in next week's European Cup semi-final at Anfield. Keegan knows all about German football from his time at Hamburg. Another English player who currently plays in Germany, Tony Woodcock, is talking rubbish. He writes that, 'Ipswich are the best in Europe'. I think he's worrying about facing them for Cologne in the UEFA Cup semi-final. Cologne have already beaten Barcelona. Haystacks thinks that both Liverpool and Ipswich will reach the European finals because English teams are so much better than the rest of the teams in Europe.

Wow, there is a chance to win a trip on Concorde. To go and see the 'North American Soccer League Super Bowl'. Apparently it is like their Cup Final. It isn't easy though. You have to match the eight famous players with the picture of the puma boots they wear. I think E is Kenny Dalglish's and Pincher is sure that C is Peter Shilton's. Spud is going for Diego Maradona as F because of the thick shin pads. He also thinks that A could be Andy Gray's as they look like his knees. This is almost impossible.

We are letting Noddy do the tie-breaker though. We have to write, in no more than fifteen words, why we like PUMA sport shoes. Noddy is the only one of us that has a pair so he seems the obvious choice. I don't like his first attempt though, 'I like Puma because it helps me score against Aston Villa'.

In the ratings part of Match Facts for the Villa game against Southampton, Dennis Mortimer got our highest score with eight out of ten. All our other players got seven except for poor Gary Williams who only got six. The game got a three star rating for entertainment.

Odd seeing Villa Park full on Sports Night and no Villa players on the pitch. At least one team is wearing claret and blue.

Even though I am still bitter about last season's FA Cup quarter-final I am still glad West Ham have taken the lead. Paul Goddard has scored. Maybe they can win their second major trophy in a year despite being a Second Division team. Plenty of time for Liverpool to come back though. Dalglish has started well.

That was some turn around. Dalglish and Alan Hansen scoring in a four-minute spell around the half-hour mark. I don't think I want to watch Phil Thompson lifting up the League Cup at Villa Park. I suppose as Villa hold the record for the most League Cup wins it makes sense that Liverpool's first league cup win would be here. Still think having three handles makes it look fantastic.

3:43pm Thursday 2nd April 1981

I didn't expect that. Grace Taylor has given me a card and a little neatly wrapped present for my birthday on Saturday. How did she know? Perhaps Bellington told her as I mentioned it at basketball training last night. No idea what the present might be. It feels soft and is so beautifully wrapped. Maybe slightly girly wrapping paper but still lovely. Can I really last two days without opening it?

5:20pm Friday 3rd April 1981

Take a bow Gary Shaw. The Villa teenager has been crowned the PFA Young Player of the Year. His fellow professionals have realised that he is the best young player in the First Division. Glenn Hoddle and Cyrille Regis are the two previous winners so he is in good company. It has been four years since a Villa player won it. That was the year greedy Andy Gray won both the PFA Player of the Year and the PFA Young Player of the Year. Gary's young enough to win it again next year. I think Tony Morley or Gordon Cowans should have won Player of the Year, instead of John Wark. Kenny Swain, Allan Evans and Gary Shaw all made it in the PFA Team of the Year. But Ipswich had four players in there. Kenny Sansom and Peter Shilton both made the team for the 5th time. I guess Villa guys have got some catching up to do.

8:49am Saturday 4th April 1981

There are good birthdays, great birthdays and unbelievable birthdays. This is an 'unbelievable' one. My 14th birthday is without doubt by best birthday ever. In my parents card was a 'We owe you an Aston Villa Season Ticket for 1981/82'. Best present ever, but second best one is an Atari Console with four games (including Space Invaders). Mum apparently got it yesterday for me and she wrapped it up. Mark and I have spent the last three hours playing on it. I have already managed to clear a whole screen of Space Invaders. The joystick with red button is so cool. I haven't quite mastered the racing car game though yet. Can't wait for my friends to come round and play on my Atari.

I have had 23 cards. The one from my grandpa and grandma even had a player wearing claret and blue on the front and they had stuck a big gold 1 and 4 on the front of it. Although the 4 is starting to peel off. Inside was a crisp one pound note. I am so lucky.

In all the excitement I had forgotten the card and present from Grace Taylor. I am going to open these now on my own while Mark has a go at Space Invaders. Love the sound they make as they go across the screen.

A nice card off Grace with some horses on the front and a tractor. Just says 'Happy Birthday from Grace' inside though. Sadly no 'love' or kisses. So what is in the nicely wrapped parcel? That is sweet. I didn't expect that. Maybe Grace Taylor does like me. It is a brand new shiny Abba pencil case. Perhaps she just feels guilty for what Bellington did to my other one. Maybe I am now too old for Abba pencil cases, but this is the first birthday present I think a girl has ever given me.

Grandpa is on the phone for me. He has managed to walk to the phonebox to ring me on my birthday. He sounds out of breath and has to put another 10p in as the pips have gone. Grandpa is telling me he has put a bet on the Grand National this afternoon for me and if it wins I can have the winnings for my birthday. The horse he has chosen because of the name is 'Another Captain'. He has put on 20p and if it wins he will win 40 times that. I tell him if it wins that we should share the money. I know he and Grandma don't have a lot.

My birthday is full of sporting events. We are watching the 127th Boat Race before the football starts. As always, it's between Oxford and Cambridge. My cousin is at Cambridge so I should really support them. Although Cambridge have won more times than Oxford in the past. Mark is supporting Cambridge so I am going to support Oxford. Just won't tell my cousin. I think Cambridge might win though as Oxford have a woman as cox. Still find it funny they're called a cox. Sue Brown is the first ever female cox in the race.

Today is obviously my day. Oxford have romped home. They have won by eight lengths. The biggest win this century. Obviously having a lady cox is the way forward. No idea why they call it a cox.

Nothing can go wrong today for me. I bet the Villa will win at Leicester and my horse 'Another Captain' will win the Grand National.

Peter Withe is back so Villa are at full strength. Perhaps harsh on David Geddis after he scored one and made another goal last week. I am sure Peter Withe will score on my birthday though. Won't leave it to chance, will have my lucky radio on from the start while I destroy these space invaders.

It wasn't supposed to be like this. A goal down to a Lynex penalty after just fifteen minutes. Ken McNaught gave it away at Filbert Street. Doesn't he know it is my birthday?

The radio is now going to concentrate on the Grand National so no goal horns for the next twenty minutes. Think I will go and watch the race with Dad on the downstairs telly.

My horse Another Captain has a jockey called Colin Hawkins. The favourite to win is a horse called Spartan Missile, but a lot of people want Aldaniti to win. Dad says Aldaniti's jockey (Bob Champion) has been very ill, with cancer and has had chemotherapy. Also his horse has suffered with chronic leg problems.

Luckily, unlike other horses he hasn't had to be shot.

First fence then and two horses have fallen already. They are Barney Maclyvie and Another Captain. There goes my share of £8. Think I will support the jockey with the cancer now.

That can't be right. The commentator, Peter O'Sullevan, is saying the jockey on the favourite Spartan Missile is 54 years old. 40 years older than me. That is ten years older than my dad. Wish I knew how the Villa were doing.

Bob Champion and Aldaniti are just ahead of a horse called Royal Mail. Why didn't Grandpa choose Royal Mail? As I had so many birthday cards arrive in the post this morning. Spartan Missile is coming back now and overtaking Royal Mail. The old man might win, but he shouldn't be allowed to whip his horse so much. How would he like it? It looks like Bob Champion is going to hold on though. Yes, he has won it. Well done Bob Champion and Aldaniti.

It's the goal horn. Unbelievable! Two goals at Filbert Street and both for the birthday boys' team. Peter Withe and Des Bremner have turned the game around. Leicester 1 Aston Villa 2. Yet another goal horn. Amazingly there are three goal at The Hawthorns. Fantastic news. It is Albion 2 Ipswich Town 1. Brazil for Ipswich, but Ally Brown and Brendan Batson with the Albion goals. Fancy Brendan Batson scoring. He might be helping Villa to go top on my 14th birthday. Yet another goal horn. Kevin Broadhurst has given Birmingham the lead at home to Boro.

When will these goal horns stop? Another one, back to Filbert Street. Come on Villa. Please have scored a third. No, disaster Lynex has scored a second against us. The reporter says it was a comedy of errors. Gordon Cowans and Jimmy Rimmer getting in each other's way. Why didn't Gordon just hoof it?

That's a better start to the second-half. Another headed goal from Peter Withe. Please keep the lead this time Villa.

I can't play any more space invaders the football is too tense. Another goal, this time in the Wolves game. Andy Gray has broken the deadlock at Sunderland. I think if we beat Leicester, Wolves will be virtually safe if they can hold on to their two points.

Yet another goal in the Villa game. Magic Morley does it again. A Cowans short free kick to Mortimer who rolled it to Tony Morley. Tony then hammered it past goalkeeper Wallington.

4-2 to the super Villans. Can really hear the Villa fans singing. Another goal horn and it is back to The Hawthorns. What a birthday this is! Baggies are beating Ipswich 3-1. Peter Barnes has scored. "We are top of the league, yes we are top of the league!!"

For once my Roy of the Rovers will have to remain unread for a bit. I have to fill in my Performance Chart and draw the line from 2nd to 1st on the League Position graph, then time to play Missile Command for the first time on my birthday Atari. Need to colour in two goal squares for Peter Withe. He has now scored sixteen league goals. The same as Gary Shaw. With Tony Morley's ten goals our three forwards have scored 42 goals. 42 the answer to life, the universe and everything.

I really am on a high and Mum has got me an Aston Villa cake with fourteen candles on. I am sure she doesn't realise that each candle represents one of the Villa heroes. Top of the league. One point ahead of Ipswich and we both have just six games to play. Now I am sure that we are going to win the League.

This special day just continues. Now it is time for the Eurovision Song Contest. Terry Wogan, as always, is telling us about each of the songs. This year it is from Dublin. Quite an old bloke in a white tuxedo is singing in French (I think) and representing Luxembourg. No idea what the song is all about but he looks very serious.

What amazing trousers the Finnish entry is wearing. They have a pink and yellow triangle pattern. His song is called 'Reggae

OK' but they are the only words that seem to be in English. Although, there aren't many other words.

Netherlands entry is quite bouncy. Pretty lady in a yellow dress is singing it. It has got my dad's feet tapping.

Finally it is us. Time for Bucks Fizz and 'Making Your Mind Up'. They are showing the group looking around the boats in Dublin Bay. I think four members is a good amount. Two boys and two girls, just like Abba. So come on Cheryl, Jay, Mike and Bobby. Let's do it for Great Britain, well, United Kingdom, for some reason.

Terry Wogan is telling the viewers that Cheryl Baker has competed before, in 1978 as part of Co-Co. The group have very colourful outfits on. I didn't know Mike was a Nolan brother. He should be a good singer then. We haven't won since Brotherhood of Man in 1975. With 'Save all your kisses for me'. I have still got that single. The boys are wearing white trousers with their colourful tops. Cheryl Baker has a long blue skirt on and Jay a long green one. Snazzy dancing. My Mum is impressed. Think we could do well. "We're making our mind up".

Didn't expect that! That got Dad's attention. The lads have just ripped the girl's skirts off. They're now wearing even shorter skirts. That must have taken some rehearsing. I bet lots of men will pause that when they play it back on their videos.

Hope the judges like it. "Don't let your indecision, take you from behind". It helps being in English. I can see this dance catching on. I can imagine Grace Taylor doing it. Swinging those hips. Maybe not the ripping the skirt off bit. Dad says he has never seen so much blonde hair on a stage in his life.

Austria, Germany and now Luxemburg have all given France twelve points (the maximum). They look like they are going to run away with it. Ireland are second and we are third. Pity we can't combine our votes with the Irish.

Twelve from Israel for Bucks Fizz. That's more like it. Only two for France from good old Denmark. Come on give us the twelve please. We buy a lot of your butter. Well, my grandad does. Ten for United Kingdom and the twelve, they give to Ireland. That puts Ireland in the lead. It is getting very close.

France never give us anything. Well, I suppose seven is better than nothing. Twelve for Switzerland though. That is two straight top scores Switzerland have got. Netherlands know their music. They have given us the twelve and just one for Switzerland. Germany and Ireland now both have 74 but United Kingdom have the lead with 83.

Ireland have given Switzerland top marks and so have Norway. Come on UK judges please don't give Switzerland top marks. If you do they will overtake us. I don't believe it we have given them the twelve points. Just nine points separate Switzerland, United Kingdom and Germany now.

Thanks to Belgium we are back in front by three. This is more exciting than the Boat Race. Now Germany and Bucks Fizz both have 120 points. Just Switzerland and Sweden left to vote. Hope Sweden don't think we are copying Abba.

Only eight from Switzerland and they haven't mentioned Germany yet. Ten to Yugoslavia so looks like twelve for Germany. Yes! The twelve goes to France. Switzerland didn't give anything to Germany. Quick Maths in my head works out Bucks Fizz only need Sweden to give us five points and we have won. Seven points to Ireland so they will end on 105, but still no mention of UK or Germany.

Bucks Fizz have won Eurovision 1981 on my 14th Birthday. Sweden have given us eight points. They give Germany twelve but we have still won by four points. So we get to see our group perform again. I wonder if they will whip the skirts off again. Well done to the four of you. Currently number five in the charts but I bet it will be number one next week. Dad says he will buy us a copy as he presses the OTR button on the video.

There go the skirts again.

A totally brilliant birthday is ending with us watching the great Aston Villa go top of the league on Star Soccer. Please Gordon Cowans, never try to dribble in your own six yard box again. I can't wait to get my first season ticket.

As I am going to bed Dad announces that he is taking me to the big Albion v Villa local derby on Wednesday night. I am really going to enjoy being fourteen.

10:36am Monday 6th April 1981

I made sure that I thanked Grace Taylor for my Abba pencil case and proudly put all my pens and things in it. Just want to put a sign on it saying, 'This was a birthday present off Grace Taylor'. I don't expect she told Bellington she bought me a present.

Haystacks is really trying to wind me up about the game on Wednesday. He says that Regis and Ally Brown are both going to score and then Albion will be just four points behind the Villa. As I explain to Haystacks, as he is putting my head under his sweaty armpit, then Albion would only have four games left and still an inferior goal difference. The Villa would have to only get three more points from their last five games and Albion would have to win all four of theirs. His response is that if Albion smash the Villa by seven then they will have the better goal difference.

Spud is trying to kid Haystacks and me that there is a new war film due out in the summer that stars John Wark, Pele, Ossie Ardiles and Sylvester Stallone. We just pretend to believe him, but Spud can tell we are not convinced. Mr Walker is suggesting Spud is right though and he heard it is called something like 'Victory' and had been filmed in Hungary last summer. Mr Walker also says that Bobby Moore was in it and Michael Caine, the actor from the Italian Job. This is obviously some kind of belated April Fools Spud and Mr Walker are playing on us. I am not going to fall for it. Mr Walker goes too far when he says that Ipswich goalkeeper Paul Cooper pretends to be Sylvester Stallone in it. They look nothing like each other. If it is real how come they didn't pick any Villa players? Gary Shaw would have loved posing in front of a movie camera dressed as a soldier.

Pincher's Match magazine this week is all about the FA Cup semi-finals at the weekend. Pincher is really pleased because his dad's company have got them both tickets to see Wolves in the Hillsborough game against Spurs. The other semi is the Ipswich - Man City one at the home of football, Villa Park. In the magazine various football stars are predicting who will win. Kevin Dillon thinks it will be an Ipswich against Wolves final. Steve Coppell thinks a Spurs - Ipswich final.

Seems everyone is having an Ipswich love-in. Manchester United defenders, Nicholl and McQueen, both say 'Must be Ipswich' for the League title. Another article on the opposite page is about how John Wark is on course to beat the European goal scoring record. He has scored eleven so far in Europe this season and the record is just fourteen.

Gerry Francis is far too good for the Second Division. In Match monthly marks for March he averaged 8.25. Next highest was a Grimsby player on 7.66. In First Division the toothless Joe Jordan won. Well, he did score against the Villa. Jimmy Rimmer and Dennis Mortimer were joint second though. Talking of Dennis Mortimer he is previewing our big game with Ipswich in his column. Strange how Match magazine comes out a week early. He should be previewing the Villa's mighty clash with the Baggies tomorrow night. If we can win both games I think we will be CHAMPIONS.

Wow, a big Peter Withe poster on the centre page. He is the 'Matchmaker Special'. Lots of facts about him. I will have to read this fast before Chemistry. He has put Dalglish, George Best and Jimmy Greaves up front in his 'Best All Time British Team'. He dislikes gardening, ignorant people and smoking. Good to hear Peter. That's interesting. His biggest influence has been 'The Doog', Derek Dougan, who Peter played with in South Africa.

Withey's pre-match meal is sugar puffs, chocolate and tea. Maybe I should have that before I go to watch the Villa tomorrow. TV show he always switches off, like me, is Crossroads. Another Villa player saying that Mark Walters is a player for the future. He must be good.

I agree with that letter in the 'Outraged' section. No, not the stupid one about having two refs, but the one titled 'Dull Ipswich'. P.A. Thomas of Heavitree, in Devon you are so right. The Charlton fans writes, "I AM sick and tired of hearing how successful Ipswich Town have been this season. The dull defensive tactics introduced by Bobby Robson have bored me to tears." That is a man who knows about football.

There's a spotlight on Kenny Hibbitt as well. Spud says he's his favourite player. Says Hibbitt used to play for Bradford Park Avenue. Hibbitt's magic moment in football was when he pulled on the England Under-23 shirt. His biggest disappointments are worrying Spud though. He lists the two FA Cup semi-finals he has lost. Spud deserves some good news. He still hasn't got over the break-up with Carrie Campton. So I hope for Spud and Pincher that Wolves don't lose by too many against Spurs on Saturday.

2:40pm Wednesday 8th April 1981

Spud cannot decide who he wants to lose the most tonight. Albion or the Villa. Pincher says he hopes it is a draw so neither team wins. Tucker and Noddy don't care who wins as long as Walsall win at Newport County. Walsall slipped into the relegation zone when they lost to Gillingham on Friday night. Only Blackpool and Hull are below them in the league now. Tucker thinks they should sack manager Alan Buckley.

Look at the queue. As me and Dad walk down the bank from Aston Hall neither of us can quite believe the length of the queue from the Holte End. It's right down Trinity Road. Still an hour and a half before the 7:30 kickoff and the walk to the end of the queue is nearly as long as the walk from the car. I really am not convinced we will get in.

Even the police are telling people in the queue about ten before us that they expect to be closing the gates very soon. The legal capacity is 48,000 and everyone is being counted in. The Villa fans are all in good voice, but I sense that like me they are feeling nervous. I manage to persuade Dad that if we don't get in we can stay and stand on the bank and a least see part of the game through the gap between the stands. They haven't closed the gates yet and we are now probably only about 100 people away from them.

Yes, through the huge turnstiles and into Villa Park. We have got in. The Holte is packed so we won't be able to get near one of the crush barriers. You can just feel what a gigantic game this is. It isn't just local pride at stake and the crown of 'Kings of the Midlands', but the League title is on the line. Ipswich failed to beat Ron Atkinson's Albion, now we have to prove that we can and prove that we are the best team in England.

From the streets below we can hear the police telling the disappointed masses of fans that the Holte End is now full and nobody else can come in. I am one of the lucky few. But then being a Villa fan makes me lucky.

Shock team news for Villa. There is no Gary Shaw tonight. David Geddis will be wearing the No. 8 shirt. Colin Gibson is also in for Gary Williams. 'Gibbo' gives us more options going forward so that change isn't a problem. But no Gary Shaw is a real blow.

Picture on the front of the programme is the Villa players congratulating Geddis on his goal against Southampton. Hope it is an omen for today.

Just reading in the 'For the Record' section of the programme about our Central League team. We are only 6th in the league a place below the Wolves, but Mark Walters has scored eight goals in his ten games. Terry Donovan continues to score as well, 17 in 28 reserve games. There is an article in the programme called AVTV. It would be amazing if one day Aston Villa had its own TV show. We are leading the way with technology. A revolutionary new closed-circuit TV camera system has been installed. It cost nearly £60,000. It's supposed to help police spot football hooligans. There is a purpose-built control room somewhere in the Trinity Road Stand. There are four cameras around the ground. Two of them are even colour cameras. They are planning to put cameras outside the ground. Not sure why. One is planned for Witton Railway Station.

Albion are making more chances than us. The crowd is so nervous. Maybe at half-time Ron will give our lads a shake=up. David Geddis just isn't involved. That is now over 135 minutes of Villa - Albion games this season and still no goals. The new scoreboard is displaying Ipswich 1 Cologne 0. I wonder if Tony Woodcock is playing.

Ten minutes to go and still no sign of a goal for either team. I suppose a draw wouldn't be disastrous. Des Bremner is playing well. The rain is coming down quite heavily now.

Less than three minutes left and oddly a few people are leaving. They can't be real Villa supporters. When I have my season ticket, next August, I will never leave until the referee blows his final whistle. You support your team right until the end.

Is Dad seriously suggesting we leave to try and beat the traffic? He can go. I am not going. I will walk home if I have to. Long punt up by Jimmy Rimmer, but straight to Brendan Batson. Albion will just keep it now until referee Shapter, from Torquay, blows his whistle. Batson rolls it back towards Tony Godden in the Albion goal. Wait a minute that's not hard enough. Peter

Withe is on to it. He's scored. Right in front of us in the last minute. We have scored. Yes!! Yes!! Yes!! Even my Dad is jumping up and down. Nobody is leaving now.

The Albion fans have gone very quiet. I am looking forward to seeing Haystacks in the morning. Just keep the ball now Villa. Nothing silly, please! It's over, the electronic scoreboard reads VILLA 1 WEST BROMWICH ALBION 0. A giant step towards our first title in 71 years. Scoreboard now showing the attendance: 47,998. Obviously a couple of season ticket holders couldn't make it. I will never miss next season. Although Dad still needs to work out how I am going to get here. Well done Peter Withe. He has now scored seventeen league goals. One more than Gary Shaw and he has played four league games less than Gary. Shaw has scored more cup goals than Withe though.

The mood walking back through the grounds of Aston Hall with the AV floodlights lighting the way really is magical. You can just tell that this is a very special night even the rain has stopped and there are bright stars in the sky. The super Villa have now taken 21 points from a possible 24 during 1981. We are the team who deserve to be top of the league. We are now three points clear of Ipswich and we have a +30 goal difference. West Brom might be 3rd but they are now eight points behind us and only have four games left. Southampton and Arsenal can't catch us so we are definitely in Europe next season. Aston Villa are back in Europe. What a great time to have my first season ticket.

Middle of the night and I just can't sleep. My head is just full of Villa. I keep seeing Peter Withe scoring the goal after Brendan Batson's mistake. I just love Brendan Batson. There should be a statue of him erected outside Villa Park. First he scores the goal that beats Ipswich then he gives Villa the goal that might win us the championship. Let me try counting to 47,998 and see if I fall asleep before I get there.

12:24pm Thursday 9th April 1981

I don't believe it Haystacks is off sick today. Where are all the Albion fans when you want to celebrate a famous Villa win? Haystacks seemed fine yesterday. Well, he can't hide forever. At least now barring Villa losing every game, Albion winning every game and a fourteen swing in goal difference I have won the bet for the highest placed Midlands team. We could have let Mr Walker in because even the great Brian Clough team can't catch us. I have never had such a fantastic week as I am having now.

9:20am Friday 10th April 1981

Grace Taylor has decided to sit by me in assembly. Her hair smells really nice today. Almost lemony. Think I might tell her that her brown hair smells lovely. Probably best not to mention the lemons. Grace's clothes always look so neat, clean and well ironed. She sits on the plastic blue chair so lady-like. Not much chance for conversation, but Grace does ask if I am going to watch the new series of Are You Being Served tonight. I just nod and resist mentioning Mrs Slocombe's pussy.

Pictures on the news of Ronald Reagan leaving hospital. He looks pretty well for somebody who was shot a few weeks ago. The main story seems to be about some major fights in London in a place called Brixton. The police all have plastic shields. A lot of police seem to be getting hit with bricks. I bet this puts Spud off joining the police. Seems conflicting stories about what has caused it. Some are saying it is racism by the police who didn't help a black lad who had been stabbed. Other people are blaming rising levels of unemployment. They are really horrible scenes. I am glad we don't live in London. Maggie Thatcher needs to start doing a better job as Prime Minister.

1:30pm Saturday 11th April 1981

Dad and Mark have gone on the Wolves coach to Hillsborough to see Wolves in the semi-final. Mum is helping Grandma look after Grandpa today. He has been very ill all week. Mum says he keeps being sick and losing blood. No idea how you can lose blood. So I am at Grandad's following the football. The Villa have a Saturday off. Bizarrely we should have been at home to Ipswich in the title decider, but instead Ipswich are at Villa Park playing Manchester City.

The back page of Grandad's Daily Express is all about Everton, even though they are not playing today. Looks like they're going to sack manager Gordon Lee. Well, they are only on the same amount of points as the Wolves. Lee is not being given another contract in the summer. Blackburn's manager, Howard Kendall, is the firm favourite to take over in the summer. Blackburn should get promotion from the Second Division.

The Wolves game has been delayed by fifteen minutes due to problems getting all the crowd into Hillsborough. Walsall are losing again, this time at home to Plymouth. They really could be relegated. Can't imagine Walsall in the Fourth Division.

Only three minutes and a goal in Wolves' semi-final. Bad news for Mark, Dad and my Wolves-supporting grandad. Spurs have scored. The reporter says there are still hundreds are Spurs fans trying to get into the Leppings Lane End. They have all pushed in from the back as Spurs have scored so quite a squash. Some fans have had to climb over the railings at the front.

Some concern about the Tottenham fans spilling onto the pitch at Hillsborough. Referee Clive Thomas is talking to the police. Perhaps the match will get abandoned. Maybe that would be good for Wolves as they are losing.

Wolves aren't losing any more. Kenny Hibbitt has equalised Stevie Archibald's goal.

I have never known my grandad so nervous. No goals in the first-half at Villa Park. But sounds like all Ipswich as usual. Come on Man City tire them out for Tuesday please.

Goal horn and the only game still not at half-time is Wolves' game. Oh dear, Glenn Hoddle has put Spurs back in front.

Liverpool are goalless with Forest at half-time. If Liverpool don't win today then they can't catch the Villa. Even if we lose every game.

Looking through Grandad's TV Times magazine for the coming week. Grandad seems to have so many more magazines and papers since Nanny died. I suppose he gets bored, despite all his technical gadgets. It says in the magazine that Robin Ellis is still trying to escape from his image in Poldark. My Mum apparently liked him in Poldark. Grandad has got the TV Times out for me mainly because there is an article about Abba in it. Anni-Frid looks very good in that extremely tight blue jumpsuit. It says in the story that Anni-Frid and Benny are planning to divorce. They say Abba will survive though because it survived the divorce of Agnetha and Benny. I hope I never get divorced. It states that if Abba ever stopped selling records that the Swedish economy would take a dive as they are the country's largest export after Volvo cars. The ones that always have their lights on even when it is sunny.

Looks like there is a picture of an old man paddling by the pier wearing an Aston Villa scarf. But clever Grandad says it is Alf Garnett and it's a West Ham scarf. I have heard of Alf Garnett. He is in a comedy that my parents can't stand.

The C&A advert has got Jingler jeans for only £5.99. Must ask Mum if I can have some of those during the Easter holidays.

Looks like Wolves aren't going to Wembley, just five minutes left and they still trail 2-1. The Villa Park clash has gone into extra-time. Still no goals and looks like it is going to a replay. This means we won't be playing Ipswich on Tuesday after all. It sounds like Manchester City are still having chances.

Penalty at Hillsborough in the last minute. Grandad cheers. Wolves have a penalty. Kenny Hibbitt was fouled although Spurs fans think he dived. Willie Carr has to take the penalty to keep Wolves' Wembley dreams alive. Grandad has his eyes closed and he's gripping the sofa. The ground seems to have gone silent. Carr steps up. What's happened? He's scored, it's 2-2. Looks like extra-time.

A goal at Villa Park now. It is all happening. Just as Metal Mickey is starting on the telly. Maybe Villa will play Ipswich on Tuesday after all. Maybe Ipswich are beatable. A free-kick played short to Paul Power and he has given Manchester City the lead in extra-time. It could yet be a Manchester City - Wolves final like it was in the 1974 League Cup.

Wolves have to replay, but Ipswich don't, they're out. So Tuesday night, at Villa Park, is now the big title decider. I am nervous already.

12:12pm Monday 13th April 1981

First day of the Easter Holidays and trying to revise for the exams when we go back, but the Villa - Ipswich game is all I can think about. Perhaps fourteen-year-olds shouldn't be watching Rainbow as they revise for an R.E. exam. Rainbow isn't as good as it used to be. It started going downhill when Rod, Jane and

Freddy became Rod, Jane and Roger. I am going to watch the more mature Crown Court, then try to do two hours revision before Five Magic Minutes with Ali Bongo is on. What a great surname Bongo is. Be a fab name for a foreign footballer in a Roy of the Rovers story.

Dad's at a Church meeting tonight, but Mum says that when he comes back they have something they want to tell me. All sounds very worrying. I wonder if it's about Grandpa. Watching The Sweeney now as I wait for Dad. A reformed criminal friend of Detective Inspector Jack Regan has won the Pools. But now he is dead.

This month just gets better and better. Dad has actually bought my 1981/82 Juvenile Season Ticket. I have seen it. He has shown it to me. It cost £40. Works out at just under £2 a game. Dad went to Villa Park to get it in his lunchtime today. He chose a seat for me. He and Mum decided a seat would be safer than being in the Holte End on my own. Dad has amazingly got me a seat right on the front row of the Trinity Stand Enclosure. Not very far from the dugout where Ron Saunders sits. I can shout instructions to the players. Tell Tony Morley when to make the right runs and instruct Colin Gibson when to make a tackle. This is the best birthday present anybody has ever had.

My parents really have thought of everything. One of the Church Stewards name Howard Hill is a Villa season ticket holder in the Upper Trinity Stand. Dad has been talking to him tonight and Mr Hill has very kindly offered to take me to all the home games next season. Dad just has to drop me off at his house each time. I don't really know Howard Hill but he must be a mighty fine chap if he has an Aston Villa season ticket. He looks quite a well-to-do gentlemen at Church. As the Villa were started by a group of Churchgoers back in 1874 it seems very appropriate that I shall be taken to games by somebody from Church.

Still more fantastic news from my dad. He really is the perfect dad. He is coming home early tomorrow night and we are going to the most important Aston Villa game in years. The game that could decide who are the Champions of England for the first time since before the First World War. Just 21 hours and 43 minutes to kick-off.

2:00pm Tuesday 14th April 1981

I am sort of enjoying Superman II at Walsall ABC with Mark, but my mind is thinking about Ron's team talk tonight. Obviously he will be demanding 110% effort from his players, but will he get Des Bremner to man-mark John Wark?

A small boy has fallen off Niagara Falls. He is lucky Clark Kent and Lois Lane are there. No idea where Clark Kent is going to find a phone box to put his tights on and still have time to put his pants on top. Superman has caught the falling boy, surprise surprise. It must be great being Christopher Reeves and pretending to fly. Even though he must get typecast. Little kid wants to do it again after Superman puts him down. Why doesn't Lois Lane realise, it's Clark without his glasses on? Oh wait, I think she has just worked it out. Taken her long enough. Get yourself out of this one Clark.

Traffic isn't too bad. Just leaving junction 6. Villa Park looks so impressive from up here on Spaghetti Junction. I have never felt this nervous before. We just have to win. We will not lose. No, we must win. We can't give Ipswich a chance of catching us. I couldn't eat my tea as I felt sick. Although I did eat a lot of popcorn at the cinema. Quite a bit of it still seems to be stuck in my teeth.

Now we have hit mega-traffic on the Aston Expressway. Dad has had to stop as the car in front braked very suddenly.

BANG!!! That really hurt my neck. Thank goodness we had clunk-clicked and had our seat belts fastened. The car behind has hit the back of us and has pushed us right into the car in front. There are at least four cars involved in the smash. All the drivers are getting out. I don't think anybody is hurt, but all the cars are damaged especially ours. I guess no match for us tonight now. At least Dad and I are fine. The driver behind should have stopped like Dad did. All the drivers are exchanging details about their cars. All of them but Dad are wearing Villa scarves.

I didn't expect that. Dad says if the car drives alright that we are still going to go. Not sure if he's just saying that to keep me happy. He looks quite shocked.

We're parked up now just by the entrance to Aston Hall Park. The car drove alright but the damage to the back of the car is quite bad. The number plate is cracked and the hatchback boot won't open. Even the 'mind your car' lad walked away when he saw the damage.

The queues were massive for the Albion game, but today they're even further down Trinity Road. I suppose we are fifteen minutes later. No sign of any Ipswich fans. Dad still looks very shocked by all the crash stuff. I don't think we will get in. Maybe the right thing to do is suggest to Dad we drive back home instead. I mean there could be damage to the car lights. Also if the car is going to break down on the way back probably better if it is earlier than later. Dad would never suggest it, but I am going to tell him that I want to go home.

Feels odd driving against the traffic going to Villa Park, but I think this is the grown-up thing to do. Probably two years ago I would have had a hissy fit if Dad had suggested we didn't stay. But now I am fourteen and seeing things differently. We just have to explain to Mum about all the dents in the car before she panics too much.

Stuck in traffic by junction 8 of the M6 now and the game has just started on the radio. They did close the Holte End but not until ten minutes before the game. We would have probably got in. It says there are some gaps in the Ipswich end so it isn't a sell-out this week.

The day gets worse, four minutes gone and Alan Brazil has given Ipswich the lead. Sounds like Ken McNaught and Jimmy Rimmer made a real mess of things. At least it's early on. I think they are missing Allan Evans. Williams and McNaught obviously don't play as well together.

Home in bed now listening to rest of Villa game as Dad tries to find out his insurance details. Mum took it better than expected and just kept saying at least we were alright. Maybe one of the reasons I came back was to put my lucky radio on. It is a pretty even game, but Villa aren't really making chances. About twenty minutes left now and still Aston Villa 0 Ipswich 1. At least Ipswich will still be a point behind us if they beat us. But we will be five points clear if we win. Come on the Villa!!!

Another mistake, this time by Bremner, and Ipswich are two-up with just ten minutes left. Eric Gates scored it and commentator says he celebrated by doing a forward roll. Even I can do a forward roll. Think I am going to turn radio off now and just go to sleep. I can't stand to hear our title slipping away. If Ipswich win all their remaining games now they will be champions. I bet Ron Saunders is livid.

Super Gary Shaw has scored a wonder goal. Come on Villa still five minutes left you can do this.

We tried, but it wasn't to be Ipswich now have 54 points from 37 games and we have 55 from 38. They have the better goal difference too. What a disastrous night.

1:04pm Wednesday 15th April 1981

Ron Saunders is on the lunchtime telly, talking about last night's game. He says even though Ipswich have five games left and we only have four, it isn't over. He asks the reporter if he would bet against us. Wish I shared Ron's optimism, I have a feeling that I will never see the Villa win the League. This was our chance. I hate Ipswich nearly as much as Birmingham City.

Mark was still moaning about Wolves replay being at Highbury when he left to get the coach just after lunch. It seems fair to me, they tossed a coin and luckily for Spurs the ground was the one nearest them. I have a feeling Wolves will win this time after their late dodgy penalty on Saturday. They will be at Wembley for the 100th FA Cup Final. At least they won't be playing Ipswich.

Deirdre Langton and Ken Barlow were causing some gossip in the Rovers Return tonight. Looks like they are going to have a fling. It looks all over for Wolves though. Garth Crooks has scored two goals in the first-half. Second one, he sprinted past several Wolves defenders. He is so quick.

Dad's friend at work sent a programme from last night for me after he heard I missed the game. Seems odd reading it now, after we lost. Ron is saying the game is as important as a Cup final in his notes. Perhaps he made the players too nervous. Reserve defender Mark Jones on Villaman page says he wants to make the first team bench this season. He will be lucky. That belongs to Eamonn Deacy and David Geddis.

Another goal at Highbury. That is it for the Wolves. The Argentinian Ricky Villa has just scored a wonder solo goal. Paul Bradshaw had no chance.

Mark is sleeping in late this morning. I don't think he was too happy when he got back in the early hours of the morning. It is the second time he has seen Wolves lose an FA Cup semi-final.

3:11pm Friday 17th April 1981

You'd think there would be better telly than this on a Good Friday afternoon. I am sure my Mum has seen this Oklahoma musical film before. It's on for over two and a half hours. Even allowing for twenty minutes advert breaks that's still a very long film. They could easily have lost a couple of songs. At least Abba – Words and Music is on next. It says in the paper that it includes live footage of their 1979 concert. How can something two years ago be live? I think I'd like to go and visit Sweden. I wonder if anybody from Sweden will ever play for the Villa. I doubt Ron Saunders would ever allow that. I can't think of any good Swedish players. There must be some, Malmo reached the European Cup Final. I bet Haystacks could name a whole team of them.

2:58pm Saturday 18th April 1981

I am getting an expert at Space Invaders now. Considering I am a pacifist I am really zapping these little aliens. Still no Allan Evans for Villa against Forest. I hope Williams and McNaught do better than they did against Ipswich. We need to make sure we get at least three points from these two Easter Midlands derbies. Mr Walker said he was going to Villa Park today. Dad was going to take me, in the Princess car that his insurance company have lent, but Grandma called from the phonebox to say Grandpa had been very poorly in the night. We really need to get them to have a phone in the house. It feels odd being here alone. I'm tempted to open one of my Easter Eggs. The Smarties one looks like I could open the foil take a bite out and then wrap it up tightly, nobody would know. I could eat half the smarties in the tube as well and then put the top back on.

Penalty to Villa after half an hour. Tim Russon is sure it was a push on Des Bremner by Scottish winger John Robertson. Come on Sid. Don't let us down now. I think he will put it to Shilton's right. Sounds like I was right. Well done Gordon Cowans. He never misses.

Double good news, Peter Nicholas has scored for Arsenal in their game at Highbury against Ipswich. So Ipswich are losing. I just want full-time now. How will my nerves take another hour of this? I am going to open the smarties Easter egg. I'll tell Mum that I was really hungry.

The letter on the smarties tube top is 'A'. How appropriate. It must be a sign that both Aston Villa and Arsenal will both win today.

Goal horn again. This time it's Old Trafford. Man U are beating the Baggies 2-0. They can't stop winning these days. Straight away another goal horn. Back to Villa Park. Oh no, Villa. Please no! Peter Withe has done it. He has headed in yet another beautiful Tony Morley cross. That's Withey's 19th goal of the season. What a bargain at half a million.

I have always liked Kenny Sansom. He has put Arsenal 2-0 up. This is a fantastic day. Ipswich are undoing all the hard work they did on Tuesday. We will be three points clear tonight if things stay the same. At this rate we could be champions a week today. Wish they had blue smarties to go with the red (nearly claret) ones. Mind you Mum always says, 'never eat blue food'.

Wolves have lost at home to Cup finalists Manchester City. 3-1. Dave Bennett scored two. Birmingham have been smashed 3-0 by Sunderland. The Sunderland player Richie scored a hat trick. Albion lost at Manchester United as well. Coventry were two up but ended up 2-2 against Stoke. Walsall got a draw at home to Barnsley, but they are still in the relegation zone. So we are the only West Midlands winners today.

Always great watching the Villa win on Star Soccer. Even Cloughie seems to be admiring our football. The Villa Park pitch is looking more like Blackpool beach each game though, but still our passing is sublime. All we have to do now is win our last three games and we are Champions of England. So Stoke away on Easter Monday, Boro at home next Saturday and then Arsenal away on the Saturday after. Ipswich still have four games to play and nobody seems to be saying when they have to play the extra game. I am not even sure who it is against. The number of games each team in the First Division has played is very mixed. Wolves have five games left, but Manchester United only have one. Wolves are three points clear of relegation. I think Leicester and Brighton will join Crystal Palace in getting relegated. One more win and Wolves are safe. Villa will have another team in claret and blue in the First Division next season, West Ham are Second Division Champions. Maybe two claret and blue champions this year. I am glad that Trevor Brooking will be playing in the First Division though. He deserves it.

3:23pm Sunday 19th April 1981

Easter Sunday and revising. I'm sure when the Jesus rose again, he didn't expect people to be revising on Easter Sunday. Wish also the Church would decide a fixed date for Easter. Around my birthday would be good. Just looking at tomorrow's fixtures and Ipswich's game at neighbour Norwich will not be easy for them. Perhaps big Justin Fashanu could do us a big favour. We just have to beat Stoke. I am starting to almost feel confident. Must update my scrapbook while the Easter Special Songs of Praise is on. Amazing how the Churches are always full when the Songs of Praise cameras are turn up. There was a really funny sketch on Not the Nine O'Clock News about it, when the vicar said how good it was to see everyone and it was a bit different to last Sunday when the congregation only had seven in and four of those had turned up a week early by mistake.

That looks a good article to cut out for my scrapbook. It says 'Shaw's better than Woodcock'. A piece on Peter Withe saying Gary Shaw is better to play upfront with than Tony Woodcock. John Barnwell (Wolves Manager) is on the same page talking about Wolves 'whizz kids'. He thinks John Humphrey,

Mike Hollifield, Colin Brazier and Wayne Clarke all have bright futures. I am not sure about Wayne Clarke. I think if he was my brother and not Allan Clarke's then he wouldn't have got anywhere near the First Division.

I didn't know that. In the 'Briefly..' section it says that Des Bremner's younger brother Kevin has signed for Colchester from Highland League side Keith. What sort of name is that for a football team? I suppose it would have been even funnier if Des's brother's name had been Keith. Kevin cost £25,000, a Highland record, and is regarded as an even better prospect than Des. I wonder if he has the same moustache and funny run.

That is a good question in 'You are the ref'. Will see if Haystacks knows that when we are back at school. Question is: A ref orders a penalty to be retaken but the initial penalty taker doesn't want to take it so one of his team mates does. Is that allowed? I thought it had to be the same person, apparently not.

The back page is about Peter Withe. He once scored all four goals when Forest beat Ipswich 4-0. Wish he'd saved some of those goals up for last Tuesday. His personal ambition is to help Villa win as much as possible and become a millionaire.

2:45pm Monday 20th April 1981

Dad cooked gammon and pineapple with Klondykes for Bank Holiday Monday dinner. That is what you call a proper dinner. Then Bird's Angel Delight for pudding and now I am nibbling on my last Easter egg waiting to hear the team news.

Allan Evans is back taking Gary Williams' place. Harsh on Gary after he was so good against Forest. Deacy is again the substitute. Adrian Heath and Lee Chapman up front for Stoke. This is our last derby of the season and we are still unbeaten in them. So far we have played thirteen Midlands derbies. We have won eleven and drawn the other two. That is impressive.

That's dreadful. It has just said on the radio that there was a fire at Tony Morley's house on Saturday night. Poor Tony. All his clothes have been burnt and his house is in a dreadful state. He had to spend last night at the Villa Hostel, but even a fire won't stop Tony Morley playing. Mind you I don't think having your house burn down would be an acceptable excuse for not playing in Ron Saunders' eyes.

Goal number twenty of the season from Peter Withe and his 19th league goal. That's two more than Gary Shaw. That's a good start by Villa. Now can we get a second? Another goal at the Victoria Ground already. Perhaps Shaw has scored. Well, that lead didn't last long. O'Callaghan has equalised for Stoke City. Oh well, only 24 minutes gone.

Trevor Francis has given Forest the lead against Wolves and the Albion are 1-1 with Sunderland. That Richie chap has scored again. Villa need a goal. Why has Gary Shaw been replaced by Eamonn Deacy? Is he injured, or is Saunders happy with a draw?

We love Justin Fashanu! Norwich City 1 Ipswich Town 0. The title is so close I can nearly touch it. Come on Villa, get the winner.

At least we didn't lose. With Ipswich's defeat we really gained a point. So just two games to go and Villa have 58 points to Ipswich's 54. The most points Ipswich can get now is 60. So we just need three points from Boro and Arsenal. It'll be very difficult at Highbury, but we could with win it before then. If we win next Saturday and Ipswich don't we are champions. Ipswich are at home to Manchester City who have won their last three games. I wish I could time travel now and go straight to next Saturday.

4:14pm Thursday 23rd April 1981

It seems like the chance of us getting jobs when we leave school is getting less by the day. Unemployment has today gone past 2,500,000 and it says in the paper that under Margaret Thatcher it could hit 3,000,000. I knew they shouldn't have put a woman in charge.

Grandpa looks really ill today. All the skin on his face looks like it is being sucked in and his eyes seem to have fallen inside his head. Dad and my uncle have put Grandpa in a bed in the front room and I don't think he has got up since. He is drinking a little water, but my mum is just holding up a beaker to his mouth. It is almost like a baby's cup. Grandpa hasn't spoken since we got here. I have never known him this poorly. This isn't the strong laughing Grandpa I know. He is making a strange croaking noise. Kind of noise I have never heard before.

Dad says he is going to take us home now and then he is coming back. I offer to stay and help, but there really seems nothing a fourteen-year-old can do. I am praying as I sit there but really struggling to know what I am asking for. I really don't want to lose my grandpa, but pretty sure he isn't going to get better.

That was not what I had expected. My grandpa has just smiled at me and said, "Looks like they've won it now". It must have taken all his energy to say that and now his eyes have closed. Dad says to let him sleep so we'll head back.

12:10pm Thursday 23rd April 1981

This is the oddest game of Subbuteo. Neither Mark nor I seem able to score. We're playing an extra five minutes each way extra-time and this is already a replay. Nearly an hour of playing and no goals. Perhaps like me Mark's mind is not really on the game. We're both just waiting for news from Mum and Dad about Grandpa. They left over five hours ago. I have retired my headless Brian Little. Mark has very skilfully painted one of the spare Coventry City players to be a Villa player. He was spare because so many Coventry sky blue men ended up broken that we disbanded the team. The only real chance in extra-time fell to George Berry (who Mark has managed to stick a large afro on). Wolves should have been winning but Berry ballooned the ball over. It ended up striking the plastic 'Motty' on the TV Camera tower. If there's no goals in extra-time then we'll take shots from the edge of the shooting area. Think I will use Tony Morley for those.

That sounds like my dad's hired Princess car pulling on to the drive. They are back. I guess we will not get to finish this game. There is a feeling of doom about what is about to happen.

Grandpa died at 10:20 this morning. He died in his bed in the front room of the terrace house where my dad was born. What had promised to be the greatest month of my life, has now become the month that my second grandparent died. My parents both now only have one parent. I have no idea how I should react. My mum is crying and my dad is just looking stunned. I guess all I can do is hug him. But it just doesn't seem enough. My 76-year old grandpa isn't going to be part of my life any more. Next April my birthday card will just say 'Love from Grandma x'. It's just wrong. Were his last words to me, "Looks like they have won it now" his last ever words? Probably best not to ask that now. What am I supposed to do now? I know, I shall offer to make my dad a cup of tea.

11:10am Friday 24th April 1981

It's good to see the boys again even if only for an hour's basketball training. The Easter holidays seem to be dragging bit. Good to get out of the house as well, so many sympathy cards and visitors. Dad has gone back to work today. The funeral is going to be next Friday. A week today at the big Church of England church in Bilston. The one with the bells. They talked about our church but it seems Grandpa and Grandma were married at the one with the bells.

Haystacks seems to have got taller and narrower during the Easter break. He's jumping higher as well and scoring some super baskets. He also took it well when I announced that I had won the bet and that Villa were guaranteed to be the highest placed West Midlands team. Good job as I'd already spent everyone's money on my Atari.

Bellington seems to be extra friendly today. He even used my first name twice. Maybe I am mellowing now that I am fourteen, but he doesn't seem too bad at the moment. Maybe he will treat Grace Taylor well after all.

Noddy and Tucker are having a pretend fight in the shower, as Spud is telling Haystacks, Bellington and me that he going back out with Carrie Campton (again). It seems Spud got her a really big Easter egg. It was one his dad had won in a raffle at work that was meant for Spud to share with his brothers. Spud was disappointed that Carrie Campton didn't offer to share any with him, but said they had spent a good afternoon listening to his collection of Gary Numan tapes.

Bellington has just claimed that he has a new girlfriend. Should I let him know that we have known about him and Grace Taylor for most of the year? Oddly the new girlfriend appears to be called Vickie. Vickie Crowe. She goes to Queen Mary's High School. Now I am confused. Is he two-timing Grace, or have they split up? And how is a 'thickie' like Bellington able to pull a girl from Queen Mary's? Nothing seems to make sense at the moment.

Spud is the brave one who brings Grace Taylor's name up.

So we'd all got it wrong for the last six months. Bellington and Grace are not an item. They have never been boyfriend and girlfriend. How could I have got that so wrong? Grace is Kenny Bellington's step-sister. Grace Taylor's mum married Bellington's dad last year. But Grace refused to change her surname as it would upset her real dad. It starts to make sense now. It's like something out of Dallas. I didn't know that Kenny's mum died two years ago from cancer. Poor Kenny. Losing my grandpa is bad enough, but to lose your mum?

I am just confirming with Bellington that there is absolutely no romance between him and Grace Taylor. The news just gets better. Trying not to look too happy though as the part about his mum was so sad. Bellington has just confirmed that his step-sister really fancies me and keeps getting upset because she thinks I don't fancy her. What a result. It is just like Peter Withe's late winner against the Albion. Grace Taylor is not only NOT going out with Bellington, but she likes me!!!

11:50am Saturday 25th April 1981

It's good to spend the morning with my last surviving grandfather, even if it means having my haircut. At least my hair will look neat for Grace Taylor on Monday at school, as well as for the funeral on Friday. I am going to have to miss the

Geography test for that. My parents gave me a choice about going, but for me there was no choice. I have to go and say goodbye to my grandpa. It will be my first funeral and hopefully my last for a few years.

The barber looks a little shaky with his scissors today. He had better not make my fringe too short. I want it to be as long as Gary Shaw's. He is quite a chatty barber. He's asking me which football team I support. Obviously he didn't notice my Villa jumper as he put the sheet round my neck. Just explaining to him that if the Villa win today and Ipswich don't win then we are champions. Also explaining that if we draw and Ipswich lose we are champions. Really, we just have to better Ipswich's result and we win our first title since 1910.

Grandad is having his hair cut now. Really isn't any on his head but he still has it cut twice a month. I suppose with my dad's lack of hair and my mum's dad's lack of hair I really haven't got any hope of keeping mine when I get older. The rain is really coming down outside. A real April shower. It will be wrecking the Villa Park pitch.

Bob Wilson on Football Focus seems to be claiming that it is a formality and Villa are going to be champions. I'm not so sure. As I remind Grandad Villa have lost the last three home games to Middlesbrough and haven't even scored a goal. We've scored a goal at Boro in the last three times we have played them away, but lost all three of them, as well. No doubt Middlesbrough are our bogey team. Hopefully Ipswich will be exhausted after having to go to Germany in midweek to beat Cologne. They've reached the UEFA Cup Final now, against a Dutch team oddly named AZ 67. Maybe they were formed the year I was born. Appropriate that they are Dutch, as so many Ipswich players are from Holland. I will support Ipswich in the final as long as we win the League. I think that is fair. Bobby Robson's team deserve to win one trophy. But winning in Europe is a lot easier than winning the First Division title. Liverpool are through to the European Cup final and they are currently 7th in the league. Although if they win their game in hand they could be 4th.

At least Villa and Arsenal are fighting at the top of the league. I bet Spud and Pincher are really worried about Wolves' game at home to Arsenal today. If they lose and Brighton win they will be 20th and be in the bottom three. It's no better for Tucker and Noddy as four go down in the Third Division and Walsall are currently 21st out of 24.

Dad wanted me to go with them to my grandparent's house this afternoon to see Grandma. I suppose in future we will have to refer to it as Grandma's house. I don't think I can do that. I certainly wasn't ready to go back there. It just wouldn't be the same without Grandpa. At least this way I can pretend he is still there.

So with Mark out at Wolves, I am getting pretty used to being on my own in the house. I suppose I could have stayed with Grandad, but I think the Villa need my lucky radio on. We just can't lose to Middlesbrough today. We have to end this jinx.

Aston Villa are at full strength it says. They seem to think that Colin Gibson is our number one left-back. It is amazing that with just one game to go we have still only used fourteen players. That would be an unbelievable achievement if we won the league. Just fourteen players and all of them heroes. Today they can become Villa legends. Emanon Deacy is sub again. Ron always seems to pick him. I suppose he can play anywhere at the back and even in midfield.

Brighton are winning at Sunderland. Not good news for the Wolves. But sounds like Wolves are playing well. Pat Jennings just made a brilliant save from Kenny Hibbitt. I still think Jennings is the best keeper in the league. If it wasn't for him then Jimmy Rimmer would probably still be at Arsenal and not in goal for us.

It is one way traffic at Villa Park, but we just can't get the ball in the net. Tony Morley is ripping the Boro defence to pieces according to the reporter.

Finally the goal horn. It is 3:25 and at last, the first goal. Even allowing for Albion's game at Leeds to be called off this is still late. The deadlock is broken at Villa Park. I fear the jinx is going to strike. No, the noise is so loud from the home crowd, can only just hear reporter saying Gary Shaw has scored. His 20th goal of the season and 18th in the league. So just one behind Peter Withe now. But that doesn't matter. It's the fact we are winning that counts. Ipswich have to score against in-form Manchester city if we hold on or the famous Aston Villa will be champions. I have got 'We are the champions' on cassette by Queen somewhere. Better find it out ready to play it full blast.

Another goal, this time at Molineux. Great news for Spud. John Richards has scored. So Wolves are also 1-0 up.

If Wolves win they can go above Coventry who will only have a game left. Coventry always seem to survive right at the end of the season, but this could be the season the Sky Blues finally go down. That would be a pity because we always seem to beat them.

All of Villa Park is applauding Villa off at half-time. It's only 1-0, but sounds like they have been brilliant. Just realised that this is the last game played at Villa Park when I won't be there. Well obviously after I die I won't be there, but hopefully for the rest of my life I will be at every Villa home game. I will be sitting on the front row of the Trinity Road Stand the next time Villa start a game at possibly the second most famous ground in England. I am putting Wembley first. Villa Park has seen more FA Cup semi-finals than any other ground and hosted the League Cup Final replay this year. Anyway it's where the League Champions play (hopefully). I wonder if I'll still get a good view of Villa Park from Heaven after I die.

Wolves are drawing 1-1 at half-time. Yet another George Berry own goal, after Andy Gray had headed the ball off Wolves goal line. Even if Brighton win though Wolves will still be outside the relegation zone, on goal difference. Good to hear half-time score at Portman Road is 0-0. If Man City can take the lead I think I will start dancing.

Walsall are now beating Swindon at Fellows Park so hopefully they can stay up. Hull and Blackpool are already relegated to the Fourth Division, but it is so close for the rest.

Peter Withe has scored his 20th league goal of the season. 2-0 up five minutes into the second-half. We can't lose this now. It was yet another Tony Morley cross. I think Tony Morley should be our Player of the Season.

That's bad news for the Wolves. Garry Thompson has just given Coventry the lead.

Another goal at Villa Park. Allan Evans this time. Seven league goals. Not bad for a centre-half. Still don't know how he's not picked for Scotland.

Maybe it won't be today. Terry Butcher has given bloody Ipswich the lead. That means we'll still need another point or hope Ipswich lose a point.

Goal horn again. Could be an important one at Molineux. Oh dear, Wolves have gone behind. Frank Stapleton has scored past former Walsall goalkeeper Mick Kearns.

The reporter at the Villa game says the Villa fans are celebrating. They seem to think Manchester City have equalised. Radio Birmingham are checking. This could be the moment, just minutes left.

Scenes of jubilation at Villa Park, but they have got it wrong. We aren't champions. Ipswich have beaten Manchester City so they're still four points behind us with a better goal difference. Ipswich have two game left and we only have one. We have to go to Arsenal next Saturday still needing a point. Go to Arsenal who have just beaten the Wolves. An Arsenal who are now 3rd in the league. An Arsenal who have won five of their last six games. An Arsenal who have not lost at home all season. Ipswich have to go to Middlesbrough who hardly even managed to get into our half today and then at home to Southampton. I don't think I can cope with this. I've really tried the last three months not to get too excited. Second is an amazing achievement, but we surely have to win it now. If we don't I am going to cry for the whole of May. Suppose that would be wrong because I haven't cried for my grandpa. I am very sad about it and have felt like crying, but for some reason the tears just haven't come. It's unusual because I do cry quite a bit. When I watched Watership Down and the rabbit Hazel died, I cried for ages. I still get tears in my eyes now when I hear 'Bright Eyes'.

It's odd that we have won 3-0 yet I still feel like we have lost. It is surely worse for Mark as Wolves lost and they are now in the bottom three. They still have three games left compared to the one that Norwich, Brighton and Sunderland have left. They all have one point more than Wolves. Leicester are now relegated mathematically.

9:05am Monday 27th April 1981

So good to be finally back at school even if we have got blooming exams. It has been a long Easter break and apart from the Villa results not a happy one. Anyway now I have the chance to get closer to Grace Taylor. I know she likes me and I know she isn't Bellington's girlfriend. This is as good as a Tony Morley cross. All I have to do is finish it off. I'd thought of a plan last night when I was supposed to be revising. The new film Gregory's Girl is out at the cinema this week. It's about a girl in Scotland who plays football. The trailer on TV last week looked really funny. So I'll tell Grace that I really want to go but I have no one to go with. Then she'll feel sorry for me and hopefully offer to come with me.

3:16pm Tuesday 28th April 1981

The History exam was tougher than I had expected. I should have paid more attention when we studied Hadrian and his flipping wall. At least it didn't stop Allan Evans, Ken McNaught and Des Bremner escaping from Scotland. I thought best not to mention them in my essay question. My wrist now aches, from all that writing. It was nice to have Grace Taylor in front of me. Her hair looked very neat at the back. I wonder if she has noticed I have had mine cut. The lads certainly did. All their comments about me losing a fight with a lawn mower and asking if they let me keep the bowl.

Grace wants to ask me about my answers in the History exam. This is my chance to mention Gregory's Girl. I am going to use the fact that it is set in Scotland. Perhaps I can say something like: I should really go and see that new film Gregory's Girl because I need to know more about Scottish history.

In the week that the Villa will hopefully win the League I have got my first EVER date. An actual going out date. Grace wants to go to the cinema with me. As long as her mum agrees. I didn't mention to her that I also need my mum to agree. That might not be as easy as it sounds. Going out on a school night in the middle of exams. Probably best not to mention to my parents that I am hoping Grace Taylor will become my first proper girlfriend. Maybe I will get my first real kiss. Full mouth on mouth action.

What had been a good day, is now anything but. Pincher has just told Noddy, Spud and me that he is leaving school on Friday. In just four days and I am not even here on Friday. That reminds me I must hand in that letter about Grandpa's funeral. Pincher is going to have to go and live in Australia. He has known for quite some time, but he's been pretending it isn't happening. His Dad lost his job so the family are all moving to the other side of the world. He will never be able to see Wolves play again, even if they do avoid relegation. His dad's brother already lives in Australia, so he's giving Pincher's dad a job on his farm. I don't know how Pincher will cope speaking Australian. I know they speak a sort of English, but it can't be the same. I suppose we can understand Richie Benaud, so he might have a chance. It's breaking up our gang. I am going to miss not having Pincher around. We have been together since first day at infant school. We were milk monitors together. Pincher bodged the holes in the top and I put the little straws in. He shouldn't have to leave the

371

country. It's all Maggie Thatcher's fault. She has to stop unemployment rising.

They didn't say on telly that Gregory' Girl was a PG. Mum says I can go as long as Dad can drop me off and pick me up, but we have to get an adult to go with us. Great! Who am I going to find to go with us? This just isn't going to happen and being dropped off by my dad is certainly going to cramp my style. Why can't we just go on the bus?

Dad's best friend who is a minister in Coventry has come round to see us. It is the first chance he has had to see Dad since my grandpa died. The Reverend is quite a character. He always says he once had a trial with the Villa and could have played for them if he hadn't got a dodgy leg. He has brought with him Saturday night Coventry version of the Pink paper. It is actually called The Pink. I think they print it later than Grandad's Sporting Star because it has got all the final scores and up to date league tables in. There's quite a lot about the Villa, even a picture of Gary Shaw on the back. He certainly looks handsome, no wonder all the girls think he is so wonderful.

Most of The Pink paper is taken up with Coventry City news and how they're almost safe. There seems a lot of rugby mentions, but I am skipping those pages. Centre pages are all about Coventry supporters protesting against their ground being turned into an all-seater stadium. It seems it's all Jimmy Hill's idea. He seems to run football these days. I don't think it will happen though as there are too many protesters.

My first date and it might go down as the worst date in history. My dad has dropped us off just outside the ABC. By us, I mean me and the responsible adult. I should have said 'no' when my grandad volunteered to come with us. What is this going to look like to Grace Taylor? My 76-year grandad coming to the film with us. He seems quite excited, he hasn't been to the cinema since Chitty Chitty Bang Bang. He has promised to buy us each an ice cream though. I can't believe that in late April my grandad is wearing so many layers. He is going to need an extra seat just to put all his discarded outer clothes on. Who wears a hat to the cinema?

Grace is there waiting for us and gives me a lovely smile. She even seems really delighted to meet my only surviving grandfather. He is an old charmer, lifting his hat up to greet the young lady. Maybe it won't be that bad after all. How can a date with Grace Taylor and a film about football ever be bad?

I never thought at my first date that I would have my grandad asking for the children's ticket and one senior citizen. How embarrassing! Looks like we are just in time the film is going to start.

Grace is sitting to my left (the top of our arms touching) and Grandad's to my right. Grace has just whispered that she hopes there are no rude bits. Me too as I have my grandad here. She also surprises me by saying, "I've been waiting for you to ask me out. Ever since I saw you horse riding in the New Forest".

No!! I don't believe it thirty seconds into the film and the nurse is stripping down to her bra. It's a nice bra, but not what you want with your grandad one side of you and your potential girlfriend the other. Don't take it off, please!! Too late in front of us are two huge breasts. Well, it isn't that the breasts are huge compared to other breasts. It's that on the giant cinema screen they look really huge. As I have little experience of breasts full stop, they might well be huge breasts. I think Barbara Windsor's were bigger. Grace Taylor has now moved several inches away from me and my grandad is making lots of tutting noises. I just hope the film doesn't continue like this. I can't wait to tell Spud and Haystacks about it tomorrow. Spud can get his brother to take him. His brother buys The Sun so knows all about huge breasts.

That was a really good film. Funny and romantic. Luckily all breasts remained covered up for the remainder of the film. Grace loved the film. Especially the space dancing bit when they were lying in the park. I even got to put my arm around Grace when Grandad fell asleep. Before I had to wake him up as the big lady in front was complaining about his snoring. Grace Taylor says she is going to call me 'Mr Spaceman' from now on. Gregory got a snog in the film, but he wasn't with his grandad and being picked up any minute by his dad.

Driving back home after we have dropped off Grandad. Strange having dad's car back. Seems a long time since the crash on the way to the Ipswich game. Dad has had a pretty rubbish

April. I think he will be more himself after the funeral. We are listening to England playing at Wembley against Romania. They just don't seem able to score. We are going to struggle to qualify for Spain at this rate. They need Peter Withe up front.

Dad says he has got some news for me. Oh no, what has happened now? Seems it is about Howard Hill the Villa fan from Church who is going to take me to the Villa home games next season. Please don't say he has changed his mind.

I am shaking. That is fabulous news. Howard Hill is wonderful. He has asked Dad if he can take me to Highbury on Saturday. To London. He has got a spare ticket for probably the most important Villa game ever. He wants to take me to Aston Villa against Arsenal. Dreams do come true. I am going to biggest game of my life.

12:33pm Thursday 30th April 1981

R.E. exam done and time to say goodbye to Pincher. Seems so odd that I am saying goodbye with the League title still to be decided and us not knowing which division Wolves will play in next season. Get the feeling we will never see each other again. Neither of us know quite what to say. They are having a little party tomorrow at school to give Pincher a proper 'Aussie-style' send-off. Wish in some way I was going to be there, but then I wouldn't get the private goodbye that we have now. At least I can tell Pincher that Grace and I are now nearly together and that Gregory's Girl has naked boobs in. I suppose as you get older school is all about saying goodbye to your friends. The 'Local Gang' of six is now down to just five. It just isn't going to be the same. It is worse for Pincher though he is about to go from six to one. I still have Spud, Haystacks, Noddy and Tucker.

The night before his dad's funeral, two days before I go to Highbury and my dad has brought us to Villa Park to see us (hopefully) win some silverware. This is Aston Villa youth team against West Ham youth team in the Final of the Southern Junior Floodlit Cup. It is a near certainty that Villa will win the cup as we are 2-0 up from the 1st leg last Monday. Tony Rees and David Norton scored the Villa goals. David Norton looks a really good player. He has plays for the England Under-18s. He can play right-back or midfield. Villa should romp this second leg on my second date with Grace Taylor. At least our chaperones are getting younger.

No goals in the first-half but I have promised Grace the Villa will score in the second-half. I can't see West Ham scoring. There are no future Trevor Brookings or Alan Devonshires in this West Ham team. It is quite high up here in the Trinity Road Stand. I am quite pleased the enclosure wasn't open. I want to save that experience until the start of the brand new season. When I sit in my season ticket seat.

Seems odd seeing the Villa players lifting a trophy when they have just lost a game 1-0. I guess we did all the hard work in the first leg. I don't know if Grace really enjoyed the experience.

Perhaps girls and football don't really mix. I am still very proud to see my team retain the Southern Junior Floodlit Cup.

Dropping Grace off and I can see Bellington peering from an upstairs bedroom window. Hopefully next time I see him, or Grace, Villa will be champions. I must admit, my mind was already at Highbury when I had that surprise kiss on the lips from Grace Taylor. She wished me all the best for the funeral tomorrow and then just planted a kiss right on the lips. Not on the cheek but the LIPS! This is real girlfriend territory.

That's harsh. It says on the radio that despite winning their last six league games, Manchester United have sacked manager Dave Sexton. Haystacks won't be happy, it is rumoured that they are interested in getting big Ron Atkinson as their next manager.

End of April Top of Division One		
Aston Villa	Pl: 41 Po: 60	+34
Ipswich Town	Pl: 40 Po: 56	+34
Arsenal	Pl: 41 Po: 51	+14
Forest	Pl: 41 Po: 49	+18
West Brom	Pl: 40 Po: 49	+16
Southampton	Pl: 41 Po: 48	+19

Villa April Results	
4th Leicester City (a)	4-2 Won (Withe 2, Bremner, Morley)
8th West Bromwich (h)	1-0 Won (Withe)
14th Ipswich Town (h)	1-2 Lost (Shaw)
18th Nottingham Forest (h)	2-0 Won (Cowans (pen), Withe)
20th Stoke City (a)	1-1 Draw (Withe)
25th Middlesbrough (h)	3-0 Won (Shaw, Withe, Evans)
League Cup Winners:	Liverpool

Chapter Ten (May)

I expect sometimes this big church seems vibrant and welcoming. But today, on this rainy day, for my Grandpa's funeral, it looks like the most depressing place ever invented. I'd have thought more people would have bothered to turn up to say goodbye to such a great man. A real gentle giant. Maybe this church is just too big for the funeral. It would fill a smaller church. This isn't what I was expecting. I can't believe that Grandpa is inside of that coffin. I bet he's looking down on us from one of the balconies. Probably wishing we would all cheer up. All these dark clothes don't help the mood. If Heaven is such a wonderful place why does everything look so thoroughly miserable, when Grandpa has hopefully gone there? I feel cheated that I will no longer have my grandpa. Will Grandma continue to buy me pants at Christmas, or was that Grandpa's idea?

Mum says most of the people here are our relatives. So how come I don't recognise many of them? It's like we have gone to the wrong funeral. I don't recognise the man the vicar is talking about either. That's not my grandpa. My grandpa was an old man who always had time for all his grandchildren. A man who did the football pools, a man who brought home sausages from the

379

market and a man who never moaned about how ill he was. So many tears in this church and none of them tears of happiness. I don't think anyone really cries because they are happy.

Seems we have to kneel to pray here. That's odd. I have got new trousers on and am going to get them dirty already. Hold on, Dad's putting his knees on that mat thingy.

What can I pray for? I suppose the real prayer is for the coffin to open and Grandpa to announce he isn't dead after all. A bit unlikely perhaps. I am sure they spend a lot of time checking people are really dead. Hope he is free from pain now. Yes, I can pray that Grandpa isn't suffering any more. I suppose as I have still got some praying time left, I can request a Peter Withe goal past Pat Jennings tomorrow.

The words of this funeral hymn are just too much. Now I am crying. Two weeks of stored up tears are now pouring from my eyes, rolling down my cheeks and on to my shirt. Now my nose has started to run. I'm so glad that Grace Taylor cannot see me now. Dad is insisting that they chose 'The Day thou gravest Lord is ended', not because it is so obviously a funeral hymn, but it was always Grandpa's favourite at the Sunday School Anniversary.

I am trying to be brave, but I just can't do this. I can't be at my grandparents' house eating sausage rolls. Why couldn't people just have gone home after the funeral? Why did they have to follow us back here? These people never came to see Grandpa when he was stuck in his bed in front room, so why are they here drinking now? Some even seem to be having fun, as if it is a party. Sharing pictures of their grandchildren and one man even has pictures of himself on Blackpool Pier. How insensitive are these people? Don't they know my grandpa has died? This is wrong. I really can't stand to be in same room with these heartless people any more. I'm going to the outside toilet. I can hide in there until everyone goes.

Terrific, Grandpa's eldest sister Sissy is already in the outside toilet and there are two elderly gentlemen queuing up outside it. At least the rain has stopped.

Grandpa's tool shed was unlocked so I came in here to hide. It all still smells of Grandpa. The familiar smell of Lifebuoy soap combined with axle grease. All now covered with spider's webs. I don't think Grandpa has been in here all year. His vice still has the piece of pipe in that he was cutting off to put under the sink, when he was taken very ill before Christmas. I have asked, but no one seems to be keen on telling me what killed him. I think it was some kind of cancer. Most people seem to die of some kind of cancer.

That's the souvenir of my grandpa I want. On the floor in the shed there is his old triangular work's pencil. This is the kind of man my grandpa was. A hardworking yet very talented man, who was a hero to me. I'll never forget you Grandpa.

Just14

The very last game of Aston Villa's 1980-81 First Division campaign. Hopefully 2nd May 1981 will be the day that the League title is decided. Ipswich can't win the title today, but we certainly can and when we do I am going to be there. London here I come. Let's write our names in history you Villa boys.

I have never known a service station so full of claret and blue. Everywhere we look there's Villa fans. All already in a party mood. Aren't some of them just little nervous, like me? Howard Hill and his son-in-law seem to be the only ones not in claret and blue. I have got my Villa rosette pinned on to my jacket. My Aston Villa scarf is on the backseat of Mr Hill's Ford Cortina. It's so kind of him to invite me along. I think we're going to get on well in the coming season. First time I have seen him without a suit on. He is wearing a cream polo neck sweater, that wouldn't be out of place fielding on the boundary at The Oval. The reason for the spare ticket is because his grown-up son had to work. Howard Hill's daughter's husband doesn't seem to be a Villa fan. I think like Mr Walker he's a Forest fan. His name is Tony, like Tony Morley, and he's very funny. He has been making us laugh all the way here. He does a really good Brian Clough impersonation. Tony also keeps apologising for his father-in-law's choice in radio music. I must admit there seems to be a lot of tunes without any words. Certainly no Bucks Fizz, or Abba.

We're having lunch in a pub, apparently it's only just ten minutes away from Highbury. Not like the pub my family normally eat in on New Year's Day. This one oddly has sawdust on the floor. I know how Snowy feels in his hutch now.

Just far too nervous to eat, but Mr Hill has got me a hamburger and chips. Feel I have to eat it to be polite. Really forcing each mouthful down. I'm feeling sick and just want to get the game started now. Most people in the pub seem to be Arsenal fans, but we can hear a group of Villa fans singing outside. Hundreds of police around.

Arsenal have had a good season. They're 3rd and only need a draw to guarantee European Football next season. It is a pity we can't both just agree a draw now. Then the Villa would be champions and Arsenal would in Europe. Everyone would be happy.

Howard Hill has given me my light blue ticket. It cost him £1.80. I bet Villa fans would have paid ten times that amount today. I need to keep it safe. It has got an 'E' in the corner. Tony says we will be in the famous Clock End. No excuse for us not knowing how long is left then.

All we need to do is draw, or if we do lose pray that Ipswich don't win at Middlesbrough.

We have only just got in the ground and I can hardly breathe. So many Villa fans and I'm really scared. What if we do lose? Is this the only chance I'll ever have me to see us win the League? I wonder if Spud is as nervous, watching Wolves at Stoke, knowing that they need a point to definitely stay in the First Division. He has gone on the coach, with his eldest brother

Norman. Haystacks is watching his Albion at home to Spurs. Albion need a win to be in Europe like Arsenal. I bet Noddy and Tucker are also feeling this sick at Bramall Lane. Where even if Walsall win, it might not be good enough to keep them in the Third Division. We all have something to play for at the end of the season, as Pincher and his family fly to Australia. But none of the prizes are as big as the potential one here at Highbury.

Villa are unchanged from last week, Deacy is still the sub. So the team who could become Villa legends today is: Jimmy Rimmer, Kenny Swain, Colin Gibson, Allan Evans, Ken McNaught, Dennis Mortimer (captain), Des Bremner, Gary Shaw, Peter Withe, Gordon Cowans and Tony Morley. A familiar line-up that has been used eleven times before this season.

The Arsenal team is: Pat Jennings, Kenny Sansom, Willie Young, David O'Leary, John Hollins, Paul Davis, Brian Talbot, Peter Nicholas, Frank Stapleton, Alan Sunderland and Brian McDermott.

Surely they can't fit anymore Villa fans in this clock end? A number of fans seem to have their transistor radios with them. Obviously not confident that we are going to get the result ourselves. I know we can do it. I think Gary Shaw will score two goals so he equals Peter Withe's twenty for the season.

Wow, this really is a special day. Pele is walking around the pitch just in front of us. The legendary Brazil World Cup player, he's just about twenty yards from us. Arms out stretched with his pale suit jacket fastened up. Well, it's quite chilly. Pele has come to see the great Aston Villa win the League. Both sets of supporters are now singing 'sign him up, sign him up'.

So many Villa flags and scarves here in this massive open end. I thought the Holte End was big, but this end dwarfs that. It hasn't got a roof on, so I hope it doesn't rain. Mr Hill is used to a seat in the stand, but he is coping well with being moved by all these stand people. All of us ready to celebrate.

The ground is now full, the announcer is saying. The bloke next to Tony has an ear-piece in his ear. He's telling us all that they are saying it's the highest League gate anywhere this decade. Over 57,000. Incredible, as Arsenal's average is only just over 30,000 this season. They have all come to see the Villa, including the great Pele.

The noise as my heroes come out, in their white tops and blue shorts, almost hurts my ears. You wouldn't think we were the away team. Howard Hill is jumping up and down already. This isn't the Church Steward Howard Hill I know, who reads the notices on a Sunday.

We haven't started well. The players look nervous like us supporters. Arsenal are full of running.

Des Bremner has given away a silly free-kick just on the edge of our penalty box, right in front of us. I have a bad feeling about this. Come on Villa keep them out. They've let Alan Sunderland win the flick-on. It's come to big ginger-haired Willie Young. No!!!!

Shouldn't Jimmy have got nearer to that? A goal down after only twelve minutes. All I can hear from the Villa fans now is Mr Hill's tutting. Opposite is just a mass of celebrating red and white. Villa, you need to start playing.

At least the last five minutes we've been putting more pressure on. Groans going around, I think Ipswich have scored. Yes, bloke with ear-piece has confirmed, Paul Mariner has given bloody Ipswich the lead at Boro. So if scores stay the same, Ipswich will just need to beat Southampton at home to be champions. Come on Morley, Shaw and Withe we need a goal.

Nearly half-time now but we are definitely playing better. Punch by Jennings and a big boot up field by Arsenal. Oh no, it's broken to McDermott on the halfway line. Only Kenny Swain is covering. Get a foot in Kenny, please!! Swain's fallen over, but Colin Gibson has got back. McDermott has beaten him too. Two nil!! Rimmer was very slow going down. I can't believe how wrong this is going. This was supposed to be our day.

Half-time and mood at the Clock End seems even more sombre than at Grandpa's funeral. The stadium announcer has confirmed that it is Middlesbrough 0 Ipswich 1. We are two goals down, we need a miracle. We need Pele on as sub in the second-half, Tony jokes. I feel so deflated and cross. I really thought we could do this. I suppose it's worse for Howard Hill. He has been following the Villa for over 50 years, dreaming of seeing them win the League. I have still got a whole lifetime of season tickets ahead of me, to see us lift that famous trophy.

Wolves are one each at Stoke. Just doing the maths but I think at the moment with Sunderland winning that Norwich are going down. They're losing at home, to already relegated Leicester. Wolves just have to better one of the Norwich, Sunderland or Everton results. Albion are 2-0 up at Tottenham so they are heading towards 4th place and the UEFA Cup. Looks like we will be playing in the UEFA Cup with them.

Come on Villa. Second-half let's make the impossible possible and turn this game around.

A bit more effort and Villa just not getting on top. Good save by Jennings from a Sid Cowans shot.

What's happened? A ripple is going around the Villa fans. They're all starting to jump up and down. They are waving their arms in the air. It has engulfed Mr Hill, Tony and me. I am wildly celebrating and I don't know why. It can only mean that Middlesbrough have equalised. Yes, yes, yes!!!

Hope these rumours are right, but everyone is now celebrating believing it is 1-1 at Ayresome Park. Mr Hill's trying to ask ear-piece man what's happening, but you can't hear a word against this tremendous noise.

Big clock says 4:35. Everyone in the Villa end seems to have stopped watching the football and we've just waiting for more news. We all seem to be swaying and shaking with nerves together.

It's happening again. The same as last time, but even more frantic and even louder this time. The whole end is screaming and going totally berserk. Is the Ipswich game over? Have we won the league?

Somebody has popped a champagne cork and we're all being sprayed with champagne. This is just totally mad. I am jumping and hugging everyone around, even Mr Hill. There's confetti and more champagne. We must have won the league. The game is still going on below us. I hope this is all true. Remember people got it wrong last week.

Yet again. A third amazing wave of excitement. This really must be it. Ipswich must have lost. The last one must have been a second Middlesbrough goal. Or maybe it's 3-1. I don't care we must have won the league. I have never known so much sheer exuberance and jubilation. Even when Peter Withe scored that late goal against the Albion, it was nothing like this. I am being squashed and drenched with what I think is champagne and I really don't care.

There goes the final whistle. We have surely done it. All these people can't have got it wrong. Thousands of Villa fans are now streaming on to the pitch and thousands of joyous Arsenal fans are running on from the other end. A line of policemen, with their helmets on, are now across the halfway line keeping the supporters apart. Everyone is so happy. Arsenal have beaten us 2-0 and they are in Europe and (I am pretty sure) we have just won the league for the first time in 71 years. I just want somebody to confirm it. The Villa players are still struggling to get off the pitch. This is just totally amazing.

That's the confirmation I needed. Now I can really celebrate. The stadium announcer has just said the final score of Middlesbrough 2 Ipswich Town 1. Ipswich might still have a game left, but they are four points behind us. It is official my Aston Villa are champions. It's also true that people do cry when they're happy. For the second time in two days I am in tears. What an incredible feeling. We have lost but this is undoubtedly the greatest day of my life.

Driving back and every car on the motorway seems to have a claret and blue scarf sticking out of it. The reporter on Radio 2 is telling us about Bosco Jankovic and how he should be given the Freedom of Birmingham. Bosco Jankovic was the reason for all the mass hysteria amongst the away fans today. Bosco Jankovic scored both the Middlesbrough goals. We love Bosco Jankovic.

Wolves have lost at Stoke and both Sunderland and Brighton won. Luckily Norwich lost at Leicester, so Wolves are safe and Norwich City go down. So my brother, Spud and Pincher (when he finds out) will all be happy. Albion beat Spurs 4-2 so Haystacks will get to see European football at The Hawthorns next season. But in my first season ticket season I will get to see my Villa playing in the biggest tournament of all, the European Cup. How good is that?

Walsall have won 1-0 at Sheffield United. That means Walsall are safe and Sheffield United are relegated to the Fourth Division. I bet Noddy and Tucker are doing cartwheels.

Back home and just want to cheer and jump around all the time. We are the champions. Filling in 'My Team's League Performance 1980-81' for the last time. I am going to keep this for ever. MATCH 42 League Position 1. We have been top after seventeen of the matches this season including the last six. Time to fill in the end of the season parts. For 'Best Home League Match of the Season' I am putting down the Liverpool 2-0. No contest on the 'Best Away League Match of the Season'. It must be the 3-1 at Everton. Now to choose 'My Player of the Season'. It has been a real team effort, but I am going to put Tony Morley. 'Top League Goalscorer' is Peter Withe with twenty goals. That is the best entry of all 'Final League Position'. I am going to write 'Division One Champions'. Last entry needs some thought. I have to give 'My Comments on the Season.' That will be 'Very Promising'.

What an unbelievable day. What a brilliant season it has been. What a fantastic manager Ron Saunders is. My Aston Villa have won the Football League with just fourteen players.

Take a bow Jimmy Rimmer, Kenny Swain, Colin Gibson, Gary Williams, Eamonn Deacy, Allan Evans, Ken McNaught, Dennis Mortimer, Des Bremner, Gary Shaw, Peter Withe, Gordon Cowans, Tony Morley and David Geddis. Every Villa fan will always know your names.

End of May Top of Division One		
Aston Villa	Pl: 42 Po: 60	+32
Ipswich Town	Pl: 42 Po: 56	+34
Arsenal	Pl: 42 Po: 53	+16
West Brom Albion	Pl: 42 Po: 52	+18
Liverpool	Pl: 42 Po: 51	+20
Southampton	Pl: 42 Po: 52	+20

Villa May Results	
2nd Arsenal (a)	0-2 Lost

FA Cup Winners:	Tottenham Hotspur
UEFA Cup Winners:	Ipswich Town
European Cup Winners:	Liverpool

Other Books by the Author

Now you've read about Jonathan Stadler in 1981 exploits, it's time to fast forward to 1986 in 'First Years: Piranhas in the Bedroom'. Released in 2012 'First Years: Piranhas in the Bedroom' was Andy Dale's successful debut novel and the hilarious introduction of Aston Villa fan, Jonathan Stadler.

'First Years: Piranhas in the Bedroom'

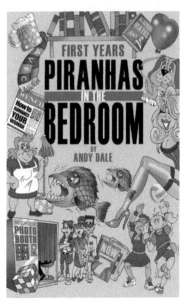

It's 1986, and 19-year-old Jonathan gets quite a culture shock when he leaves home to start his First year teacher training at Derbyshire College of Higher Education. Living in a large white (unmissable) student house full of lads, ranging from a posh boy from Kent to a northerner with anger issues, he must negotiate the perils of student life, which include seven-legged pub crawls in the dead of winter, fishnapping raids and cereals in the bedsheets, all at the same time as trying to woo a pretty blonde from Rochdale.

Set in a time when cassette players were cool, contact with home was a red phonebox, but alcohol, lingerie and high jinx were still the order of the day, First Years: Piranhas in the Bedroom is written with a great British dry wit. Its nostalgia for all things 80s as well as its "will-they-won't-they" romantic comedy gives it a really broad appeal: The Young Ones meets High Fidelity.

Find out more about Andy Dale and his books by visiting his website **andydalewrites.com**

Lightning Source UK Ltd.
Milton Keynes UK
UKHW051641191121
394140UK00009B/340